Dhows & the Colonial Economy of Zanzibar

T0313608

EASTERN AFRICAN STUDIES

Dhows & the Colonial Economy of Zanzibar

1860–1970

ERIK GILBERT

Assistant Professor of History
Arkansas State University
Jonesboro, Arkansas

James Currey
OXFORD

Gallery Publications
ZANZIBAR

Ohio University Press
ATHENS

EAEP
NAIROBI

ISBN 978 0 85255 486 9 (James Currey cloth)
ISBN 978 0 85255 485 2 (James Currey paper)
ISBN 978 0 8214 1557 3 (Ohio University Press cloth)
ISBN 978 0 8214 1558 0 (Ohio University Press paper)

Transferred to digital printing

James Currey
www.jamescurrey.com
is an imprint of Boydell & Brewer Ltd
PO Box 9, Woodbridge, Suffolk IP12 3DF, UK
and of Boydell & Brewer Inc.
668 Mt Hope Avenue, Rochester, NY 14620, USA
www.boydellandbrewer.com

Gallery Publications
PO Box 3181
Zanzibar

Ohio University Press
19 Circle Drive, The Ridges
Athens
Ohio 45701

E.A.E.P.
PO Box 45314
Nairobi

Library of Congress Cataloging-in-Publication Data is available
from the Library of Congress

A CIP record for this book is available from the British Library

This publication is printed on acid-free paper

Contents

Illustrations & Maps

Figures

Illustrations & Maps

Maps

Glossary

A Compendium of Foreign, Nautical
or Otherwise Unfamiliar Words

Bêche de mer	The sea cucumber. These are common in the tidal zones of Zanzibar's beaches, and are gathered and exported to China where they are eaten with great relish. No Zanzibari would put one in his mouth.
Boriti	The Swahili word for a mangrove pole intended for use as a rafter. Also called a *chandal* in Persian, or sometimes *mambore* after a village in the Lamu archipelago that produces especially good rafters.
Bum-boat	Small paddled or rowed boats used as water-taxis.
Carvel	Planking on the hull of a ship where the edges of the boards are flush instead of overlapping or clinkered. All western Indian Ocean craft are carvel-built.
Chief Secretary	Second most important colonial official after the Resident. He was responsible for the daily administration and functioning of the government.
Come About	The most desirable way for a sailing craft to change tack, executed by turning the vessel into the wind.
Copal	A resinous substance found in the earth around certain species of trees, used in the manufacture of varnish.
Fore-and-aft Rig	Sails attached to mast and set lengthwise rather than from yards. Opposite of square-rigged.
Frasila	Unit of measure. Equal to 35 lbs.
Godown	A warehouse or storage area.
Lateen Sail	Traditionally used in the Mediterranean and the Indian Ocean. It is triangular or near triangular in shape and hangs from a yard that attaches along the hypotenuse of the triangle described by the sail.
Lighter	A barge-like, shallow-draught vessel used to transfer cargo to and from ships too large to approach a wharf.

Glossary

Maria Theresa Dollar	Standard currency of the nineteenth-century East African coast, and widely used throughout the western Indian Ocean. MT$1 was worth about £4.75 sterling.
Nakhoda	The Swahili and Arabic term for the master of a ship.
Paying	As a noun, substance used to waterproof and protect the hull of a wooden vessel. As a verb, the act of applying this substance. The most common paying used on traditional craft in the western Indian Ocean is a mixture of burnt lime and cow fat which turns into a hard, bright white coating as it dries.
Pratique	Certification that the crew and passengers of a vessel are not suffering from communicable disease.
Resident	Chief representative of the British Government in Zanzibar during the colonial era.
Serang	The second-in-command on a dhow or the leader of a group of stevedores.
Seyyid	Title used by the secular rulers of Oman and Zanzibar. Seyyid Said was incorrectly called the 'Imam' by the British, a title that had been used by elected religious leaders of Oman in the eighteenth century. The Royal Navy even had a ship named after Said called the *Imaum*.
Sifa	Shark oil used to waterproof and preserve the hulls of sailing craft in the western Indian Ocean. Quite pungent, the location of official *sifa* storage areas in Zanzibar town was a subject of great debate since nobody wanted to live near a *sifa* godown.
Ton	Measurement of the size of a ship. Depending on the way tonnage is measured, it can refer to the amount of water the hull displaces, the cargo capacity of the ship or, most often, the total volume of the hull.
Wear	To change tack in a sailing-ship by turning downwind and then looping back up into the wind on a new tack. Used by lateen rigged vessels and considered less desirable than coming about since a ship that wears loses ground each time it changes tack. Near shore the lost ground can mean the difference between going ashore and staying at sea.
Yard	Spar that supports a sail.

Preface

In the summer of 1992 I made my first trip to Tanzania since the mid-1980s. I was attending a summer Swahili programme and I had a small grant from Boston University to do three weeks of pre-dissertation research in Tabora in central Tanzania. In Tabora I was going to look at the effects of the nineteenth-century caravan trade on local farming and the environment. My plans changed abruptly during the Swahili training course. We spent the second three weeks of the course at the Tasisi ya Lugha in Zanzibar. By the time those three weeks were over, I had abandoned my original dissertation topic and concluded that whatever topic I pursued, it was going to be researched in Zanzibar. I still was not sure what the topic would be, but I knew exactly where I wanted to spend my (then highly speculative) Fulbright year. The topic came to me a few weeks later when the language group made a trip to the old port of Bagamoyo. I wandered away from the group and stumbled on a boat yard. There I found a huge boat being built. The boat's owner, Sheikh Adam Ali, was there and politely let me interrogate him for a while in my halting Swahili before switching to his impeccable English. It later came out that he also spoke Russian, Italian, Arabic and Somali. He was a Somali refugee whose family lived in Norway. He had learned Russian while studying electrical engineering in the USSR and was at the time of our meeting in the import–export business. His boat was to be used to trade between Tanzania, Somalia and Yemen. My topic hit me then and there.

At the time I still imagined that my study of the dhow would be what environmental historians call a 'declensionist narrative'. I also imagined that it would be a fairly local project researched almost entirely from Zanzibar and Dar es Salaam. I was wrong on both counts. Sheikh Adam's cosmopolitan curriculum vitae should have tipped me off that this would not be a purely local study. Eventually my research included a Fulbright to Tanzania, a month in Salem, Massachusetts at the James Duncan Phillips Library of the Peabody Essex Museum paid for by a grant from the

Museum, four months in Yemen courtesy of the American Institute for Yemeni Studies, and most recently a month in Kenya thanks to a Faculty Development Grant from Arkansas State University.

The last two of these trips happened after my dissertation was completed. Their main effect on this, the book version of my dissertation, is that the Kenya and southern Yemen coasts brought home to me just how much of a coherent region the western Indian Ocean littoral is. In both places I started my trip in a highland city that seemed very unfamiliar and concluded it on the coast, where I felt very much at home. This was most pronounced in Yemen. Sana, Yemen's capital, is an amazing place full of multi-storey mud buildings and home to Yemen's only traffic-light. It was like nothing I had ever seen in my life. It was intensely traditional and heavily armed. While Sananis are no longer allowed to carry their rifles in town, the bodyguards of the many visiting tribal sheikhs are. Because of the prohibition on rifles, a large percentage of men carry pistols. As people get in and out of taxis or perform other operations that pull their jackets up, you see flashes of pistol.

After about a month in Sana, I went to Aden. In Aden I felt immediately at home. Aden is in many ways like a big Zanzibar or a small Dar es Salaam. It has the same Indo-colonial architecture that graces much of the East African coast. Its inhabitants include Somalis, Ethiopians, Hindu and Muslim Indians and even a few Chinese. I met people who could speak Swahili and who had relatives in Zanzibar. There were even a few Parsees and a tower of silence. I had my morning tea in a place called the Tanzania Restaurant, where they served a fine milky tea and what looked and tasted like mandazis (a sort of Swahili doughnut). Sana was a tense place; everyone was on guard against something. Aden had the familiar louche quality of an East African port.

Mukalla also had an intensely familiar feel to it. Shop-fronts had many of the same family names on them as one might find in Zanzibar – Baharoun, Bahormuz and Bakathir. There were *kangas* and *kofias* for sale in the streets. People strolled along the waterfront at night and ate ice-cream, a scene reminiscent of Fordhani Gardens in Zanzibar or Oyster Bay in Dar es Salaam.

I had a similar experience in Kenya. After a week or two in Nairobi – where I nearly froze to death – I went to Lamu and then Malindi and Mombasa. Again the transition from highlands to coast took me from the alien to the familiar. My post-dissertation travels have convinced me that there really is a western Indian Ocean world. It may not go much past the coast, but it is there. So, if there is a critical difference between the book and the dissertation, it is that in the dissertation I was less confident of commonalities across the region that result from trade.

Because the research and writing of this book have encompassed ten years and three continents, there are many people to thank. At Boston University, Jean Hay and Jim McCann directed the dissertation from which this book derives and have since written innumerable letters on my behalf. At the University of Vermont (UVM), Al Andrea not only lent me the book that first sparked my interest in the Indian Ocean, but he also found work for me at UVM at a crucial point in the writing process. In Zanzibar, my greatest debt is to the staff of the National Archives. They bent over backwards to track down missing files, helped me to buy a bike and even retrieved my watch after it went to the vault in a file. Zameer Rashid did me a great service by introducing me to his father and other former clove merchants. Abdul Sheriff's interventions helped me to get my research clearance. Bill Bissell and Dodie McDow spent hours letting me bounce ideas off them under the lunch tree at the Archives and were also conscientious participants in the daily dhow observations from the Starehe Club. In Yemen, David Buchman answered my many perplexed questions about highland Yemen, taught me to distinguish among the various varieties and qualities of qat, drove me around in his truck, taught me most of what I know about Sufism, and introduced me to *sheesha*. In Aden, Captain Roy Facey got me into the Port Office, introduced me to all sorts of people, showed me the best places to eat lunch in Tawahi and let me use his photocopier. In Kenya, Jeremy Prestholdt kindly let me use his apartment in Mombasa and Athman Lali gave me access to the library and photo archive of Fort Jesus, in addition to leading me to Jeremy's flat. I would also like to thank the three anonymous readers of the manuscript whose criticisms helped me to sharpen my argument. Of course, none of the above parties are implicated in any of the book's failings of evidence or argument.

Thanks to the Peabody Essex Museum for permission to use the photographs on pages 22, 23, 41 and 48, as well as for permission to use the last of these on the cover of the book. Unless otherwise stated the remaining photographs were taken by myself.

Finally the members of my family, both nuclear and extended, played a huge role in this project. My parents introduced me to the African continent in 1966 when they took me to live in Ghana at the age of two. We later lived in Nigeria, Cameroun, and Tanzania. They have since lived in the Sudan and Ivory Coast also, giving me opportunities to visit those places as well. My wife Donna, to whom this book is dedicated, took a year off from her job to come to Zanzibar with me. She again took time off to watch our boys while I was in Yemen and again when I went to Kenya. Our boys, Oscar and Hans, have put up with my occasional travels and are now urging me to find a new research project somewhere with good snorkelling.

One

Introduction

All the earth made by God is holy; but the sea, which knows nothing of
kings and priests and tyrants, is the holiest of all ... the spirit of liberty is
on the waters.

Joseph Conrad, *Nostromo*

The steamer wharf in Zanzibar port is a quiet place. There are two deep
water berths, a few mobile cranes, one or the other of which is usually
engaged in moving a container from one stack to another, a lot of hangers-
on and little bustle. Seventy-five yards away the dhow harbour is chaotic
with activity. *Jahazis*, the standard coastal craft of the late twentieth century,
jostle for room at the wharf. Stevedores sweat, curse and strain to shift the
sacks of cement and lime, boards, flour, laundry soap, mattresses, car tyres,
and occasionally cars from the boats to the wharf, and from the wharf into
the fleet of ancient Bedford and Leyland lorries that carry the dhows'
cargoes to shops, godowns and construction sites. It does not take long to
see that the modern side of the port is running well below capacity, while
the traditional side is booming.

The continuing economic importance of dhows surprised me when I first
came to Zanzibar in 1992. Since virtually every book about the dhow
economy, whether written in 1940, 1958 or 1978, has claimed to be
documenting the final gasp of an ancient trade, I fully expected to find that
dhows were only in use in the most marginal sectors of the economy.[1]
Instead I found that the President's son was having a big motor dhow built,
and a prominent Somali merchant was building a monstrous 300-ton vessel
with the intention of using it to carry tea to Somalia, livestock to Yemen
and undisclosed 'sundries' back to Tanzania. It was clear that the dhow

---

[1] Esmond Bradly Martin and Chryssee Martin, *Cargoes of the East*, (London: 1978), D.N.
McMaster 'The Ocean-going Dhow Trade to East Africa,' *East African Geographical Review*,
4 (1996), A.H.J. Prins, *Sailing from Lamu* (Assen: 1965) and Allan Villiers, *Sons of Sinbad*
(New York: 1969).

1.1 Jahazis in the dhow harbour at Zanzibar, c. 1985

economy represented more than an anachronism and that its survival and continued dynamism were worth investigating.

This book is the result of that investigation. It is first and foremost an attempt at historical reconstruction, an attempt to tell the story of the world of the dhow – an economy that has often preferred picturesque obscurity to centre stage. The protagonist in this narrative is not a person, a family or even, except in the broadest possible sense, a social or economic class. Rather, our hero is the dhow, a ship that brought Zanzibaris, mainland East Africans, Arabs, Indians, Greeks and the colonial state into a shifting series of alliances and conflicts from the middle of the nineteenth century until the present.

In addition to being a good story, the reconstruction of the commercial world that was predicated on dhow transport gives us a window on the colonial attempt to modernize and control the economies of East Africa. It shows how local entrepreneurs resisted those efforts and gives us some notion of the extent to which these efforts succeeded. The premise of this work is that the 'dhow trade' was in many respects the creation of colonial ideas about modernity and tradition. The colonial state saw the dhow as traditional and so something to be replaced by modern steamships or at least kept out of the modern sectors of the economy. The result was the conversion of the nineteenth century dhow economy into a colonial-era informal economy, which was structurally almost identical to its precursor. Like its nineteenth-century parent, the dhow economy of the colonial era continued to participate in a larger regional economy, keeping Zanzibar firmly embedded in the economy and culture of the western Indian Ocean throughout the colonial period.

2

1.2 A ship at the main wharf in Zanzibar, 1994

The continuing survival and real importance of this regional economy during the colonial period brings into question some common assumptions about colonial-era economic history. Did modern technology introduced and encouraged by colonial regimes really drive out indigenous technology? Were pre-colonial trade patterns superseded as colonial authorities reoriented their new possessions towards cash-crop production for the metropole? Were local entrepreneurs allied with or enemies of the colonial project? Was the advent of colonialism the crucial watershed in African economic history or did that rupture come later?

That the answers to these questions are different for Zanzibar than for much of Africa is attributable to the economic importance of the dhow economy in Zanzibar and the difficulty of exerting control over a seaborne trade. The low cost of dhows, their ability to use virtually any beach as a port and the informal economic linkages they created between the various colonies of the western Indian Ocean made the dhow economy deeply subversive of the colonial project in Zanzibar, giving the colonial era a different flavour there from that in colonies that lacked the ability to carry on a locally controlled international trade.

Modernity and tradition

Modernity in the form of steamships, capitalism and colonialism was supposed to spell the end for the dhow trade. Virtually every study of East Africa in the nineteenth century or earlier begins with an explanation of the monsoon system and a description of how this wind pattern brought

3

Arab and Indian ships to East Africa, thus connecting East Africa to a larger Indian Ocean trading world. Authors working on the nineteenth century refer to those ships as 'dhows' (a word not usually used to describe the same ships before the nineteenth century).[2] Apparently most authors believe that the burgeoning presence of Western sailing-ships and steamers in the East Africa trade ought to have rendered 'dhows,' those other sailing-ships, increasingly irrelevant, because by the late nineteenth and early twentieth centuries all attention shifts to the struggle between Arab, Indian, African and European for economic and political control of the coast.[3] Dhows, the monsoon system, and regional trade – disappear from the historical consciousness as if surgically excised and the dhow ceases to be the subject of the serious historian and instead becomes beloved of the antiquarian and the anthropologist.[4] The former seeking links between the sewn ships of ancient Rhapta and Menuthias and the nineteenth-century *mtepe*, while the latter use the dhow as a way of understanding the Swahili mind. But serious historians look elsewhere, preferring the colonial economy, capitalism and other apparently more central currents in the stream of history.

Students of the broader Indian Ocean world have been explicitly dismissive of the economic importance of the dhow trade. Chaudhuri, a leading light in Indian Ocean studies, says that 'Modern technology is intolerant of the living past going beyond ... the 1850s,' and 'If Kwaiti booms and their Indian fellow-vessels continue to cross the Arabian Sea, they do so ... either as part of a backward economy or because their owners are not rational beings.' The ultimate source of the demise of the regional trade system to Chaudhuri's mind was 'the invention of the steam-engine'.[5]

Partially bucking this trend, a recent work by Rajat Ray argues that what emerged in the nineteenth century was less a total victory for European capital than a situation where Asian capitalists were 'strongly affected by the European colonial supremacy' but none the less resisted adopting

---

[2] Norman Bennett, *A History of the Arab State of Zanzibar* (London: 1978) and *Arab versus European* (New York: 1986), M. Reda Bhacker, *Trade and Empire in Muscat and Zanzibar* (London: 1992), Frederick Cooper, *Plantation Slavery on the East Coast of Africa* (New Haven, 1977), C.S. Nicholls, *The Swahili Coast: Politics, Diplomacy and Trade on the East African Littoral, 1798–1856* (London: 1971), and Abdul Sheriff, *Slaves, Spices and Ivory in Zanzibar* (London: 1987).

[3] Bennett, *Arab versus European*, Frederick Cooper, *From Slaves to Squatters* (New Haven: 1980), Jonathon Glassman, *Feasts and Riot* (Portsmouth, NH: 1995), L.W. Hollingsworth, *Zanzibar Under the Foreign Office, 1890–1913* (London: 1953), M.F. Lofchie, *Zanzibar, Background to Revolution* (Princeton: 1965) and Abdul Sheriff and Ed Ferguson, *Zanzibar Under Colonial Rule* (London: 1991).

[4] Neville Chittick, 'Sewn Boats in the Western Indian Ocean, and a survival in Somalia,' *International Journal of Nautical Archaeology and Underwater Exploration*, 4 (1980), W. Facey and E.B. Martin, *Oman, a Seafaring Nation* (Muscat: 1979), C.W. Hawkins, *The Dhow* (Lymington: 1977), J. Hornell, 'The Sea-going *Mtepe* and *Dau* of the Lamu Archipelago,' *Mariner's Mirror*, XXVII (1941), and A.J.H. Prins, 'Uncertainties in Coastal Cultural History: the *Ngalawa* and the Mtepe', *Tanganyika Notes and Records*. 53 (1959).

[5] K.N. Chaudhuri, *Trade and Civilization in the Indian Ocean* (Cambridge: 1985), p. 221. A similar but slightly more guarded position is found in Kenneth McPherson, *The Indian Ocean* (Delhi: 1993) pp. 225-36. The heading that begins this passage is 'Capitalism Triumphant?'

European business methods. Instead they relied on a variety of paper monetary instruments that let them transfer money over long distances. These merchants and bankers functioned in a largely autonomous middle tier of a three-part economy, sandwiched between European capital on the one hand and the world of retail pedlars on the other.[6] While Ray is right that this class of Asian capitalists kept its autonomy and that there were links between these merchants and the 'earlier maritime world of the Indian Ocean', he is as dismissive as Chaudhuri of the role of dhows and the people who used them. Unlike Chaudhuri, he sees the steam engine as only a secondary cause of the demise of traditional seafaring. More important, to his mind, is that the Arabs and 'the African tribesmen of the Swahili–Somali coast' (along with the Malays, Bugis and Dyaks of the eastern Indian Ocean) all lacked the experience and skills needed to handle money over long distances, and so could not function in a world increasingly dominated by telegraphs, steamships and banks.[7]

Historians are not alone in their tacit belief in the triumph of modernity over tradition. In the early decades of the colonial era, annual reports and returns published by the Protectorate government in Zanzibar usually noted that the numbers of native vessels calling at the port were declining. As late as 1928 the Zanzibar Port Officer said of the dhow that 'this class of carrier is gradually but surely dying out'.[8] And this was as it should be. The Ports Department had built a modern harbor and was running a steamship service, and how could dhows compete with that? What the officials making these predictions about the demise of the dhow were overlooking was the tenacity of the surviving dhow fleet. Even as government officials predicted the decline of the dhow, their steamers ran virtually empty and dhows carried the bulk of the cargo between points served by the government steamer service. Like our historians, colonial officials were so wedded to their faith in modernization that they were blind to economic reality. When everybody from rank empiricists to Marxist historians to colonial officials agree about something, in this case the triumph of one economic system over another, something strange is afoot. What all of these parties have in common is a Whiggish notion of progress. That colonial officials saw Western technology as the embodiment of progress and modernity comes as no surprise. What is perhaps more surprising is the extent to which scholars have embraced this perspective. It is doubly surprising because most of them, I am sure, if asked if they saw western technology as progress and modernity would answer 'no'. I claim no immunity to this preconception: witness my original intention, when I set out to document the decline of the dhow trade as a result of the introduction of the steamship, a project as thoroughly wedded to progressive notions of modernity as one might hope to find.

These progressive notions are not confined to scholars. A dhow builder

---

[6] Rajat Ray, 'Asian Capital in the Age of European Domination: the Rise of the Bazaar, 1800–1914,' *Modern Asian Studies*, 29 (1995), p. 551.

[7] Ibid., pp. 501–2.

[8] ZNA BA36/1 Zanzibar Government, *Port and Marine Annual, Report, 1928*, p. 1.

I met in Nungwi made a distinction between work done '*kiswahili*' (in the Swahili manner) and work done '*kizungu*' (in the Western or 'white' manner). The implication was that his *kiswahili* work was inferior to *kizungu* work. Here was a man building beautiful, handmade boats, many of them destined for use by dive shops, beach hotels or other manifestations of the tourist trade (surely the most modern aspect of Zanzibar's economy), disparaging his own work as outdated. The universality of this notion is attested to by Amitav Ghosh's *In an Antique Land*, Ghosh's brilliant account of what he really did while he was supposed to be researching a thesis on Egyptian agriculture. While being quizzed by Egyptian peasants about life in India, Ghosh was asked if, like them, Indian peasants still used oxen to plough their fields and still built their houses with mud. Ghosh was struck by their use of the word 'still' which implies that these things are anachronisms waiting to be superseded by modern technologies.[9] These ideas then seem to be fairly universal, Zanzibari boat-builders and Egyptian peasants joining the ranks of colonial officials and historians.

In reality, steamers did not replace dhows during the colonial era. Rather the two reached an uncomfortable accommodation, wherein both economies continued to function in the same geographical area, each mostly confined to and defined by its own commodities, means of transport and organization, but with a few points of contact and often intense conflict between the two. These points of contact and conflict are illuminating. The colonial government was usually content to leave the dhow economy alone, so long as it behaved in a traditional manner. Carrying salt, dried shark, dates, mangrove poles, grain, coconuts, carpets, ghee, rose-water and suchlike was a perfectly acceptable thing for dhows to do, since these activities did not interfere with the attempt to modernize Zanzibar. Indeed the state often encouraged this type of trade, partly because they realized that it was economically useful, but perhaps also since it provided an anachronistic counterpoint to their carefully cultivated modern sector. The dhow world was never satisfied with this narrow idea of what they should be doing and constantly encroached on the official, modern economy.

What was intolerable to the colonial state was that dhows should try to participate in or interfere with the elaboration of the modern economy. Even before the British had declared a protectorate over Zanzibar they had identified dhows as an enemy of modernity. In the second half of the nineteenth century, when Britain decided that it was time that traditional slave labour be replaced by modern wage labour in East Africa, dhows bore the brunt of the anti-slave-trade efforts. The stigma of involvement in the slave-trade clung to dhows long after the slave trade disappeared and much of the colonial era regulation of the dhow trade was rooted in nineteenth-century attempts to control the slave-trade.[10]

---

[9] Amitav Ghosh, *In an Antique Land* (New York: 1992) p. 200.

[10] Even now, over a hundred years since the regulations meant to prevent dhows from carrying slave were first concocted, many of these regulations are still in effect. Apparently these regulations still serve the needs of a state that is just as suspicious of dhows as their former colonial masters were.

Likewise, when it came to modernizing the clove industry, the principal source of tax revenues and Zanzibar's only significant cash crop, dhows were identified as one of the problems facing the industry and the state made a costly and ultimately unsuccessful attempt to drive dhows out of the clove carriage trade. When motorized schooners, which, like dhows, were legally native vessels, tried to get into the business of hauling cargoes destined for international export from Tanganyika there was a similar hue and cry, which was not resolved until legal dhow cargoes were carefully defined to exclude coffee, sisal and cotton. If modern steamers, with their standard fares, regular schedules and dry holds, were inherently superior to dhows, one wonders why they needed the coercive force of the state to prevail, when indeed they did prevail. In the case of the clove trade where the state made a huge investment in infrastructure, subsidized a steamer service and took regulatory steps to put dhows at a disadvantage, steamers still could not compete and eventually the government had to back down. The struggle over the clove carriage trade was a clear defeat for the champions of modernity and a victory for the informal sector created by their efforts to marginalize the dhow economy.

In Zanzibar, the advent of colonial control in 1890 was not a turning-point in terms of the technologies used in seaborne trade. Steamers had been a factor in Zanzibar's external trade almost since the steamship was invented, and the colonial regime, despite its modernizing tendencies did little to change the relative importance of dhows and steamers. Steamers continued to control trade with the Atlantic and Bombay, while dhows controlled most of the trade with southern Arabia, the Red Sea, the Persian Gulf and the local trade. Dhows were as important to the economy of colonial Zanzibar as they were to nineteenth-century Zanzibar, and the blindness of historians to this continuing importance suggests that they too have accepted the premiss that modern technology naturally drives out older technologies, whether or not the rest of the economy has been transformed by modernity. This is not to deny the importance of steamships to the colonial project. Steamships played as important a role in the age of high imperialism as did the Maxim gun.[11] It is not surprising that both the colonial state and historians have focused on the success of the steamer, but steamers never captured the entire commercial economy. Zanzibaris lacked the means to stand up to the Maxim gun, but they had the means to resist the steamship. This perhaps is the key point. Steamers could not supplant dhows until Zanzibar's economy and the regional economy in which Zanzibar functioned had been fundamentally transformed and the structures of the monsoon economy had been finally and completely changed. Since Zanzibar was not cut out of the monsoon economy until after independence, the dhow economy remained an important force in Zanzibar during the colonial era.[12]

[11] Daniel Headrick, *Tools of Empire* (New York: 1981).

[12] For current critiques of modernization theory see Bruce Berman, 'African Capitalism and the Paradigm of Modernity,' in Bruce Berman and Colin Leys (eds), *African Capitalists in African Development* (Boulder: 1994), Sara Berry, *No Condition is Permanent* (Madison, WI: 1993)

Zanzibar and the western Indian Ocean region

Zanzibar was firmly integrated into a western Indian Ocean regional economy from the late eighteenth century until the mid-1960s. Dhows and this regional economy were mutually supportive. Dhow transport kept this economy alive while the opportunities offered by the regional economy helped to keep dhows in business. The two were virtually inseparable and their combined influence made Zanzibar what it was – a cosmopolitan, polyglot microcosm of the western Indian Ocean.

Zanzibar and the Swahili world in general have long posed a problem for African studies. Africanists have never been quite sure whether East African coastal society was African or somehow alien. Early archaeological work on the coast assumed that the coast was as much Arab or Persian as African and that the flowering of urban culture in East Africa was rooted in trading colonies created by Arab or Persian settlers. Many East Africans who are not from the coast agree.[13] The Kenyan archaeologist Chapurukha Kusimba describes, in his childhood, reading textbooks that pictured the Swahili as alien invaders and slave hunters.[14] His work as an archaeologist has been devoted to refuting this contention. His work, and that of other archaeologists, has demonstrated that that the rise of cities on the coast was a primarily local phenomenon. They have found that Swahili cities did not just spring forth *ex nihilo* as one would expect if they were trading colonies built by Arab colonists. Instead, these cites grew out of fishing villages that grew over centuries into cities as they became more involved in trade. Furthermore, pottery styles common to both the early coastal settlements and sites over a hundred miles from the sea suggest that the inhabitants of the early coastal settlements were the coastal branch of a larger East African cultural group.[15]

Scholars approaching this debate from the linguistic or historical angle have also declared Swahili culture, language and urbanism to be African. The Swahili language is a member of the North Coast Bantu family of languages. Modern Swahili contains many Arabic loan words, but this is attributed to recent changes in the life of the coast. They assert that it is only in the nineteenth century that large numbers of Arabs, the source of all the loan words, have been incorporated into the Swahili world. Before the nineteenth century, they argue, the Arabian world served the Swahili in much the same way the Greeks did the Romans, as a model from which

[12] (cont.) and Lynn Mytelka, 'The Unfulfilled Promise of African Industrialization,' *African Studies Review*, 32 (1989).

[13] Neville Chittick, *Kilwa: An Islamic Trading City on the East African Coast* (Nairobi: 1974), James Kirkman, *The Arab City of Gedi* (London: 1954) and *Men and Monuments on the East African Coast* (London: 1964).

[14] Chapurukha Kusimba, *The Rise and Fall of the Swahili States* (London: 1999) pp. 13–15.

[15] Mark Horton, 'Asiatic Colonization on the East African Coast: the Manda Evidence,' *Journal of the Royal Asiatic Society*, 2 (1986), 'Early Muslim Trading Settlements on the East African Coast: New Evidence from Shanga,' *Antiquaries Journal*, 67 (1987), and *Shanga* (Nairobi: 1996) and Mark Horton and John Middleton, *The Swahili* (Oxford: 2000).

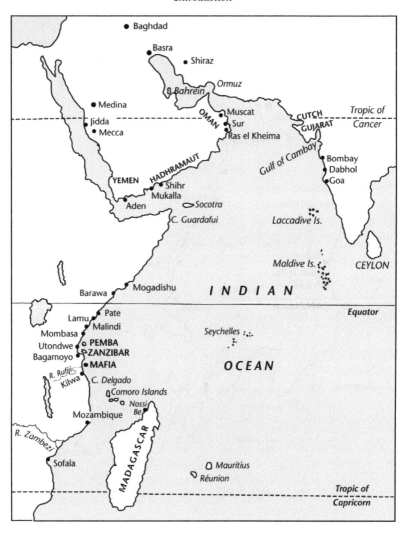

● Baghdad

● Basra
● Shiraz

Ormuz

ᑎ *Bahrein*

Muscat

● Medina

Jidda
● Mecca

O
M
A
N

Sur
Ras el Kheima

CUTCH

GUJARAT

*Tropic of
Cancer*

YEMEN

H
A
D
H
R
A
M
A
U
T

Shihr
Mukalla

Aden

Gulf of Cambay

Bombay
Dabhol
●Goa

⌒Socotra

C. Guardafui

Laccadive Is.

Maldive Is.

CEYLON

Barawa ●

Mogadishu

I N D I A N

Equator

●Pate

Lamu
Malindi

Seychelles

Mombasa
Utondwe ● o **PEMBA**
Bagamoyo **ᑎZANZIBAR**
● **MAFIA**

O C E A N

R. Rufiji
Kilwa

C. Delgado

ᑎComoro Islands
ᨆo Nossi
Be

Mozambique

R. Zambezi

M
A
D
A
G
A
S
C
A
R

Sofala

ᑎ *Mauritius*
ᑎ *Réunion*

*Tropic of
Capricorn*

*Map 1.1 The western Indian Ocean
(based on John Gray* A History of Zanzibar *London: 1962 p. v)*

9

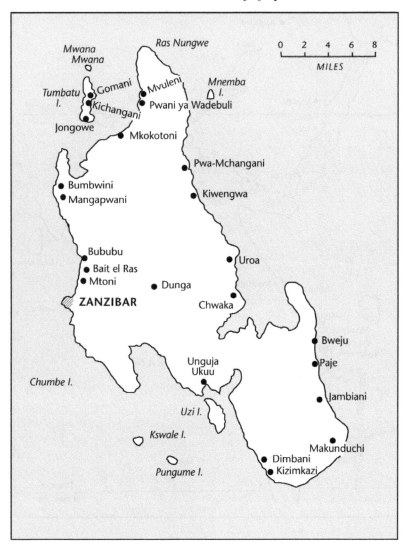

Map 1.2 Zanzibar – Island of Unguja
(based on Gray History of Zanzibar *p. vi)*

10

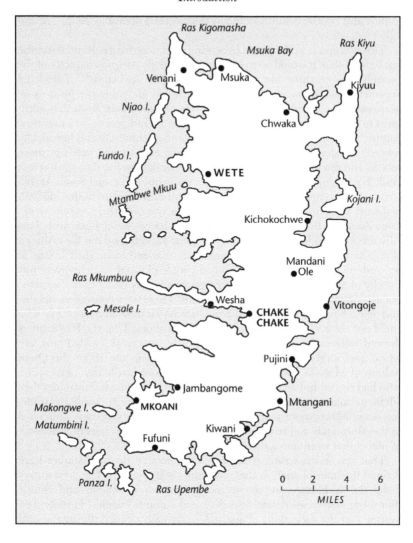

Map 1.3 Zanzibar – Island of Pemba
(based on Gray A History of Zanzibar *p. vii)*

to pick and choose cultural elements that seemed desirable (Maps 1.2 and 1.3).[16]

This position is in danger of becoming a bit doctrinaire. Rene Barendse has written that 'it would seem as if the "essentially African character of the Swahili" is something like a mantra among the specialists'.[17] I find the argument that the origins of the Swahili world are primarily local to be persuasive, but I find some of the possible extrapolations from that argument to be less convincing. First, what is 'local' or 'indigenous' in a maritime culture? Should we see contiguous bits of land as culturally and historically related? Or should we see areas connected by easy-to-cross water as more related and interconnected than areas with contiguous but difficult-to-cross land? For example, one could argue that the people of coastal South Arabia have at least as much in common with coastal East Africans as they do with highland Yemenis. The port city of Mukalla was only three to four weeks from Zanzibar by boat. People in Mukalla shared Shafii Islam with East Africans, dressed in *futas*, which are the local variation on the East African *kikoi* (a sarong-like wrap skirt for men), ate rice and made their livings at sea and/or as migrants abroad. Only a couple of hundred miles away was the city of Sana. Sana may have been geographically closer than Zanzibar, but as a practical matter it was quite distant. There were miles of mountains and desert between Mukalla and Sana, much of it inhabited by people who could not always be relied upon to welcome visitors. Thus the Highlanders dressed differently, spoke Arabic differently, practised Zaydi Islam, ate wheat and sorghum and rarely travelled. When in the 1930s the Quati Sultans of Mukalla, themselves the descendants of Hadhrami mercenaries who had served Indian princes, set out to hire talented administrators they felt they could trust, they hired Zanzibaris. Where there are boats and trade, the sea connects more than it divides. So, when regional trade flourished in the nineteenth and twentieth centuries, Zanzibar was part of a network of places that were simultaneously distant and local.

That this seems wrong is the result of the way the area studies have defined the units of analysis that constrain most research. The area studies divide the world into components mostly based on continents, and assume that those continents define historical and cultural realities. Further they assume that the these units of analysis – originally defined during the cold war as a means of apportioning research money – make sense now and make sense deeper in the past.

Zanzibar and the rest of the Swahili coast are part of Africa as defined by the area studies world. If you want a Fulbright or SSRC grant for

[16] The best example of this position is Derek Nurse and Thomas Spear, *The Swahili* (Philadelphia: 1985). See also John Middleton *The World of the Swahili* (New Haven: 1992), who has a similar but more subtle take on the issue, and James de Vere Allen, *Swahili Origins* (London: 1993), who is firmly in the African camp. Glassman, *Feasts and Riot*, has taken a slightly different approach and sees Swahiliness as more of a class identity than an ethnic one. For a recent review article on the subject, see Thomas Spear, 'Early Swahili History Reconsidered,' *International Journal of African Historical Studies*, 33 (2000).

[17] Rene Barendse, *The Arabian Seas* (Armonk, NY and London: 2002) p. 6.

1.3 The port city of Mukalla, 1997. This was a major port of the Hadhramaut region of Yemen, and one of Zanzibar's main trading partners

Zanzibar you apply through the African studies wing of both agencies. If you want to do some sort of regional or comparative study, you are welcome to apply for regional studies grants that encourage you to compare Zanzibar with Lesotho or Gambia, but if you want to do research that involves work in Zanzibar and Yemen or Oman you have a problem. There are regional studies grants for Africa and regional studies grants for the Middle East and South Asia, but neither permit recipients to cross the area studies boundary between Asia and sub-Saharan Africa. Disciplinary boundaries have lumped Zanzibar in with Cameroun, Ghana, and Angola, while separating it from its much nearer neighbours in the Indian Ocean world. Perhaps the most interesting critique of the area studies' use of continental units of analysis is in Lewis and Wigen's *The Myth of Continents*. They argue that these continentally defined units make little sense from a cultural perspective and that they rely on essentialized visions of cultural and civilizational uniformity. They argue for new, less continental units of analysis, but they fail to consider the possibility that bodies of water may at times make good units of analysis.[18]

In this book I shall argue that the dhow trade made possible a Zanzibar that was part of a world of cultural interactions and creation that cut across the continental divisions between Africa and Asia. This does not mean that Zanzibar was exclusively Arab or Asian either. I am not arguing for a return

---

[18] Martin Lewis and Karen Wigen, *The Myth of Continents* (Berkeley:1997).

to the idea that coastal people are aliens. Instead I am arguing for a more nuanced definition of what 'African' or 'Arab' means and a broader sense of the local. For the time period I am dealing with – the middle of the nineteenth century until the middle of the twentieth century – I contend that is it just as useful and valid to look at Zanzibar from the perspective of the western Indian Ocean world as it is from an African perspective. Again, this is not to say that there were no African elements in Zanzibar: it is only that those African elements were caught up in the context of a commercial and cultural world that spanned the western Indian Ocean. Furthermore, I am not saying that Zanzibar's more distant past and perhaps even its present and future are not 'African', only that during this one period in Zanzibar's history the island was part of a western Indian Ocean region that brought together people from places as far apart as India and Central Africa, and in the process created something new and vibrant, though not without strife and contentiousness.

In this study, Zanzibar and the East African coast will be treated as part of an economically and socially integrated region that stretched from Madagascar to the Red Sea to the Persian Gulf to the southern tip of India. To be sure, Zanzibar had trade connections that reached from Salem to Marseille to Singapore to Canton, but these waxed and waned as demand for ivory, copra, cloves, copal, shark fins and *bêches-de-mer* came and went. While these external trade connections fluctuated, the structures of the western Indian Ocean's monsoon economy remained the rock-solid foundation of Zanzibari life, dictating what people would eat and wear and how they would shelter from the elements.

The idea that the Indian Ocean rim constitutes a unified culture area is not a new one. A number of Braudel-influenced studies of the Indian Ocean exist, but these tend to ignore East Africa's role in the economic and cultural life of the Indian Ocean. Moreover, they rarely extend this concept beyond 1750, or at the latest 1800, since by 1750 European capital is thought to have so transformed the Indian Ocean as to make this unity inconsequential. The neglect these works show for Africa has not inspired Africanists to write East Africa into the history of the Indian Ocean. This book aims to show that East Africa was indeed part of a larger Indian Ocean world and that historically important commercial and cultural continuities and connections between the lands that fringe the western Indian Ocean survived beyond the traditional 1750 cut-off date.[19]

It was this Indian Ocean world that gave Zanzibar its ethnic diversity. Zanzibar was, and to a lesser extent is, home to people from all over the western Indian Ocean rim. Although there are now only a few people in Zanzibar who claim Malagasy descent, there was formerly a quarter of Zanzibar town known as the Malagash quarter, and the tidal creek at Funguni is sometimes referred to as the Malagash inlet. Much, but not all, of the rural population of Zanzibar descends from slave and wage labourers

---

[19] K.N. Chaudhuri, *Trade and Civilization* (Cambridge: 1985) and *Asia before Europe* (Cambridge:1990), a notable exception is M.N. Pearson, *Port Cities and Intruders* (Baltimore: 1998).

brought from deep in the East African interior to work the coconut and clove plantations. Bajuns, from the Lamu archipelago, are present both as urban-dwelling shipowners and in rural communities, where they descend from migrant mangrove pole-cutters who settled near the swamps they came to work. Somalis are also a factor in Zanzibari life. Several Somali merchants were resident in prerevolutionary Zanzibar, where they acted as dhow agents to the annual influx of dhows from Somalia, whose crews added a Somali flavour to town life for the six months of the north-east monsoon. Yemenis, known in Zanzibar as Shihris after the main port of the Hadhramaut region of Yemen, were an important presence in Zanzibar, serving as coffee sellers, porters, merchants, religious scholars and dhow agents. As was the case with Somalis, the dhow season brought an influx of Shihris that numbered in the thousands. Likewise, Omanis and other Gulf Arabs, known locally as Wamanga, were present in droves, controlling most of the clove plantations and of course the precolonial government. In smaller numbers we would also find Persians and Baluchis (most of whom served in the Sultan's army). From India came Cutchis, Gujaratis and Goans. The Indian component in Zanzibar came from a bewildering variety of backgrounds, ranging from Parsees to Isamailis to Roman Catholics, giving Zanzibar representatives of virtually every world religion, including Buddhism.[20] All this mass of humanity came from an area defined by the monsoon. All these people came from places that were in the range of a single monsoon-season, round-trip journey by dhow. People from outside this zone were either not present or temporarily present in small numbers in pursuit of a specific commodity. Americans were present for about fifty years in search of ivory. The Chinese have come in very small numbers seeking *bêches-de-mer* and shark fins; a handful have stayed on and now run small factories that produce vermicelli for local consumption. Despite the fact that Indonesia was a major market for Zanzibar's cloves, nary an Indonesian is to be found. Zanzibar's ethnic patchwork is clearly the result of the monsoon-based dhow economy.[21]

So who are the real Zanzibaris? The traditional answer to this question is the Swahili. The Swahili are conventionally seen as an African people who have adopted Islam, who live in cities and towns along the coast and whose patrician class was deeply involved in regional trade. In Zanzibar the term is used to designate people of slave descent and it is currently hard to find a self-identifying Swahili on Zanzibar. Most people whom anthropologists would call Swahili call themselves something else, either Shirazi, which means that they claim decent from Persian settlers, or Hadimu or Tumbatu, both of which are groups of fishermen and farmers that claim to be original inhabitants, although it is clear that much of the former slave

---

[20] Robert Gregory, *South Asians in East Africa* (Boulder, CO: 1993) is the only thorough treatment of the history of Asians in East Africa.

[21] This position is not too far from that of Middleton, *World of the Swahili*, pp. 20–23, who sees the Swahili world, especially its patrician components, as defined by their position in Indian Ocean trade networks.

population, which of course hails from the mainland, has been absorbed into these groups. Other people who would normally be called Swahili, since they have dark skins and speak Swahili, call themselves *Warabu* or Arabs, a category which is distinct from that of *Wamanga*. So the true indigenes, the original Zanzibaris, are elusive. To be sure there is a Swahili culture, in that there is a language, a style of dress, a cuisine and a body of literature that are called Swahili. But participation in this culture is not a function of ethnicity or race. Some Asians speak Swahili at home, most self-described Arabs speak Swahili at home, and everybody enjoys a good *sambusa*, the Zanzibar variation on the Indian samosa. Whatever or whoever the Swahili once were, over the last two hundred years or so Swahili identity has incorporated much from the broader Indian Ocean world.[22]

In all likelihood only a very small percentage of Zanzibar's nineteenth-century population was indigenous in the strictest sense of the word. Almost all Zanzibaris are the descendants of immigrants, some from the African mainland and others from the western Indian Ocean region. Neither type of immigrant should be seen as having greater legitimacy than the other. To see Zanzibaris of Indian or Arab descent as alien is to misunderstand what it is to be a Zanzibari.[23] Likewise, the cultural contribution of immigrants from the mainland to the creation of a Zanzibari identity has only recently received the attention it deserves. In *Pastimes and Politics* Laura Fair argues that many of the basic elements of twentieth-century Zanzibari culture – particularly styles of dress and music, for instance – were the creation of former slaves who were trying to carve out a social niche for themselves in Zanzibar. In both instances, in creating these new ways of being Zanzibari, the former slaves drew on models that derive from the broader region. The *taarab* music of Zanzibar was created by borrowing Arab instruments and musical styles but singing in Swahili. *Taarab*'s popularity then spread out of Zanzibar and into other parts of the western Indian Ocean. The new clothing styles devised by former slaves, the *kanzu* and the *kanga*, were meant to allow their wearers to meet Islamic standards of modesty in dress.[24] These too have spread to other parts of the Indian Ocean world. *Kangas* are sold in South Arabia, complete with the mandatory pithy and sometimes suggestive sayings in Swahili on them. The western Indian Ocean region is not something that only acted upon East Africans: they also affected it.

---

[22] Cooper, *Slaves to Squatters*, p. 159, correctly points out that the essence of Swahili identity is its vagueness.

[23] David Himbara, 'Domestic Capitalists and the State in Kenya,' in Berman and Leys, *African Capitalists*, argues that the nature of the Kenyan economy has been profoundly misunderstood because 'sheer force of ideology' has made Kenyans of Indian descent an alien and hence insignificant force in the Kenyan economy. For the Zanzibari economy the opposite is true – Indians have been seen not as insignificant, but merely as exploitative. See for example Lofchie, *Zanzibar*, and Sheriff and Ferguson, *Colonial Rule*. In a similar vein, Bennett, *Arab State*, p. 252, points out that Zanzibari Arabs are no more alien in Zanzibar than blacks are in the Americas.

[24] Fair, *Pastimes and Politics*.

Thus, while Zanzibar is African in the geographical sense, culturally, economically and ethnically it also has a regional identity. And this regional identity is just as important to an understanding of what Zanzibar is about as is Zanzibar's African identity. So, whenever possible, I call Zanzibaris Zanzibaris and do not try to put them into the traditional Arab, Indian and Swahili pigeon-holes. To be sure, Zanzibaris have always divided themselves, or in some cases others have divided them, into a number of ethnic groupings. When these categories are important to understanding the flow of events (which is often the case), I use them, otherwise I try to avoid them.

Interestingly, the coastal merchant class was as ethnically diverse as the regional economy would allow. Zanzibar's trade encompassed the entire rim of the western Indian Ocean, and representatives of most of the region were active in Zanzibar's trading community. Occupying the heights of the economy were merchants of Indian extraction. They, depending on the time in question, bought and sold cloves, ivory, copal and slaves. They were also the main financiers of the clove industry – much to the consternation of the colonial state. When Omani Arabs ruled Zanzibar, Indian merchants also ran the sultanate's custom-house, and so were also the main financiers of the state. Arabs, of both the *manga* and *mwarabu* varieties also took part in commerce. They rarely had the financial depth to engage in the clove business, so instead they dealt in more mundane items – copra, dried fish, naval stores and mangrove wood. Even a few Somali merchants lived in Zanzibar, where they acted as agents for Somali dhows.

Informality, statism and regional trade

By now the concept of the informal economy has become a widespread and popular way of understanding the functioning of contemporary African economies. As the state-sponsored formal economies of modern African states have atrophied, a vibrant, reactive and often illegal informal sector has begun to fascinate students of Africa and other developing regions.[25] The result has been a burst of studies of the informal sectors of modern African economies. While in Latin America informal-sector studies have tended to look at firms that operate on a relatively large scale in the informal sector, in Africa attention has focused on individual initiatives or small firms engaged in smaller-scale enterprises, such as beer brewing, food preparation, construction and car repair.[26] Large-scale informal activity or activities

---

[25] Keith Hart, 'Informal Income Opportunities and Urban Employment in Ghana,' *Journal of Modern African Studies*, 11 (1973) was the first of these. More recently, T.L. Maliyamkomo and M.S.D. Bagachwa, *The Second Economy in Tanzania* (London: 1990), Janet MacGaffey (ed.), *The Real Economy of Zaire* (Philadelphia: 1991) and Janet MacGaffey, 'State Deterioration and Capitalist Development: The Case of Zaire,' in Berman and Leys, *African Capitalists*.

[26] Hernando de Soto, *The Other Path* (New York: 1989) and J.J. Thomas, *Informal Economic Activity* (Ann Arbor, MI: 1992) treat the activities of firms operating in the informal sector in the USA and Latin America, many of which operate transnationally. Sara Berry, *Fathers Work for their Sons* (Berkeley and Los Angeles: 1985), Deborah Brautigan, 'African

that transcend national boundaries are often ignored, in part, I expect, because this is often the province of immigrants rather than 'real' Africans. A related body of work treats the question of African entrepreneurship and capitalism, but since these works use a narrow racial definition of 'African,' immigrant entrepreneurial groups have been all but ignored.[27]

The other area that has been entirely overlooked by studies of informal activity is the colonial era. This is surprising in that the colonial state equalled or exceeded its independent successors in its heavy-handed dirigism. African governments come by this honestly; they inherited it from their colonial predecessors. In Zanzibar this antipathy to private initiative emerged early in the British attempt to reorganize the clove industry around a government marketing board, the purpose of which was to eliminate private clove shippers, whose profits, they believed, belonged by rights to the state.

That colonial regimes foreshadowed the statism of their independent successors is hardly a major revelation, but the existence of a second economy during the colonial era is seldom mentioned. Resistance to the colonial state's economic polices is widely studied, but private capitalists and entrepreneurs outside the farming sector rarely figure in the literature. This failure to recognize the existence of a colonial-era informal sector stems from a fundamental shortcoming of most contemporary work on the informal sector. Work on contemporary African economies assumes that the rise of the informal sector is the result of the failure of the official sector since independence.[28] The tacit assumption seems to be that the official economy worked much better during the colonial era, that the modernity that has eluded independent Africa worked for the colonial state. In Zanzibar this was not the case at all. If anything, the relative prosperity of the colonial period was the result of the colonial state's failure to modernize, not its success in that direction. That Zanzibar's clove economy flourished (when it did flourish) had much more to do with the efforts of the informal sector than with the success of colonial dirigist policies. Far from not existing during the colonial era, the informal sector probably played a larger role in Zanzibar's colonial economy than it has in the postcolonial economy.[29]

Since there has been no work on the colonial-era informal economy, the role of merchants and entrepreneurs in resisting the colonial state has gone unnoticed. In Zanzibar the most important locus of economic resistance to

---

[26] (cont.) Industrialization in Comparative Perspective: the Question of Scale,' in Berman and Leys, *African Capitalists*, Hart, 'Informal Income,' and McGaffey, *Real Economy*, all of which deal with the African informal sector, tend to focus primarily, though not exclusively, on a small-scale enterprise and rarely deal with transnational trade or firms.

[27] John Iliffe, *The Emergence of African Capitalism* (Minneapolis: 1983) and Paul Kennedy, *African Capitalism: The Struggle for Ascendancy* (Cambridge: 1988). Himbara, 'Domestic Capitalists and the State,' in Berman and Leys, *African Capitalists*, is a notable exception to this trend.

[28] See, for example, MacGaffey, 'State and Capitalism,' in Berman and Leys, *African Capitalists*.

[29] Timothy Welliver, *The Clove Factor in Colonial Zanzibar, 1890–1950* (unpublished PhD thesis, 1990), argues that the colonial state's efforts to shape and direct the clove industry were a total failure. He sees all innovation in the clove industry as deriving from the efforts of Zanzibaris.

the colonial state came not from farmers resisting incorporation into the cash economy (Zanzibaris had been producing cash crops for the world market since the 1840s); rather, it came from the merchant class. While the colonial state tried to modernize and control Zanzibar's economy, Zanzibar's merchants and merchants from other parts of the western Indian Ocean regional economy maintained an international (intercolonial?) trade, using their own capital and technology. In doing so they prevented Zanzibar's economy from depending entirely on one crop, created opportunities and work outside the clove sector and saw to it that Zanzibar had an economic safety net in the form of the regional economy. In times of economic crisis in the formal economy, during the Second World War, for instance, Zanzibar's links to the regional economy provided economic opportunity and critical food when other parts of East Africa went hungry.

Perhaps most importantly, Zanzibar's merchants never conceded control of the clove industry to the state. They fought hard to keep their share of the clove shipping business and succeeded. In the sector of the economy most important to the colonial state, Zanzibar's merchant class never let go of their control over the transport of cloves, which in turn made them the main source of capital in the clove industry. So, by maintaining a diversified regional economy and by retaining control over the critical cash-crop sector, the informal commercial sector succeeded in subverting the colonial state in a way no other element of Zanzibari society could.

The difference between the 'success' of colonial economic policy in mainland East Africa and its failure in Zanzibar is interesting. Here Richard Roberts's work on the regional cotton economy in French West Africa is illuminating.[30] There he has noted that the French originally justified their colonial acquisitions in the West African Soudan on the grounds that the metropolitan economy needed a steady supply of cotton. So capturing and directing the cotton economy was a major colonial priority. Roberts argues that ultimately none of the schemes to turn the Soudan into a source of cheap, high-quality cotton succeeded, in part because the integuments of the regional economy were too strong to be easily overwhelmed by the colonial state. He also suggests that this more developed regional economy in West Africa may explain the differences between the highly interventionist 'strong' colonial state in East Africa and the 'weak' colonial state in West Africa.[31] Certainly the colonial state in the Kenya highlands was 'strong' and interventionist. The farming and herding peoples its settlers came to dominate were only on the fringes of regional systems of exchange and hence more vulnerable than their economically more sophisticated counterparts in West Africa. But Zanzibar and the Swahili coast are a different story. On the coast the strong regional economy, like that of the western Soudan, made colonial domination difficult.

[30] Richard Roberts, *Two Worlds of Cotton* (Stanford: 1996).
[31] Ibid., p. 286.

The Dhow

The key to understanding the success of Zanzibar's (and much of the rest of the coast's) commercial classes in remaining independent of the state and subverting the colonial project is the dhow. From a practical perspective, dhows provided the low-cost transport that held the regional economy together. They moved goods and people in patterns that defied both the chronological and political boundaries of colonial states, allowing capital and labour to be mobilized in ways that escaped colonial control. Dhows provided a means of transport that was ideally suited to the monsoon economy. That dhows were less reliant on ports than steamers, letting them trade profitably in areas where steamers could not go or would not go, allowed marginal areas that would have withered in a steamer-centred economy to remain functional and occasionally thriving components of the western Indian Ocean's regional economy.

On a philosophical level, dhows and the sea trade they fostered struck a blow for liberty. The sea-lanes of the Indian Ocean have rarely been effectively controlled. The nineteenth and twentieth centuries have been no exception to this rule. While there were intermittent attempts at naval supervision of East African waters in the second half of the nineteenth century, these were never completely effective and dhow captains rapidly found ways of subverting them. During the twentieth century the British abandoned their attempts at patrolling the sea-lanes and tried to control the sea-lanes from the land. This worked for steamers, which are dependent on ports, which is where the regulating authorities are found, but did not succeed in bringing dhows, which are less reliant on ports, under control. The sea-lanes were free from state control and have remained that way. No matter how hard colonial and postcolonial governments have tried to suppress private economic initiative and personal freedom, dhows and the access they provide to the uncontrolled sea have undermined those efforts. As Conrad tells us, 'The spirit of liberty is on the waters.'

Two

The Dhow Trade
in Nineteenth-century Zanzibar

> Throughout the age of sail – that is, for almost the whole of history – geography had absolute power to determine the limits of what man could do at sea. By comparison, culture, ideas, individual genius, or charisma, economic forces and all other motors of history meant little. In most of our traditional explanations of what has happened in history there is too much hot air and not enough wind.
>
> Felipe Fernández-Armesto (forthcoming)

Zanzibar in the mid-nineteenth century was a boom town. A stroll down the waterfront at mid-century would reveal a harbour choked with dhows, both local and from distant parts of the Indian Ocean, sailing-ships from New England, the Sultan's fleet of small steamships, British men-of-war, fishing canoes, bum-boats, lighters, hulks, consular yachts and all the flotsam and jetsam that so many vessels might produce. Ashore we would find gangs of labourers unloading and loading lighters, *hamali* porters carrying goods to and from the custom-house, that in those days was a long low building which lay parallel to the water-front. Inside the custom-house would be merchants from Bombay, Gujerat and Cutch auctioning ivory and gum copal they have brought from the mainland, and Yankee sea captains bidding on copal or trying to hurry their own cargoes of cotton, kerosene and sundries through customs.

Just to the north of the custom-house we would find the Sultan's palace, an ice factory and the Hotel Afrique. A little to the south were the homes of the resident European merchants and consuls. Right on the beach were the O'Swald House, the John Bertram Agency and the British Consulate. A little way back from the beach was the French Consulate and the warren of narrow streets that constituted Zanzibar town.

Further to the north we would find Zanzibar Creek. Here we would see dhows loading and unloading mangrove poles brought from the mainland and destined to be incorporated into houses in Zanzibar or the Persian Gulf. Other dhows would have been dragged further up the creek so as to

*2.1 The Zanzibar waterfront painted in the mid-nineteenth century.
On the left is the custom-house with the fort behind it. Consulates and merchant
houses cover the rest of the waterfront. Under sail in the harbour are a large
sea-going* bagala *and smaller* mtepe
(Photograph courtesy Peabody Essex Museum, catalog no. 15,600)

be left high and dry when the tide was out. Local craftsmen or the dhow crews would be caulking the hulls with cotton soaked in shark oil or paying them with a mixture of beef fat and lime. Here too we would find ships' boats coming to collect water from the springs that made Zanzibar famous as a watering spot.

Back in town we might find British sailors staggering out of a grog shop, Baluchi mercenaries from the Sultan's army, raw slaves on their way to the clove plantations, the two English concubines of the Sultan's sailing master[1] or a sixteen-year-old midshipman from the barque *Elizabeth Hall* out of Salem as he chased a 'whole parcel of black girls'.[2] Zanzibar was where East Africa, the Indian Ocean and the world economy met.

A hundred years earlier the site of all this activity had been a sleepy fishing village. As late as 1834, the commander of HMS *Imogene* visited Zanzibar and reported that:

> The port of Zanzibar has little or no trade, that to Bombay consists in the export of a little gum and ivory brought from the mainland, with a few

---

[1] ZNA AA1/3, Hammerton to Aberdeen, 2 Jan. 1844. In this letter Hammerton is reporting on the population of Zanzibar. There are, he says, nineteen white residents, who are American or European traders, and the two 'English women concubines', who apparently fall into a different conceptual category than the other white residents.

[2] PEM, Log of the *Elizabeth Hall* 1851–52.

cloves, the only produce of the island, and the import trade is chiefly dates, and cloth from Muskat to make turbans. These things are sent in small country vessels which make only one voyage a year, the trade is consequently very trifling.[3]

The commander of the *Imogene* probably underestimated the amount of trade at Zanzibar in the early part of the nineteenth century. As early as 1827 Salem ships had been calling at Zanzibar and only three years after the *Imogene*'s visit there was an American Consul, one Richard Waters, resident at Zanzibar. Still, his account stands in contrast to the bustle of mid-century Zanzibar. By 1859 the trade done at Zanzibar was worth £1,664,577, putting it ahead of both Kurachi and Aden. In the same year, 80 European-style ships (i.e. steamers and sailing-ships; about 10 per cent of these were under Arab registration and were probably the Sultan's ships), representing 23,340 tons, called at Zanzibar. These ships carried MT\$967,650 (MT\$=Maria Theresa thalers, one of the preferred currencies of the western Indian Ocean) in exports to Atlantic ports, while another MT\$886,100 worth of exports, carried mostly by dhows, went to Indian Ocean ports in Arabia, British India and Cutch.[4]

While Zanzibar's entrepot trade had been pioneered by the Indian Ocean-based merchants, this mid-century explosion of trade was due to the expansion of the industrial economies of the Atlantic and their growing demand for East African produce. Zanzibar was where the Atlantic obtained East African produce, and where the Indian Ocean and Atlantic economies met and mingled.[5]

Zanzibar's rise to importance

Trade in the western Indian Ocean is an ancient phenomenon, but it was not until the later part of the eighteenth century that Zanzibar began to play a major role in that trade. As early as the second century AD Greek merchant vessels had made their way to already existing trade towns on the East African coast. The *Periplus of the Erythrean Sea* (*c.* 100 AD), a set of sailing directions that describes the coast of East Africa, indicates that this early trade was mostly in the hands of Arabs. By 1000 AD a string of city states on the coast from Sofala to Mogadishu were carrying on a busy trade in gold, ivory, slaves, wax, civet, and other African products with Arabia and India. Unguja[6] was clearly part of this Swahili world. There are ruins on the island

[3] Quoted in ZNA AA2/4, Rigby to Sir C. Wood, 1 May 1860.
[4] ZNA AA2/4, Rigby to Sir C. Wood, 1 May 1860, ZNA AA2/4, Rigby to Russell, 16 May 1860.
[5] The two best accounts of this era in Zanzibar's economic history are Frederick Cooper, *Plantation Slavery on the East Coast of Africa* (New Haven: 1977) and Abdul Sheriff, *Slaves, Spices, and Ivory in Zanzibar* (London: 1987). For political history see Norman Bennett, *A History of the Arab State of Zanzibar* (London: 1978).
[6] The term 'Zanzibar' refers to different things at different times. It can refer to either the town of Zanzibar, the polity which comprises the islands of Unguja (which is where the town of Zanzibar is situated) and Pemba, or often it is used (slightly inaccurately) to describe the island which is called Unguja by its inhabitants. I shall use the term 'Unguja' to describe

2.2 A photo, c. 1890, showing dhows beached by the custom-house, with the O'Swald house in the background. Note the presence of what appears to be a gas lamp, or possibly an electric lamp at the far end of the custom-house (Photograph courtesy Peabody Essex Museum catalog no. 6,088)

2.3 The Zanzibar waterfront in 1994, about 200 metres north of where photo 2.2 was taken

that date from this period and a mosque which is still in use which dates from the twelfth century, but it is equally clear that the island did not attain the commercial importance of a Kilwa or a Mombasa. When the Portuguese began to meddle in the affairs of the coast in the sixteenth century, it was Sofala, Kilwa, and Mombasa that attracted their attention while Zanzibar rated little comment.

During the seventeenth century, Oman began to challenge the Portuguese hegemony on the Swahili coast and in these struggles Zanzibar changed hands several times. In 1744, there was an Omani governor in Zanzibar, although, in a move that presaged later British indirect rule in Zanzibar, the Omanis allowed the Mwinyi Mkuu, Shirazi leader of Unguja, to oversee the affairs of his subjects.[7]

Although it appears that the Omanis would have preferred to make Mombasa their principal East African port, the truculence of the Mazrui, Mombasa's leading family, forced them to concentrate on Zanzibar.[8] This was a serendipitous turn of events, since Zanzibar was remarkably well suited to the needs of the trade that would dominate the East African coast in the nineteenth century.

Once in Omani hands, Zanzibar's rise to commercial prominence was the result of the combined forces of geographical advantage and legal compulsion. The most basic of the physical factors was Zanzibar's position in the monsoon system. The monsoons were the driving force of Indian Ocean commerce, affecting the rhythms of life and trade both at sea and on the land. The north-east monsoon begins late in November and blows steadily until late February. It is a hot, dry and predictable wind that lets dhows from India and Arabia sail to the East African coast with the wind at their backs. In March the winds become variable and the rains come. Then in April the south-west monsoon begins and continues until September. The south-west monsoon is more violent than the north-east, and so most ships choose to sail either as the monsoon builds or as it wanes. At the peak of the monsoon in late June and July, the seas are so rough that dhows remain in sheltered water. An interesting reflection of the respect in which the sea is held at this time of the year is the fact that in India insurers will not underwrite dhow voyages taken then.[9] In late September and early November, the winds again become variable and the short rains come to the islands.

These winds have carried ships from the north to East Africa since at least the time of the *Periplus* and, even in the mid-nineteenth century, when steam was beginning to make itself felt, still dictated the rhythms of trade on the coast and at Zanzibar. Caravans from the interior timed their departures so as to reach the coast in time to meet dhows that had come down on the north-west monsoon.[10] American vessels timed their arrival in

---

(cont.) the island when it needs to be distinguished from Pemba and 'Zanzibar' to mean either the town or the larger polity.

[7] Sheriff, *Slaves, Spices and Ivory*, p. 26.

[8] Ibid., p. 26.

[9] Interview with Sherali Haji Rashid, 16 August 1994.

[10] C.S. Nichols, *The Swahili Coast* (New York: 1971), p. 76.

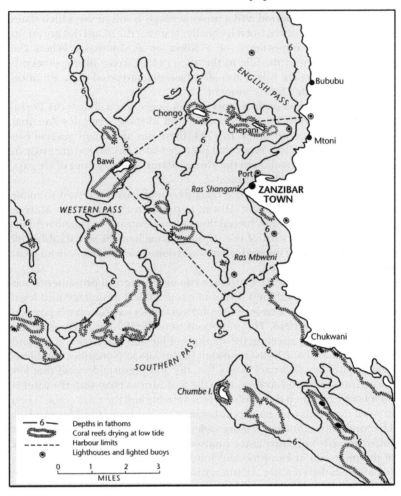

Map 2.1 Zanzibar Town
(based on B.D. Hoyle Seaports of East Africa *Kampala: 1967, p. 102)*

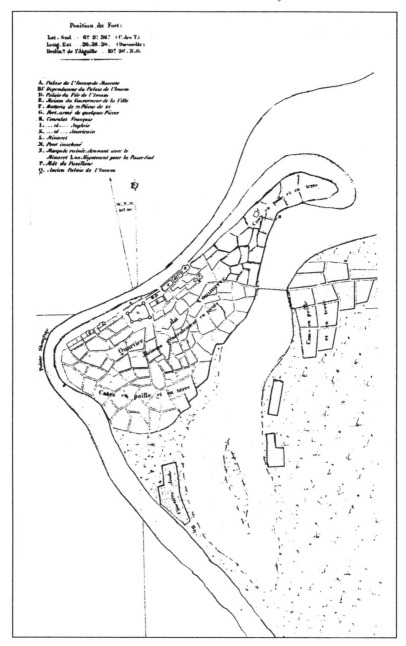

2.4 *A map of Zanzibar town made in the mid-nineteenth century. Note the creek at Funguni that was used to careen ships and has since become an area closely associated with sailors and their work (Source:* Guillain, Album, *1856, PL 9)*

Zanzibar so that they could ride the tail-end of the south-west monsoon to Arabia and then catch the beginning of the north-east monsoon for the voyage back to Zanzibar and home.[11]

The monsoons reach as far south as Madagascar, but the further south one goes the less certainty there is of getting all the way home in just one year, and so northern ships seeking produce from the south have preferred to use intermediate ports as way stations. Several of the cities of the Swahili coast owe their importance to this phenomenon. When Sofala gold was still flowing north to the Muslim world, it was obtained first in Mogadishu and later in Kilwa, since Arab *nakhoda* (dhow captains) were leery of sailing so far south. Like these earlier entrepôts, Zanzibar is squarely in the monsoon system. A vessel that comes to Zanzibar and goes no further south is certain (barring disaster) to make it home. Zanzibar is also close enough to the most productive part of the coast for coasting vessels to be able to reach the ports and roads of the mainland in either monsoon, and so Zanzibar was used to stockpile goods from the mainland throughout the year to meet the sudden burst of demand that occurred during the dhow season. It was this monsoon-driven trade that dictated the economic and cultural patterns or structures of Zanzibar life until the middle of the twentieth century.

One might ask why dhows did not simply go directly to the coast to trade and cut out the middlemen that an entrepôt trade involved. This did occur, especially in respect of the slave trade, but for the most part these smaller ports often lacked the capacity to absorb large amounts of trade goods rapidly or to provide full return cargoes for large numbers of ships. Furthermore, the mainland offers only very poor ports, as at Kilwa Kivinje, or more often open roadsteads, as at Bagamoyo.

This was not the case in Zanzibar. On the contrary, the island is almost perfectly designed to serve as an entrepôt for the East African coast. The island sits 6° south of the equator about 25 miles offshore. It is about 50 miles long and 30 wide. The east coast of the island receives the full force of wave and weather off the ocean and has been pounded into relative uniformity. A barrier reef runs from Ras Nungwi at the northern tip of the island to Ras Kizimkazi at the southern tip. Occasional breaks in the reef permit small vessels to get in and out, but in general the reef has discouraged navigation. The east coast's only indentation occurs at Chwaka Bay. Chwaka Bay is large, almost 5 miles across at its widest point. It is hemmed in to sea by coral and to land by mangrove swamps. Though Chwaka was never a significant port, dhows used it in the twentieth century, and most probably in the nineteenth century, as a place to collect mangrove poles for sale in Zanzibar town. At least one Western ship, a Spanish slaver, called there in the nineteenth century, so apparently the Bay was accessible to European shipping.[12] Chwaka Bay might well have served as a major port, except that it faces away from the African continent.

---

[11] I base this on an examination of about twenty logs of Salem ships that went to Zanzibar. Most but not all managed to time their voyages to coincide with favourable winds.

[12] ZNA AA2/4, Rigby to Wood, 28 August 1860.

2.5 Ras Shangani, the tip of the triangle that is Zanzibar town. Ships were and are moved from one side of the point to the other depending on the season

It was on the west coast of the island that maritime trade found its niche. Zanzibar town, which lies nearly on the mid-point of the western coast, is a triangular peninsula that is surrounded by a circle of small islands. Each island has its own fringe reef with the result that the area enclosed by the islands and their reefs remains fairly calm, but the gaps between the islands let ships pass through easily. The water is deep in the passes between the islands and remains deep close to shore so ships can come within a few yards of the beach at high tide.[13]

There was no wharf at Zanzibar until the 1890s. Before the wharf was built, dhows landed their cargoes by beaching themselves along the waterfront, while sailing-ships and steamers worked their cargoes with their ships' boats in the early years and later with lighters owned by the various merchant houses in town. Hoyle has suggested that dhows used both the northern and southern side of the peninsula on which the town is built to work their cargoes, using the southern side during the north-east monsoon and the northern side during the south-east monsoon.[14] This suggestion is borne out by the observations of James Christie, who wrote in 1876 that 'Zanzibar has thus ... two harbours, the one being safe to shipping during the north-east monsoon, and the other during the south-west monsoon. The two harbours are separated by the heel or angle [of the peninsula] ... but both are filled with native craft during the respective seasons.'[15] In

[13] ZNA AA1/3, Hammerton to Brown, 11 August 1844.
[14] B.S. Hoyle, *The Seaports of East Africa* (Nairobi: 1967) p. 100.
[15] Quoted in John Gray, *History of Zanzibar* (London: 1962) pp. 6–7.

contemporary Zanzibar there are still reminders of this practice – the navy shifts it gun boats from one side of the peninsula to the other as the monsoons shifts and the boats of the town's two dive shops, which load passengers from the beach, also favour one side or the other depending on the season.

As a harbour, Zanzibar had more to offer than just shelter. It had fresh water that was famous for its pleasant taste, purity and abundance. It also offered a creek just north of the town where vessels of up to 300–400 tons could be careened.[16] Nearby was a beach where mangrove poles could be landed and stored while waiting for local buyers or transshipment to the Gulf.

Thus, as a harbour and as a commercial centre, Zanzibar had much to offer to dhows and to European vessels. For European ships it offered a sheltered harbour that could be entered easily and where even heavily laden ships could draw near the shore to unload. It offered a reliable and safe water-supply and access to the African produce which the dhows brought from the mainland. For dhows it offered a safe anchorage, a good beach for landing mangrove poles (these poles were a critical cargo for monsoon dhows in both the nineteenth and twentieth centuries) and access to the world economy.

That Zanzibar became the principal entrepôt of the East African coast was not due entirely to its physical qualities. A certain amount of compulsion was involved. Trade on the Mrima coast, which lay opposite Zanzibar, was legally limited to subjects of the Sultan. This meant that American and European vessels had to trade in Zanzibar – cutting out the middlemen was not an option for them. Furthermore, there was a system of graduated duties for goods coming to Zanzibar from the coast. Goods from the more distant ports paid lower duties than those from the ports directly opposite Zanzibar. The effect of this was to encourage merchants from more distant places, who might be tempted to ship through some other entrepôt, to ship their goods through Zanzibar. Meanwhile goods from the Mrima were heavily taxed since they had no outlet other than Zanzibar. The nature and extent of this system of taxation and the trade monopoly on the mainland are not entirely understood, but for our purposes it is sufficient to know that these initiatives by the Omani rulers of Zanzibar contributed to Zanzibar's importance as an entrepôt.[17]

---

[16] ZNA AA2/4, Rigby to Wood, 1 May 1860.

[17] The intricacies of this system are explained in more detail in Sheriff, *Slaves, Spices, and Ivory,* pp. 125–6 and Nichols, *The Swahili Coast,* pp. 80–81. Phillip Northway, 'Salem and the Zanzibar–East African Trade, 1825–1845,' *Essex Institute Historical Collections,* XC (1954), p. 139, maintains that this system of differential taxation was the determining factor in Zanzibar's rise to entrepôt status, and that Majunga in Madagascar could just as easily have served the needs of the Atlantic trade had it not been for the high level of taxation there.

Zanzibar and the Indian Ocean trade

During the mid-century boom, the Atlantic and the Indian Ocean trade systems met and mingled at Zanzibar, but if we look at the very early years of the nineteenth century we see a time when the Indian Ocean trade nearly monopolized the trade of the East African coast. Nearly but, to be sure, not entirely. The French were buying slaves in Kilwa and Zanzibar on either side of 1800, and a certain amount of the African produce that made it to Bombay was transshipped to Britain. It is not my intention to suggest that the 'traditional trade' of the western Indian Ocean was static and untainted by outside influences until upset by capitalism and colonialism in the later nineteenth century. Rather, I would like to describe the position of Zanzibar in the larger structures of the Indian Ocean trade in the years before the Atlantic economy had fully penetrated. I do this in order to show how long-lived these basic patterns were and how deeply embedded in those structures the Zanzibar trade was. The patterns that had evolved around the monsoon economy by the early nineteenth century were tenacious and continued to shape life and commerce in Zanzibar well into the present century.

In the early part of the nineteenth century, Zanzibar produced little but coconut products.[18] Thus most of what was exported from Zanzibar was produce from the coast. Smee and Hardy reported in 1811 that in 'some seasons' more than one hundred large vessels from northern ports called at Zanzibar. At the time of their visit (the last month of the north-west monsoon) fifty vessels were in the harbour. These included:

> Two ships, two snows [small brigs], three ketches, 21 dows, 15 buglas, four dingeys, ten small boats of sizes, besides a variety of country boats constantly arriving and departing, and two large boats building.[19]

These ships brought a variety of goods to Zanzibar. Vessels coming from northern ports brought cloth from Cutch, iron, sugar and rice from Bombay, ghee and salt fish from Socotra and dates from the Persian Gulf. These goods were carried to the coast in the 'country boats', which came back with slaves, ivory, beeswax, tortoiseshell and 'a small quantity of drugs', to make up the return cargoes of the monsoon traders.[20]

Cloves are not in this list since the island was not yet producing them in quantity. Copal is also absent, probably the result of an oversight. Interestingly, the only other commodity that would later play an important role in the Zanzibar trade that is not listed here is mangrove poles. Either they were overlooked or at this time it was possible to obtain them closer to Arabia.

[18] This is a bit misleading in that coconut products are remarkably useful. The fronds were used to make roofs, temporary walls and sails. The nuts furnished a tasty drink, milk for cooking, meat for eating, oil and coir for rope making. The trunks provided wood that was used for furniture. Indeed, coastal society still lives by the coconut.

[19] Captain Smee and Lt. Hardy, 'Observations during a Voyage of Research on the East Coast of Africa...' in Appendix III of R.F. Burton, *Zanzibar: City, Island and Coast* (New York: 1967) Vol. II.

[20] Ibid.

The goods brought from the north for sale in Zanzibar can be divided into goods destined for use as trade goods in the interior and goods intended for the coastal market. Beads, iron, and cloth were used as trade goods. The other goods – dates, fish, ghee and grain, cannot have been intended for use in the trade with the interior on account of their low value and high bulk. Thus it would appear that there was a coastal market for dried fish, dates, ghee and other foods brought by dhows from the north.

The other inference we can make from these glimpses of the coastal trade is that there was a local dhow trade as well as a long-distance trade. If one hundred large seagoing vessels called at Zanzibar each year there must have been a significant number of smaller 'country boats' that distributed the goods brought from the north and collected the African produce that these larger vessels took home with them. It is not clear who these local trading vessels belonged to, nor is the volume of the trade apparent from the sources.

According to Nichols, the goods brought by the Arab and Indian trading vessels were worth approximately Rs.1,200,000, but it is not clear what percentage of this was goods for coastal consumption and what percentage goods for trade with the interior.[21] Presumably the value of the export goods was about the same as the value of the import goods, but again whether this was 80 per cent ivory and 20 per cent slaves is impossible to say. According to Sheriff, Bombay imported Rs.231,000 worth of ivory from East Africa in 1811–12.[22] It cannot be said for sure whether all of this ivory came from Zanzibar (some probably came from Mozambique) and it is certain that ivory also went to other Indian ports in Cutch and Gujarat, but this statistic would let us guess that ivory constituted more, probably much more, than 20 per cent of the total volume of the export trade in these early years.

For the early part of the century, the above is about all that can be said about Zanzibar's trade. Patterns of ship ownership, finance, organization and so on remain obscure. Nor is there much information available about the ships themselves or their crews. It is worth noting that, early in the nineteenth century, a discrete 'dhow trade' did not exist. Smee and Hardy mention the presence of ships they call 'dows' but they do not see them as part of a separate economy. Rather they are simply one type of vessel participating in the commerce of Zanzibar. Smee and Hardy do not give a separate tally of modern European-style ships calling at Zanzibar or describe which type of ship carries which type of cargo. The modern/traditional dichotomy was not yet part of their mental landscape, at least in respect of Indian Ocean shipping.

By the middle of the century, the western Indian Ocean was swarming with European and American ships. Their presence changed the conditions and patterns of the trade, but it also created a richer and more complete body of information about their own activities and those of their

[21] Nichols, *Swahili Coast*, p. 82.
[22] Sheriff, *Slaves, Spices, and Ivory*, p. 249.

fellow seamen on dhows than exists for the early years of the nineteenth century. It was this new presence in Zanzibar that began the process of creating a discrete and partly marginalized dhow trade.

The Atlantic economy

Before the 1830s there was little trade between the East African coast and Europe and the Americas. The French had bought slaves in the late eighteenth and early nineteenth century at Kilwa and Zanzibar, but these slaves had been taken to Bourbon and Ile de France and so remained within the Indian Ocean. The sugar they produced found its way to Europe, so in a small, indirect way they had entered the Atlantic economy. An occasional Spanish or Portuguese slaver took slaves around the Cape to South America, but the mortality rate must have been frightful, and the numbers of slaves transported this way seems to have been small.[23]

Direct trade with the Atlantic at Zanzibar was pioneered by American vessels from Salem, Massachusetts. Salem's Zanzibar trade seems to have grown out of the Mocha coffee trade. The brig *Ann*, which made one of the first voyages to Zanzibar by a Salem vessel, had initially been involved in the coffee trade from Mocha.[24] The *Ann*'s next voyage was a commercial exploration of the East African coast. In 1827 she called at Madagascar, Johanna, Ibo, Lindi, Zanzibar, Mombasa and the Benadir ports of Merka and Brava. From the log of this voyage it is apparent that *Ann*'s master had only the most rudimentary idea of where he was going and how to get there. To find his way into Zanzibar he followed a dhow. At Mombasa he met a French slaver from Bourbon. On the way from Mombasa to Lamu he had an unpleasant encounter with some Muscat dhows. After escaping and reaching Lamu he was told that the dhows that had threatened him were on their way to try to capture the French slaver he had seen at Mombasa. The log is full of detailed navigational advice and mentions that the 1824 survey of the East African coast by Owen was substantially correct. The Salem Marine Society thought the information in this log important enough for them to arrange for its publication.[25]

From this humble beginning the Atlantic trade with Zanzibar grew steadily. Salem vessels brought cargoes that heavily favoured cotton cloth, so popular that brown sheeting came to be called *merikani* in Swahili, but also included a broad variety of consumer goods. Take, for example, the cargo carried by the barque *Bhering* on an 1844 voyage to Zanzibar. The total value of this cargo was US$38,052, of which $30,000 was cotton cloth. The remaining $8,000 was made up of sugar, rosin, tobacco, earthenware, sperm-candles, cider, butter, cheese, pilot bread, pork, flour, soap and

---

[23] Paul Lovejoy, *Transitions in Slavery* (Cambridge: 1983), p. 151, put the numbers at about 10,000 for the whole East Africa to the Americas trade in the first decade of the nineteenth century, rising to 100,000 by the fourth decade, and falling to almost nothing thereafter.

[24] PEM, Log of the brig *Ann*, 1826.

[25] Ibid., 1827.

muskets.[26] That there was a market for pork is strong evidence of the growing importance of the Atlantic economy in Zanzibar. Given that salt pork is not a preferred food of either Muslims or Hindus, we must assume that the pork sold by Salem vessels in Zanzibar was bought by the growing community of Westerners there or was intended for resale as ships' stores. For return cargo the Salem ships carried ivory, gum copal and hides. Other things, such as cloves, turtle shell, ebony, orchilla weed and aloe, also show up in return cargoes, but the first three mentioned goods, especially ivory, were by far the most important. These first three items owed their importance to the emerging industries in New England. Ivory was the nineteenth century's version of plastic, gum copal was used to make varnish and hides fed the Salem area's tanning industry.

Shortly after the Americans began coming to Zanzibar they were followed by the French, the Germans and, to a lesser extent, the British. The French bought edible oils which they paid for mostly with specie. The Germans were best known for their trade in beads and cowrie shells, which they exported in vast quantities to West Africa, where cowries were used as currency.[27]

The trade with the Atlantic rapidly became the most important thing going on in Zanzibar. Seyyid Said, ruler of Oman and Zanzibar, seeing where the money was, attempted to trade directly with the Atlantic with mixed success. Eventually he confined his trade to the Indian Ocean after American merchants threatened to challenge his monopoly on the Mrima coast if he did not desist.[28]

The Atlantic challenge to the dhow trade

In 1859 the volume of Zanzibar's trade with the Atlantic had increased to the point where it was a shade larger than Zanzibar's Indian Ocean trade. Zanzibar exported MT\$967,650 to the Atlantic, while the Indian Ocean took MT\$886,100 in Zanzibari exports. Of the Indian Ocean trade, MT\$ 467,500 went to British India and MT\$313,400 to Cutch, while Arabia took only MT\$105,200.[29] Almost all of this trade moved in dhows, though how many dhows were involved is not clear. Rigby tells us that '[t]he trade with Bombay, Cutch, and Arabia, is almost entirely carried on in dhows and buttelas, of which no return is kept.'[30] Guillain, a French officer who visited the western Indian Ocean between 1847 and 1850, reported that roughly one hundred and twenty large trading vessels and one hundred smaller vessels visited Zanzibar each year from northern ports.[31] If these figures are correct, the volume of the long-distance dhow traffic coming to Zanzibar

[26] PEM, Michael Sheppard Papers, Box 1, Folder 5, 'Invoice of goods shipped on board the bark *Bhering*, 8 April 1844.
[27] Sheriff, *Slaves, Spices and Ivory*, p. 99.
[28] Ibid., p. 101.
[29] ZNA AA2/4, Rigby to Russell, 16 April 1860.
[30] ZNA AA2/4, Rigby to Wood, 1 May 1860.
[31] M. Guillain, *Documents sur l'histoire, la geographie, et le commerce de l'Afrique Orientale* (Paris: 1856), Vol. 2, pp. 357–8.

in the 1850s had more than doubled since Smee and Hardy visited in 1811, despite the rapid increase in the Atlantic world's share of the Zanzibar trade.

The volume of local shipping would also have expanded in these years. Since the local vessels were kept busy supplying the needs of both the Atlantic and the Indian Ocean economies, there must have been a dramatic growth in the local fleet. Photos and paintings from this era show the waterfront crowded with dhows, some large and obviously ocean-going, most small and probably local.[32] Guillain says that in 1848 fifty local craft were involved in the trade between Zanzibar and the coast and that these were supplemented during the monsoon by *bedans* from Muscat.[33] No record of this local fleet was kept until the 1890s when local vessels were required to register. In 1893 it was reported that 414 local craft were registered at Zanzibar 'representing a tonnage of 9,164 tons, and manned by 2,943 men and boys'.[34]

The expansion of trade that resulted from the Atlantic economy's penetration of the Zanzibar trade had a mixed effect on the dhow trade. The Atlantic economy, for example, took over the supply of the caravan trade. Cotton goods, which were the principal trade good carried by the caravans, had at the beginning of the century been supplied by dhows, which brought cloth from India. By 1859, Indian cloth imported to Zanzibar was worth MT\$242,000, while the Americans were bringing in MT\$421,850 in cloth and MT\$169,700 worth of English cloth made it to Zanzibar.[35] Thus the Indian Ocean economy's share of the cloth market had dropped to 29 per cent of the total.

The other staple of the caravan trade was beads. The beads were made in Italy and had been brought to Zanzibar by dhow from the Red Sea.[36] Once European vessels began to call regularly at Zanzibar, the Red Sea bead trade was undercut by direct shipments from Europe, and another caravan good was lost to long-distance dhows.

But the news was not all bad for the dhow trade. Dhows had been largely cut out of supplying the caravan trade, but they continued to supply the needs of coastal society. As commerce expanded in Zanzibar and on the coast in general, the number of people with the money and desire to

---

[32] See, for example, PEM, Ropes Collection 'Zanzibar: Battery and house of Mess. Wm. O'Swald & Co.', which shows a cluster of beached ships, and a painting of the Zanzibar waterfront, also at the PEM, bearing the number 15,600.

[33] Guillain, *Documents*, Vol. 2, p. 357.

[34] ZNA BA110/1, *Diplomatic and Consular Reports on Trade and Finance: Zanzibar, Report for the Year 1893*, p. 8.

[35] ZNA AA2/4, Rigby to Russell, 16 May 1860. For an account of the role of Omani-produced textiles and their role in the regional economy see, M. Reda Bhacker, *Trade and Empire in Muscat and Zanzibar* (London: 1992), pp.132–5. Bhacker says that the Omani export textile industry flourished during this period, riding the wave of the regional economy's expansion.

[36] Richard F. Burton, *The Lake Regions of Central Africa* (New York: 1961), Vol. 2, pp. 390–94. The appendix of this volume goes on in obsessive, Burtonian detail about the different types of beads used in the caravan trade and exactly how much each type was worth in different parts of the caravan route.

consume Arabian and Indian goods increased. Thus what long-distance dhows lost in the cloth and bead markets must have been made up in dates, salt, dried fish, dyes, drugs, coffee and other consumables. Doubtless there was less profit to be made in the dried-fish business than in cloth, but it cannot have been all that bad or the volume of the dhow trade would not have doubled in 45 years.[37]

More significant than the question of whether dried fish was more or less profitable than Surat cloth is the direction in which the dhow economy was being pushed. At the beginning of the century dhows had dominated the Zanzibar trade. By mid-century the long-distance trade was already becoming marginalized. Although Indian dhows continued to supply some 30 per cent of the cloth market, for the most part the dhow trade had become a supporting player.[38] The dhow trade supplied the needs and wants of Zanzibar and the coast, it brought essential goods from Africa to Arabia and it continued to ferry goods wanted by the Atlantic economy to Zanzibar from the East African coast. While dhows were not able to hold on to their dominant position during the boom and certainly relinquished the near monopoly they had at the beginning of the century, the overall volume of dhow traffic increased during the course of the great expansion of the mid-nineteenth century.

The dhow economy gave ground to the Atlantic economy in the first half of the nineteenth century, but it was a tactical retreat, not a rout. The position it fell back on was a position of strength. The markets that dhows controlled in 1860 were, with some exceptions, markets they would still control in 1960. Dhows and their owners may have been pushed to the margins of the world economy, but they clung to their position on the edge with remarkable tenacity.

The emergence and prosperity of the Atlantic trade in Zanzibar was a critical first step in the creation of the dhow trade as a discrete entity seperate from the general trade of Zanzibar. While dhows remained an essential component of the Indian Ocean trade and the collection of goods for the Atlantic trade, by 1860 dhows were begining to carry cargoes that were different from those of the Atlantic vessels, to ply different routes, and to appear on British trade reports as 'country craft'. While there was still a great deal of interpenetration between the Atlantic economy and the dhow economy, the first steps towards the separation of the two trades and the creation of a 'dhow trade' were under way.

The Dhow trade *c*.1860

Zanzibar's dhow trade in the 1860s comprised two categories: the monsoon trade, which brought Indian and Arabian goods to Zanzibar and

---

[37] For the changing nature of dhow cargoes in the 1860s, see ZNA AA12/8, Steart to Consulate, Zanzibar, 4 September 1862, ZNA AA 7/3, Proceedings of the Zanzibar Vice Admiralty Court, 14 April 1869 and 1 May 1869, and various notes of protest in ZNA AA 12/13, although these last only reflect insured cargoes.

[38] ZNA AA2/4, Rigby to Russell, 16 May 1860.

carried African goods back to India and Arabia, and the local trade, which carried goods from Zanzibar to the coast and vice versa. This is a somewhat arbitrary division, since monsoon dhows usually engaged in local trade while they waited for the monsoon to change and local vessels occasionally switched roles and made monsoon voyages. Another arbitrary aspect of this division is that the further north on the coast you go, the more monsoonal the trade became. Zanzibar to Mombasa was possible in almost any state of the monsoon, Zanzibar to Lamu was more monsoon-dependent and dhows from Somalia's Benedir coast were part of the seasonal influx of dhows in Zanzibar.

The principal differences between the two categories of dhows were size, style and the residence of the owner. Most of the owners of the long-distance dhows lived in the northern ports rather than in Zanzibar, while the owners of the local vessels lived in Zanzibar and often owned their coasting vessels to facilitate their own trade. The vessels preferred for local trade were smaller. Using the 1893 statistics on the local trading boats, we find that the average tonnage for a local vessel was 22 tons. Vessels in the long-distance trade were usually in the 50 to 150 ton range and sometimes reached 350 tons.[39]

Exceptions to these generalizations abound. Indian merchants in Zanzibar would occasionally dispatch one of their vessels to Bombay or Cutch. An anti-slave-trade patrol that descended on the Somali port of Brava in 1869 captured a dhow that belonged to the Sultan of Zanzibar's sister. Thus some Zanzibar-based owners, both Indian and Arab, were involved in monsoon trade. Likewise, the size of these vessels varied. Some rather large vessels were used in the local trade, especially to carry slaves, and some tiny vessels, really boats rather than ships, made the voyage from Arabia to Zanzibar.[40]

This brings us to the question of ship types. 'Dhow' is an English word that has come to be used to describe the various types of 'native vessels' used in the western Indian Ocean. It is not used either by Arabic or Swahili speakers to describe indigenous craft as a group. In Arabic *sambuk* is sometimes used for this purpose, but only because *sambuks* are such a common type of vessel. At the beginning of the nineteenth century 'dow' was used to describe a particular type of sailing craft, possibly the *betil* (see Smee and Hardy quotation above). By the second half of the nineteenth century the term 'dhow' was a generic term for any 'traditional' East African, Arab or Indian ship. The changing use of this term appears to be related to changing ideas about the differences between modern shipping and traditional shipping.

---

[39] ZNA BA110/1, *Diplomatic and Consular Reports on Trade and Finance, Report for the Year 1893*, p. 8, Guillain, *Documents*, Vol. 2, p. 357, and P.H. Colomb, *Slave Catching in the Indian Ocean* (London: 1873), p. 35.

[40] ZNA AA1/7, Lt. Cameron to Commander of HMS *Star*, 9 Aug. 1869, enclosed in Commander of HMS *Star* to Heath, 10 January 1870. Guillain, *Documents*, Vol. 2, p. 357, mentions that *bedans* as small as 12 tons (probably 20 or fewer feet long) made the annual voyage from the Gulf to Zanzibar.

2.6 and 2.7 *Two plates made by the Guillain expedition. Compared to the beautiful etchings that make up most of the images produced by Guillain's expedition, these paintings of dhows are almost cartoonish. In plate 2.6 there are vessels that include*

elements of the bagala *and the* ganja. *The vessel in the middle of page 38
looks like a* dau la mtepe. *The top boat on page 39 appears to be a bedan, the
second from the bottom in the same plate appears to be an* mtepe

In the long-distance trade *bagala* is the most often-encountered ship type. *Bagalas* and a few other closely related types seem to have constituted the bulk of the ships engaged in the monsoon trade. The *bagala's* design may derive from the caravels that brought the Portuguese to the Indian Ocean. They carried two and sometimes three forward-raking masts. Atop each mast was a large spar, from which hung a triangular sail. Virtually all the Indian Ocean craft we shall be considering here carried this type of sail, which is called a lateen sail. In the West ships are described by their rig. Since all dhows have the lateen rig, their hulls rather than their rigs are used to differentiate them. A high stern with five elaborately decorated windows in it distinguishes the *bagala.*[41]

Related to the *bagala* are the *kotia* and *ganja.* These are for all practical purposes the same as a *bagala* except for variations in decorations, and the number of windows in the stern. Villiers considers them to be more Indian than Arab and because of their less elaborate decoration, they were a bit cheaper to make.

Comparable to the *bagala* in popularity was the *betil.* The *betil,* unlike the *bagala,* was double-ended and was elaborately decorated at both bow and stern. One naval officer who did several tours on the anti-slavery patrol claimed that the *betil* was the largest of the dhows.[42] Not much is known about *betils* compared with some of the other types of dhow since they did not survive in large numbers into the twentieth century and few pictures have survived.

The *bedan* is a smaller boat, often used for fishing in the Gulf but also used for long-distance trade. The design is unusual in that the hull is shearless (i.e. its cross-section is shaped more like a V than a U) and the rudder is controlled by means of an elaborate system of ropes and pulleys, rather than a tiller. The mast too is different from most of the masts seen on dhows since it is upright rather than forward-raking. Despite its unusual mast, it carries a lateen rig.

At some point in the second half of the nineteenth century the *betil* and to a lesser extent, the *bagala* began to be replaced by the *boom* and the *sambuk.* Since neither of these latter were elaborately decorated, they were cheaper to build. Moreover, the *boom* required less timber per ton than the *bagala,* allowing for further savings. Nineteenth century sources never mention the *boom,* but by 1939 the *boom* had completely replaced the *bagala* in Kuwait and the *sambuk* was doing likewise in Oman.[43]

There is no collection of shipping returns on which this list is based. My assertion that these were the types of vessels used in the long-distance trade is based on their frequent mention by European observers of the area and the prevalence of these types of ships in Zanzibar's vice-admiralty court adjudications. It is not always clear that the European observers knew all

---

[41] Descriptions of the different types of dhows used in the nineteenth century are taken, unless otherwise noted, from Allan Villiers, *Sons of Sinbad* (New York: 1969), pp. 395–7.

[42] G.L. Sullivan, *Dhow Chasing in Zanzibar Waters* (London: 1873), p. 102.

[43] Villiers, *Sons of Sinbad,* p. 396.

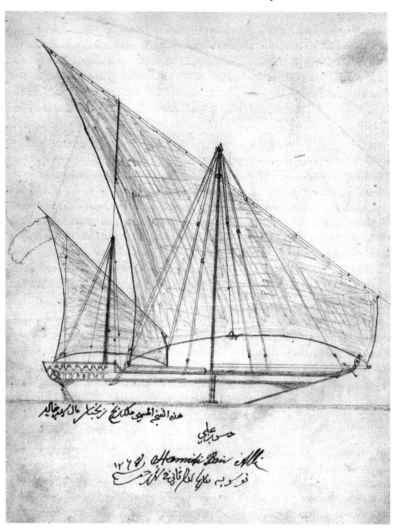

*2.8 A sketch from the logbook of the 'William Schroder' c. 1847 shows a bagala.
Note the high and decorated stern. This is a much more sympathetic rendering of a
dhow than the contemporaneous paintings in 2.6 and 2.7
(Photograph courtesy Peabody Essex Museum, catalog no. 30,165)*

that much about dhows. Even in the case of the vice-admiralty court cases, the identification of the captured dhow was made by the officers who captured it, who were not always that clear on the distinctions between the various types themselves.

As for the more social side of the monsoon dhows, there is not too much we can say about them. Their crews were probably mostly 'Arabs', in the sense that they resided in the Gulf or southern Arabia, but it is just as probable that their crews included sailors of East African extraction. Naval vessels searching dhows for slaves often had trouble distinguishing between slaves and crewmen of African appearance, and East African slaves had served as sailors in the Arab world since at least the sixteenth century.[44] It also seems that most of the captains or *nakhodas* did not own their own vessels, although some did.

Few accounts of voyages by vessels engaged in the long-distance trade in the nineteenth century exist. The closest thing to such an account comes from depositions made at the vice-admiralty court in Zanzibar. One such account is that of Hammad bin Sahel, the *nakhoda* of a *bedan* that was captured and burned by boats of the HMS *Nymphe* in 1869. The *bedan* belonged to Salim bin Seif of Sur in Oman and had left Sur two years before its capture with a load of dried fish. These were sold in Zanzibar and the resulting MT$100 profit sent to the owner in Sur. Then when the monsoon changed, he carried a load of grain to Socotra, where he bought more dried fish and some ghee. These were sold at Zanzibar. At a loose end in Zanzibar while they waited for the monsoon to shift, they decided to go fishing. This was not a good idea, since it was while fishing that they were found by the *Nymphe*'s boats, seized and burned. His crew consisted of fourteen men, of whom four were blacks and spoke little Arabic. The case was decided in his favour, and the *Nymphe* was ordered to pay MT$709 as compensation for his lost bedan.[45]

From this rare account of a long-distance trading voyage there is much we can learn. Hammad's *bedan* was engaged in a mixture of trade on the ship's account, as when it carried dried fish, and the carriage of cargo for freight charges, as when they carried the grain to Socotra. It also looks as if Hammad's obligations to his owner were limited. He mentions having sent the proceeds of the sale of the first load of dried fish to his owner, but there is no mention of what happened to the $80 he made by carrying the grain to Socotra. Possibly this was his to keep and divide with the crew. Most probably, any proceeds of the fishing voyage would also have been theirs to keep. Also of interest is the make-up of his crew and the value of his vessel. The boat was a *bedan*, 86 feet long and 176 tons. This was big for a *bedan*, and it had a small crew for so large a vessel.

---

[44] Ralph Austen, 'From the Atlantic to the Indian Ocean: European Abolition, the African Slave Trade, and Asian Economic Structures,' in David Eltis and James Walvin (eds), *The Abolition of the Atlantic Slave Trade* (Madison, WI: 1981) pp. 134–5, has a table that lists references to the presence of East African slaves in the Gulf shipping and pearling industries from 1200 to 1907.

[45] ZNA AA7/3, Proceedings of the Zanzibar Vice Admiralty Court, 1 May 1869.

It is hard to say how representative this voyage was, since there is so little information of this type available. It is a pity that more *nakhodas* did not come and argue their cases at the vice-admiralty court, since those who did often had a fairly easy time challenging the case against them and because they would have created a broader pool of information on which historians of the future could have drawn.

As for how these vessels were handled at sea, there is again not too much we can say. What little we know comes from the experience of Horace Putnam, a sailor from Salem who left his ship at Nossi-be in 1847 and rode a dhow to Majunga in Madagascar. The dhow was somewhere between 150 and 200 tons. Dhows this size carried crews of twenty to sixty men, Putnam says. He also asserted that one Yankee was worth four Arab sailors, noticing, in effect, that the more sophisticated rigging carried by American and European ships allowed them to carry fewer men per ton of ship.

The dhow had a compass on board, but no charts or other navigational equipment. They found their way by going from one known landmark to the next. If they were blown off course, they had to hunt around until they found a known landmark to get their bearings. He also indicates that they tried to avoid sailing at night, and only did so when he offered to help them stay on course. He reports that both the *nakhoda* and the men took their turn at the wheel, a practice that seemed dangerously democratic to him. They made Majunga in three days. It was a small world even in 1847. At Majunga he met his brother, apparently unexpectedly, who had just arrived on another Salem ship, the *Emily Wilder*. In general, he was impressed by the sailing qualities of the dhow, but pointed out that they cannot come about and must wear round instead.[46]

This brings us to some of the technological disadvantages the dhow sailor laboured under. First there were the limitations of the lateen rig. Well-suited to a following wind, the lateen rig does poorly when going to windward. Because the yard (the wooden pole to which the leading edge of the sail is attached) must be shifted from one side of the mast to the other every time a lateen-rigged vessel changes tack, it cannot come about (turn up into and across the wind) like a square-rigged or fore-and-aft-rigged boat. Instead it must fall off the wind and, while its stern is to the wind, manoeuvre the yard to the other side of the mast. This is called wearing round and requires that the ship make a little downwind loop. If this were not done and a lateen-rigged ship were to try to come about, the yard and the sail with it would be trapped on the windward side of the mast. In a strong wind this could be disastrous. Thus a lateen-rigged vessel loses ground every time it changes tack. This is a minor consideration in the open ocean where a boat might change tack once or twice a day but close to land with an onshore wind it can make a threatening situation a desperate one, since the ground lost in changing tack might be enough to put the vessel aground. The lateen rig also helps to explain the large crews that dhows carried compared with comparably sized European vessels. Since lateen rigged vessels carry one

[46] PEM, Log of the barque *William Schroder*, 1847.

large sail per mast rather than several smaller sails per mast, the size and weight of the main yard is often tremendous. This weight and the poor quality of the tackle used to handle it mean that large crews are necessary to raise the yard. An observer in the 1930s reported that, on a 150 ton Kuwaiti boom, it took sixty men 30 minutes of brutally hard work to raise the main yard.[47]

The second area of technological disadvantage that Putnam mentions is navigation. At one time Arab mariners had had the equipment and knowledge to find latitude, and open sea voyages had been common. When Vasco da Gama first arrived in East Africa *en route* to India, he was able to find a pilot who took him directly to Calicut. A crude sort of quadrant, called a *kamal*, allowed navigators to find latitude. It consisted of a collection of rods, each tied to a piece of cord. The cord was held at the observer's eye and the stick was held as far from the face as the string would allow. The bottom edge was held at the horizon and the top edge on the pole star. Each string and stick combination represented the latitude of a known port. Thus a sailor trying to make Bombay from east Africa would sail East and adjust his course northward if the pole star was below the top of his Bombay stick and southward if it was above.[48]

By the nineteenth century this device was no longer in use. Indian dhows, however, continued to make open sea voyages, probably because they had better access to European navigational equipment and training, and in the twentieth century, Arab *nakhodas* who wanted to make an open sea voyage would hire an Indian navigator.[49]

According to Putnam, the dhow he sailed on had a compass. He does not elaborate on this, but if the nineteenth-century practice was the same in the twentieth century, then these compasses were probably salvaged from European ships. Their accuracy was probably somewhat suspect. According to Alan Villiers, who sailed on a dhow in the 1930s, no attempt was made to correct for compass deviation caused by iron in the ship or the difference between magnetic and true north. The compass was used more as a general guide to keep the ship on a precise heading.[50]

Despite these disadvantages the vessels used in the long-distance trade were adequate for their intended purpose. That it was difficult to tack in them did not make that much difference since they usually sailed with the wind. It should also be noted that European sailing-ships, which were easier to handle while sailing to windward, rarely did so for long periods of time. Sailors making the Atlantic crossing knew that by changing their latitude they could usually find a tail wind for both the outward and return voyage. The difference in the Indian Ocean was that it was not necessary to venture far from land to find a favourable wind. It was just a question of waiting until the monsoon became favourable.

---

[47] Villiers, *Sons of Sinbad*, pp. 209–10.
[48] K.N. Chaudhuri, *Trade and Civilization in the Indian Ocean* (Cambridge: 1985), p. 134.
[49] Villiers, *Sons of Sinbad*, p. 186.
[50] Ibid., pp. 270, 398.

The other disadvantage of the lateen rig – that it is hard to handle due to the huge sails and heavy yards – was less of a disadvantage in the western Indian Ocean than it might have been elsewhere. During the sailing season the winds and seas are fairly predictable and steady, and so the sort of rapid adjustments to the sails which were commonplace in European vessels sailing the much rougher North Atlantic were rarely necessary.

The dhow's biggest advantage was its cheapness of construction. They were built mostly of teak, which was brought from India to the Gulf for the construction of Arab boats. Teak is an oily wood that is ideal for boat making since it resists the ravages of the salt-water environment better than most others. Because they were not built to take the kind of abuse that vessels intended for use on the Atlantic were, they did not need the massive timbers that their European competitors did, and so used less wood in their construction. The hull was held together with nails, which, at least in the early part of the twentieth century, were imported from India to the Gulf. The planking was carvel and caulked with cotton soaked in shark oil. The inside of the hull was also painted with shark oil to help waterproof and preserve the wood. The outside of the hull was payed with a mixture of lime and beef fat, to help keep the shipworms out. The cordage was usually made of coconut coir, the sails of Indian cotton. Other than the compasses, which were of European manufacture, the material used to build dhows derived entirely from the western Indian Ocean and was made just sturdy enough for the relatively benign waters in which they sailed.[51]

While our knowledge of the long-distance trade is based on little glimpses afforded by the memories of visitors or the court cases of sailors unfortunate enough to have run foul of the Royal Navy, some statistical records for the local trade exist. The British Consuls in Zanzibar kept records about the movement of dhows belonging to British subjects. The British had decided that the Indians of Zanzibar were British subjects. The Indians in Zanzibar had other ideas about this, and in fact many of Zanzibar's Indian residents were from Cutch or Muscat and so, strictly speaking, were not British subjects, but British opinion and power prevailed.[52] A by-product of this unwelcome protection granted to Zanzibar's Indians was that the consulate kept a record of at least some of the voyages made by their ships.[53] The list begins in August 1863 and continues for 350 entries until May of 1867. The list simply exists. There is no accompanying documentation that explains why it was started or why it stopped. Nor is it clear whether it was intended to record all or just some of the voyages. And of course it only tells about the activities of the Indians and excludes other Zanzibaris who were no doubt also engaged in local trade.

What information the list contains varies with time. Different clerks seem to have had different ideas about what types of information were worth

[51] Interview with Fundi Ali, 4 April 1994. Villiers, *Sons of Sinbad*, pp. 397–400.

[52] Bhacker, *Trade and Empire*, p. 196, sees the British insistence that Cutchis were 'British Indians' as part of a larger effort to undermine Omani power by directing Zanzibari trade away from Oman towards British India.

[53] ZNA AA2/4, 'Returns of British Shipping at Port of Zanzibar,' no date.

2.9 *Stitching on a sewn boat. Shihr, Yemen, 1997*

2.10 Sewn boats on the beach at Shihr, Yemen, 1997.
Note the oculus, a small charm that hangs from the bow

recording. Also, no two clerks seem to have agreed on how to spell anybody's names. The list offers a very narrow and impressionistic window on the local dhow trade, but it is the only window we have.

The local trade as carried on by Zanzibar Indians in the 1860s used the same ship types that are mentioned in the long-distance trade and a few additional types as well. *Bagalas, betils, ganjas* and *bedans* are all mentioned in the list. Two other types that are not mentioned in the long-distance trade are also present. These are the *mashua* and the *mtepe* or *dau la mtepe*.[54] The *mashua* is a small boat, more or less a smaller version of the *jahazis* that now predominate in East African waters. It has a nearly vertical stem and a transom stern. The *mashua* appeared to represent about one-third of the local (Indian) dhow fleet and was used exclusively for trips between Zanzibar and the mainland or Pemba.

The second type, the *mtepe*, appears in the list as 'dhow'. The only plausible explanation of this, since every other major hull type is represented in the list, is that 'dau' was being transcribed as 'dhow'. The *mtepe* is one of the more interesting types of vessel used in East Africa. It is especially associated with the East African coast. They are considered to be one of the icons of Swahili culture and by the twentieth century were used only in the Lamu archipelago. The *mtepe* was a sort of living fossil. It retained qualities that had once been common in Indian Ocean craft, but had mostly died out by the nineteenth century.

Foremost among these anachronisms was the fact that they were built without nails; instead, the double-ended hulls were sewn with leather or cord. Prior to 1500 most western Indian Ocean craft were made in this way, but the arrival of the Portuguese in ships with nailed hulls caused a rapid abandonment of this technology. The hulls were designed to flex and move with the sea rather than to be rigid and to resist the sea. The flexing made them leak enough for their crews to include enough young boys to bail full-time. At least one Royal Navy vessel lost a captured *mtepe* when it was left overnight with no one on board to bail.[55] Other odd features of the *mtepe* were its sail, which was made square rather than lateen like most other Indian Ocean craft, and even odder was the fact that it was made from palm matting rather than cloth. The decking was made by thatching over part of the hull, a technique not seen on Arab or Indian ships, but still seen on the Zanzibar *jahazi*. Its final odd characteristic was that it was made, at least in Lamu in the twentieth century, from mangrove wood. Everything, from the mast to the planking and even the plugs that were driven into the holes the lashings passed through, was fashioned from mangrove wood. The result was an inexpensive, shallow-draught and entirely locally produced craft.[56] These characteristics, as we shall see in later chapters,

---

[54] The *mtepe* and *dau la mtepe* are actually two different craft but they are so often confused that it is not likely that a clerk at the consulate would bother to distinguish between the two. For our purposes they can be conflated since they were used in quite similar ways.

[55] ZNA AA12/8, Wilson to Secretary of the Admiralty, 10 November 1861.

[56] E.B. Martin and C. Martin, *Cargoes of the East* (London: 1978) p. 94, and A.H.J. Prins, 'The *Mtepe* of Lamu, Mombasa, and the Zanzibar Sea,' *Paideuma,* 28 (1982).

2.11 A photo taken in the 1890s at Funguni in Zanzibar. It shows an mtepe
*either loading or unloading a cargo of mangrove poles. Visible on the prow are the
oculus, the* ndevu *or beard of grass fibre, and three small flag poles.
On top of the thatched deck house is the matting sail. Note other boats
and sheds holding mangrove poles in the background
(Photograph courtesy Peabody Essex Museum, catalog no. 30,104)*

made the *mtepe* an ideal boat for working the mangrove swamps and a
handy slave-smuggling boat.

The uses to which the owners of the local fleet put their vessels is
interesting because the patterns of ownership, the origins of the crews and
the routes sailed persisted into the second half of the twentieth century
and in some respects are still with us. Zanzibar's Indian shipowners came
from a broad band of the economic spectrum. One name that figures
prominently in the list is Jairam Sewji. Jairam Sewji and his descendants
farmed the customs at Zanzibar for most of the nineteenth century and in
his time Jairam was the wealthiest of Zanzibar's merchants. Over the three-
year period covered by the records, Jairam's ships made eighteen recorded
voyages. The orthography of the list is so variable that it is hard to say to say
how many different vessels were in his fleet, but it looks as if it numbered
about four or five. On coastal duty he had the *Oshiar Kutch*, a *betil*, which in
1864 made two or possibly three voyages to the coast. Also in 1864, three
other ships belonging to Jairam were sent to the East African coast. Also in
his fleet was a *ganja* called *Sajee* which went to India once a year.

Other prominent dhow owners were Ibrahim Waljee, who was more involved in the Arabian trade, and Damoder Munjee. Between 1864 and 1866 Ibrahim Waljee sent eight ships to southern Arabia and seven to the coast or Pemba. Damoder Munjee seems to have owned around six or seven vessels. These mostly plied the waters between the coast and Zanzibar, but, like Jairam Sewji, he sent one vessel a year to India.

But the big men who owned these large fleets and dispatched an annual ship to India are the exception rather than the rule. The average Zanzibar Indian dhow owner seems to have owned just one or two vessels and most of them went to the East African coast or Pemba.

While the vessels were owned by Indian merchants, the crews were virtually all locally recruited. The list of *nakhodas'* names is rich in Jumas, Hamisis and Alis, Swahili or Arab names it would seem. Interestingly, vessels bound for Arabia or India are more likely to feature a *nakhoda* whose name includes a patronym, i.e. Ali bin Said rather than simply Ali, which is how the *nakhodas* bound for the coast are described. In the final twenty entries of the list the ethnicity of the crewmen is described as is their status as free men. In almost every case the crews are composed of 'people of Tumbaat' or just 'Tumbaat'. Tumbatu is an island just off the north west of Zanzibar. Today it still furnishes a high percentage of the crews of local dhows, and it is interesting that the Tumbatu have dominated the business for so long. The exception to this Tumbatu domination is in vessels bound for Arabia or India. In the case of Ibrahim Waljee's 'Munsoor' which sailed for the Persian Gulf in late April of 1867, the *nakhoda* was Salim bin Rashid and his crew consisted not of Tumbatu but of '5 free Arabs, 16 black Arabs'. Three days later the 'Fullel Khan' which belonged to Ebjee Sewjee set out for Bombay under the command of Raja (presumably Indian) with a crew of eleven Cutchis.

Many of the crewmen on the local dhows with owners who were not British subjects were probably slaves. In 1846 Captain Cogan, an English friend of Seyyid Said's, had been granted the right to mine the guano on an uninhabited island south of Zanzibar. He wanted to hire local sailors to mine and transport the guano. Hammerton, the Britsh consul in Zanzibar, refused him permission to do this on the grounds that there were no free sailors in Zanzibar and Cogan as an Englishman could not legally hire slaves.[57]

British Indians were also forbidden to engage slaves, and it is noteworthy that the our list of dhow activity by British Indians always specifies that the crews were free. That this was necessary would indicate that at least some sailors were slaves. Most of the slaves involved in this type of work belonged to a category of slave called 'vibarua'.[58] These were slaves that often did unsupervised work for wages, a portion of which they turned over to their owners. Two slave crewmen on a dhow captured by the HMS 'Daphne' in 1873 were each paid a dollar per voyage. It is not clear what portion of this they turned over to their masters.[59]

[57] ZNA AA1/3, Hammerton to Aberdeen, 10 March 1846.
[58] Cooper, *Plantation Slavery*, p. 186, Burton, *Zanzibar*, p. 467.
[59] ZNA AA1/2, Kirk to Foreign Office, 1 Sept. 1873. See also Cooper, *Plantation Slavery*, p. 188.

2.12 and 2.13 Two jahazis photographed near Lamu, Kenya in 2000. These were and are the standard vessels used in the coastal trade in the twentieth and twenty-first centuries

How different the situation would have been for dhows belonging to Zanzibaris who were not British subjects is hard to say, since the Sultan's governments were less interested in record keeping than the British Consulate. What glimpses we have of the Zanzibari local trade come from slave captures, and with these it is often difficult to tell whether the vessel in question is locally owned or a monsoon dhow that was captured in local waters. In all likelihood dhows flying the Sultan's flag were very similar to local dhows flying British colours. They used similar technology, had similar crews (although they were allowed to carry slave crews for a few more years than British dhows) and carried similar cargoes.

The cargoes

Perhaps the best way of getting a feel for the manner in which dhows participated in Zanzibar's mid-nineteenth-century economy is to look at the specific cargoes they carried. Doing this will help shed light on the complex way in which dhows were able to participate in the Atlantic economy and the Indian Ocean economy, the local trade and the long-distance trade, the 'legitimate' trade and the 'illegitimate' trade.

Let us begin by looking at the cargoes brought to Zanzibar by the monsoon dhows. From Arabia the monsoon dhows brought dried fish, salt, ghee, Muscat cloth, mats, livestock, coffee, dates, shark oil and passengers. From India came furniture, salt, rice, onions, Surat cloth and passengers. And, finally, from Somalia came hides and oil-seeds.

Virtually all the imports from Arabia were consumed in Zanzibar or on the coast and all were basic goods – not necessities perhaps, but not luxuries. It is not possible to say in what quantities these goods came to Zanzibar from Arabia, but some of the goods are mentioned so often that it is safe to assume that they were a significant part of the trade. Of these commodities, dried fish is one of the more interesting. While coffee and dates may have been minor luxuries, dried fish was mostly consumed by the poor.[60]

At first glance, bringing dried fish all the way from Arabia to East Africa has a sort of coals-to-Newcastle quality to it. Fish are not exactly in short supply in East African waters, and shark, which constituted the bulk of the dried fish that made it to East Africa, are not uncommon. None the less, dried fish from Arabia was a staple in Zanzibar until the mid-1960s. That this trade was economically viable was probably due to the ideal environment offered by southern Arabia for fish drying, the fact that the humidity of the East African coast makes drying large fish a bit more difficult and, probably most importantly, that tastes acquired in Arabia were retained by emigrants from there and probably spread to indigenous coastal East Africans.[61]

---

[60] Burton, *Zanzibar*, Vol. 1, p. 104.
[61] Even today market towns in the interior of Oman sell dried shark to the bedouin, so even Arabs who have never seen the sea may have a taste for the 'goût of Zanzibar'.

Fish, and shark in particular, were plentiful off the southern Arabian coast. J.F. Osgood, who travelled to Muscat in the 1850s, observed that the local fishing fleet ranged from bedans of up to 50 tons down to catamarans made from three or four logs lashed together and paddled by a single fisherman whose feet dangled over the sides. Most of the fishermen specialized in catching shark, the flesh of which was cut into strips and dried, the livers were rendered for oil and the fins were sent to China.[62] Doubtless it was easy to dry shark in the hot, dry climate, and the salt-pans and marshes would have made salt plentiful and cheap. Thus the Arabian fishing industry provided the dhow trade with two important commodities. One was dried shark, for which there was a mass demand in East Africa. The other was shark oil, which was used to waterproof the timbers in dhows and was an important export to East Africa.

The islands off the southern coast of Arabia also produced dried fish. Socotra, as we have seen from the voyage of Hammad bin Sahel, which was described above, was a source of dried fish for export. Southbound dhows also stopped at the Kuria Muria Islands, which lie off the south-western coast of Oman, to buy fish. Here fishing was the only business. The Kuria Muria Islands were so desolate that all of their inhabitants, human as well as bovine, lived on fish. This apparently gave the milk a distinctive flavour.[63]

Both shark oil and dried shark are pungent substances. Once while visiting a dhow yard, trying to show off my knowledge of dhow construction, I asked a man who was daubing a clear gooey substance on the inside of a dhow if he was using shark oil. He informed me that it was varnish and, had it been shark oil, I would not have been standing close enough to him to ask such a foolish question. As for the odoriferousness of dried shark, we have the testimony of a colonial officer stationed in Pemba at the turn of the century. Commenting that there must be a shortage of fish in Pemba waters to explain the large quantities of dried shark that are imported from the Gulf, he offered this aside:

> I may remark, incidentally, that until one has happened to find oneself close to leeward of a dhow laden with dried shark one has yet to learn the full significance of the word 'stench,' and the fact that men survive a voyage from the Persian Gulf to these latitudes in a dhow laden with that inexpressibly foetid commodity constitutes an impressive object lesson as to the limits of endurance latent in the human organism.[64]

I include this mostly because it is funny, but also because it offers some insight into the harshness of life on board a dhow. As we shall see later, when given the opportunity to lead easier, though less romantic, lives, dhow sailors jumped at the opportunity. And surely the grimness of some of their cargoes contributed to their willingness to abandon the sailor's life.

[62] John Felt Osgood, *Notes of Travel* (Salem: 1854) p. 56.
[63] ZNA AA2/1, Fremantle to Clarendon, 18 July 1854.
[64] ZNA BA110/3, *Africa: Diplomatic and Consular Reports; Report on the Island of Pemba for the year 1900*, p. 21.

2.14 A shark fishing boat in Shihr, Yemen

2.15 Two boys display the result of a shark fishing trip in Shihr, Yemen

2.16 The island in the harbour at Aden where dried shark was stored for export

Dates from Oman and coffee from Mocha were also common dhow cargoes. Dates and coffee are not essentials, but they go a long way towards making life more pleasant. Since they are so important a part of life in southern Arabia, it seems likely that there was a steadily increasing demand for them in the nineteenth century as immigrants from Oman and the Hadhramaut came in increasing numbers to East Africa.

The types of products that came from India were a bit different from those that came from Arabia. The cloth that came from India was intended to feed the caravan trade, while the cloth that came from Muscat was intended for use on the coast (it was mostly used for making the tightly wrapped turbans worn by Omani men of substance). While the Indians had lost a major portion of the cloth market to American cottons, they used some ingenious methods to try to recapture their share of the market. Beginning around 1880, Indian merchants began to import an imitation of the brown sheetings that were made in the USA. These American sheetings, known in Swahili as *merikani*, were the staple of the caravan trade. Each was sold in a bolt 30 yards long with 30 folds and stamped with a '30'. In India some enterprising cotton manufacturer began to produce brown sheetings with 30 folds, and the '30' stamped on them, but with only 27 yards of cloth. How successful this was is hard to say, but in 1884 F.M. Cheney, the American Consul in Zanzibar, wrote that the price of the Indian counterfeits was so low that 'it is impossible to sell American Sheetings at a profit, and unless the price of cottons at home falls very low, American cottons will be driven from the market'.[65]

Other Indian imports such as furniture were probably consumed mostly on the coast by a small elite who could afford such luxuries. Rice, on the other hand, often came in larger quantities intended for consumption by less elite mouths. Rice is mentioned second after cloth as an import from India in the American trade report of 1884.[66] Onions and other foodstuffs also appear to have come to East Africa from India, often as deck cargo.

Hides came by dhow to Zanzibar from Somalia. The hide dhows came each year during the monsoon season. In 1884 122,749 hides were exported through Zanzibar to the USA and Europe.[67] The Somali dhows came on the monsoon, like the Arab and Indian dhows, but, unlike them, they had a cargo to sell that was of direct interest to the Atlantic economy.[68]

The cargoes the monsoon dhows took home with them came mostly from the mainland, and most of these were brought to Zanzibar by local dhows, which also supplied the needs of the Atlantic economy. Ivory, slaves, gum copal, orchilla weed, mangrove poles and food all came to Zanzibar by dhow. Cloves also came by dhow to Zanzibar from Pemba, especially after the hurricane of 1872 wiped out the Zanzibar plantations and the focus of clove production shifted to Pemba.

---

[65] F.M. Cheney, *Trade Report on Zanzibar June 30, 1883–June 30, 1884*, in Norman Bennett, *The Zanzibar Letters of Edward D. Ropes, Jr. 1882–1892* (Boston: 1973) p. 121.

[66] Bennett, *Ropes*, p. 120.

[67] Ibid.

[68] PEM, Ropes Papers, E.D. Ropes Jr to his Parents, 1 May 1883.

The Dhow Trade in Nineteenth-century Zanzibar

Ivory was probably the single most important commodity exported from Zanzibar in the mid-nineteenth century. Ivory was the nineteenth-century equivalent of plastic and was in great demand in the USA and Europe. It was also widely used in India for making bangles for brides and any number of other ornamental objects. East African ivory is 'soft' and so is easily worked compared with the more brittle ivories found in other parts of the world.[69] Early in the nineteenth century ivory was obtained quite near the coast, but as the demand for ivory increased the ivory frontier moved steadily westward.

Caravans were pushing into the lakes region by the mid-century and by the 1880s were well into present-day Zaïre. At Tabora and Ujiji towns had sprung up with a definite Swahili flavour to them. Ivory from the northern caravan route, which passed through Tabora, usually ended up in Bagamoyo, where a quick dhow trip brought it to Zanzibar. The more southerly route terminated in Kilwa, where a longer dhow trip brought it to Zanzibar. At Zanzibar the ivory was bought either by European or American merchants, who shipped it home, or by Indian merchants, who shipped it to Bombay or Cutch. It is possible, though not certain, that this ivory was shipped by dhow. The major Indian merchants in Zanzibar shipped their goods to India by steamer and by dhow, with a heavy emphasis on the latter. Letters from Tharia Topan's son, Jaffa Tharia, to E.D. Ropes in Salem indicate that much of the produce shipped by Tharia Topan to Bombay arrived by dhow.[70] Tharia Topan was the wealthiest Zanzibar merchant of his era and it seems probable that, if he found dhows to be a sensible way to transport his goods, despite the increasing steamer traffic between Zanzibar and India, others did too. Ivory would seem to have been a sensible cargo to ship by dhow since it does not suffer damage from wetting.

Copal was another African product that was moved by dhow from the coast to Zanzibar, but most of the copal was destined for the American and European markets. Gum copal is a natural resin that is found in the earth around certain types of trees. Copal was mined on the coast and shipped by dhow to Zanzibar. In Zanzibar it was cleaned or 'garbled' and then exported to the Atlantic or, in smaller quantities, to India. Copal was used to make varnish and so, like ivory, was in great demand in the industrializing West.

Cloves, which unlike Zanzibar's other exports, were actually produced in the islands, became an increasingly important commodity as the nineteenth century wore on. The Atlantic economy took part of the clove crop, India, Indonesia and the Gulf the rest. Those cloves that stayed in the Indian Ocean economy may have been transported by dhow, but it seems likely that cloves, which lose value when wet, were among the cargoes most likely to be transported by steamer. In 1873 the Sultan's steamer *Nadir Shah* was lost *en route* to Bombay. Her cargo included 2,196 bags of cloves with

---

[69] G.S.P. Freeman-Grenville, *The Medieval History of the Coast of Tanganyika* (London: 1962), p. 75.
[70] PEM Ropes Papers, Jaffer [*sic*] Tharia to E.D. Ropes, 13 June 1871.

140 pounds of cloves to the bag.[71] So it looks as though cloves going to India were sent in steamships when they were available. Whatever the attraction of steamships for the long-distance shipping of cloves, dhows remained the preferred way of shipping cloves from Pemba to Unguja.

Slaves worked the clove plantations and slaves came to Zanzibar in dhows. In August of 1845, the brig *Richmond* saw twenty-one slave dhows arrive in Zanzibar, carrying some 2,000 slaves.[72] In 1844, Hamerton estimated that Zanzibar imported 20,000 slaves per year. Twenty years later Rigby estimated that 16,000 to 20,000 slaves a year arrived in Zanzibar.[73] These numbers are a bit suspicious, since it seems unlikely that anybody in their right mind would give the British Consuls, who were known to oppose slavery, accurate figures about the slave trade. It seems equally likely that Hamerton and Rigby would be inclined to believe higher rather than lower figures. However foggy the numerical data about the slave trade, it is certain that large numbers of slaves came to Zanzibar to work on the clove plantations. A smaller number were shipped north to Arabia, where they became domestic slaves or ended up in the date plantations. As late as the 1860s, Spanish slavers were coming to East Africa seeking to take slaves around the Horn to Cuba.[74] In fact, Rigby's principal slave-trade concern seems to have been with this type of traffic, rather than the trade to Arabia, which later became such an obsession with the British. The slave-trade will be looked at in more detail in the next chapter, but for now it is sufficient to say that, although there were a succession of treaties, each restricting the scope of the legal slave-trade more than the last, the slave-trade between the mainland and the islands and between the islands and Arabia was an important part of what dhows did until roughly 1880.

Slaves were moved between the mainland and Zanzibar in vessels that carried nothing but slaves and these in large numbers. The crew of the *Richmond* saw a dhow with 360 slaves on it arrive at Zanzibar from Kilwa.[75] The passage between the coast and the islands was relatively short and water and provisions for large numbers of slaves could be carried for these short distances or even done without. In the northern trade, it seems to have been more common for a ship to take a few slaves as part of a mixed cargo. This simplified matters when it to came to food and water and meant that the risk of slave revolt was relatively minor. Later, as the anti-slaving patrols were stepped up, risking the capture and destruction of a vessel over just two or three slaves began to make less sense, and slaving became a specialized business. Slaves were carried north in batches as large

---

[71] ZNA AA1/12, Kirk to High Court, Bombay, 31 August 1873.

[72] While one might question a visiting American's ability to find out how many slaves had arrived while his ship was in port, it is worth remembering that New England ship captains were not unfamiliar with the business of slave running and the *Richmond*'s captain might have been capable of judging the capacity of the boats he saw.

[73] PEM, Log of the brig *Richmond*, 1845, ZNA AA1/3, Hammerton to Brown, 11 August 1844, and ZNA AA3/20, Rigby to Bombay, 14 May 1861.

[74] ZNA AA2/4, Rigby to Wood, 28 August 1860.

[75] PEM, Log of the Brig *Richmond*, 1845.

as 150–200.[76] If it looked as if the dhow was about to be captured, the dhow would be run ashore and the slaves chased on to the beach and then marched overland to the next port. The slave cargo was worth so much more than the boats that carried them that the possibility of losing a dhow in the process of running a cargo of slaves was considered an acceptable risk.[77]

Ivory, copal, cloves and slaves were used in both the Atlantic and the Indian Ocean economies. Other East African products were used in only one or the other. Orchilla weed, a dyestuff, was brought to Zanzibar by dhow, but used only in the Atlantic. Other products such as mangrove poles, remained entirely in the Indian Ocean economy.

Mangrove poles were one of least noticed, but consistently important, cargoes carried by dhows returning to Arabia. Southern Arabia and the Gulf are timber-poor, and so most building was done with mud bricks or coral blocks, which require little or no timber. Ceilings and roofs, however, must be reinforced with something, and in these areas the mangrove pole was the standard rafter. Mangrove poles remained in steady demand in the Gulf until the early 1960s. In Yemen the use of mangrove poles continued into the 1970s. Mangrove wood was the East African analogue of the dried fish brought by southbound dhows. It was a low-value, high-bulk cargo of great social and economic importance within the Indian Ocean economy and of little economic importance outside the Indian Ocean.

It is significant that the dhow trade between Zanzibar and Arabia was based upon staples like dried fish and mangrove poles. Although the trade between East Africa and Arabia was small compared with the vastly larger trade between Zanzibar and the Atlantic or Zanzibar and India, in its own way it was as important as the other more glamorous trades. The Arabian trade dealt in essentials – food and building material. The Arabs exchanged dried fish, something easily produced in their dry and salty climate, for mangrove poles, which were produced in abundance in the much wetter climate of East Africa. The trade was rooted in ecological differences between the two regions. The two regions were so economically and socially intertwined that each depended on the other for essential elements of daily life. As a result, this trade endured through booms and busts until the middle of the next century and its ending marked an important historical rupture for both regions. The Indian dhow trade, which dealt in trade goods and other commodities that were more valuable than fish or poles but not as essential to either side of the exchange did not fare as well in the long term as the Arabian trade. By the twentieth century, the Indian trade had shrunk to about a quarter the size of the Arab trade, and the final end of the Indian dhow trade did not mark an important change in the life of India or East Africa.

---

[76] ZNA AA3/20, Rigby to Bombay, 14 May 1861.
[77] Colomb, *Slave Catching*, p. 194, note 1.

Conclusion

By the middle of the nineteenth century a pattern had been established that was to persist in modified form well into the twentieth century.[78] Two economic systems coexisted in Zanzibar. One was devoted to funnelling raw materials to the industrial economies of the Atlantic. It was this economy that caused the mid-century Zanzibar boom. The other economy was that of the Indian Ocean. Zanzibar had been the principal East African port for the Indian Ocean economy before the Atlantic economy took an interest in East Africa. As the Atlantic economy increased the pace of economic activity in Zanzibar, the Indian Ocean economy's trade at Zanzibar grew, but its share of the total trade decreased. India managed to keep a small share of the business of supplying the trade with the interior; Arabia was cut out of that sector entirely and left with supplying the wants of coastal society.

Dhows kept a foot in both worlds. They carried most of the trade within the Indian Ocean and most of the goods that left Zanzibar in steamers bound for the factories of New England and Europe had crossed to Zanzibar in a dhow. Between feeding African commodities to the Atlantic trade in Zanzibar and Arabian and Indian goods to the coastal population, dhows were able to cash in on the Zanzibar boom and this period was probably the heyday of the East African dhow trade.

At the same time dhows and the Indian Ocean economy they supported had been partially marginalized, and the Arabian segment of the trade more so than the Indian. The forces that by 1860 had pushed Arabian dhows to the far edges of the trade and Indian dhows at least part way there were economic. In the next fifty years a whole new array of forces – political, military and bureaucratic – would be unleashed on Zanzibar and the Indian Ocean. The structure of East Africa's international trade would be profoundly changed and the boom created by the Atlantic economy's entrepôt trade came to a halt. For the Atlantic economy Zanzibar was transformed from an entrepôt to a backwater. For dhows and the economy they supported, this transformation was far less upsetting. Since dhows had long since been cut out of the key sectors of the entrepôt trade, the end of the Atlantic entrepôt trade was less of a shock. Their marginal position protected them from the full force of the changes that swept Zanzibar in the last years of the nineteenth century.

---

[78] Frederick Cooper, *From Slaves to Squatters* (New Haven: 1980), p. ix, states that although slavery was abolished in 1897 in Zanzibar, the social relations associated with slavery survived into the twentieth century. The same might be said of the nineteenth-century dhow economy. Although in some ways superseded by steamers and the global economy, it remained an important social and economic force in Zanzibari life until the revolution.

Three

The Creation of a Colonial Economy
Dhows in a Changing World
1872–1914

For elegant and excellent was the pirate's answer to the great Mace-
donian Alexander, who had taken him: the king asking him how he
durst molest the seas so, he replied with a free spirit, 'How darest thou
molest the whole world? But because I do with a little ship only, I am
called a thief: thou doing it with a great navy, art called an emperor.'

St. Augustine, *The City of God*, Book IV, Chapter IV[1]

By the middle of the nineteenth century the dhow trade, though
flourishing, was being edged towards marginality by the vigour of the
Atlantic economy. The second half of the nineteenth century saw the
dhow trade transformed into a second economy – an informal sector that
in some cases existed on the fringes of the new colonial economy or,
more often, was completely separate from it. This transformation was
caused by three related political phenomena.

The first of these was the slave-trade suppression campaign waged by
the Royal Navy from the late 1860s until the 1890s. The campaign
disrupted commerce in the western Indian Ocean and gave dhows a
pariah status in the eyes of the authorities, be they colonial or postcolonial, from which dhows have not entirely recovered. The second of
these was the separation of Zanzibar's mainland territories from the
islands. The Germans took the Mrima and the British the Kenya coast.
This gradually put an end to the entrepôt trade through Zanzibar.
While Zanzibar continued to be the entrepôt for some dhow cargos, it
ceased to be the transshipment point for the valuable and glamorous
trade goods that had interested the Atlantic economy. For dhows, this
ended the lucrative business of hauling East African produce to Zanzibar. The final blow, which came close on the heels of the loss of

[1] Quoted in Anne Perotin-Dumon, 'The pirate and the emperor: power and the law on
the seas,' in James Tracy (ed.), *The Political Economy of Merchant Empires* (Cambridge:
1991), p. 196.

Zanzibar's mainland territories, was the declaration of a British protectorate over Zanzibar in 1890. The pariah status dhows had acquired in the slave suppression campaign was translated into a bureaucratic effort to regulate and control the dhow trade. This meant a host of new regulations and dhow-specific rules, which served to separate dhows legally and conceptually from the emerging colonial economy. The British, realizing that Zanzibar's days as an entrepôt were over, began the process of making Zanzibar into a place more dependent on cash-crop production than on trade. Clove production became the heart of the new, formal, colonial economy and, as the British envisioned it, dhows would have no part in this modern economy. Excluded from the economic mainstream, dhows and the transport they offered remained at the heart of Zanzibar's unofficial economy.

Slave suppression

From early in the nineteenth century, the British had been pressuring the Omanis to restrict the slave trade. The Moresby Treaty of 1822 restricted the movement of slaves in the western Indian Ocean to a region west of a line drawn between Cape Delgado and Diu. This was adjusted westward in 1839 to the eastern edge of the Persian Gulf, which meant that it was legal to export slaves to Arabia but not to India.[2]

Then in 1845 Atkins Hamerton, the British Consul in Zanzibar, bullied Seyyid Said into completely outlawing the northern trade. The new treaty limited the legal slave trade to the movement of slaves from Zanzibar's coastal possessions to the islands of Unguja and Pemba. In 1873 even the local slave trade was outlawed in a treaty signed by Sultan Barghash (ruler of Zanzibar 1870–88) under threat of blockade by the Royal Navy. From then on, the movement of slaves over water was illegal, no matter where they were going. The slave markets in Zanzibar were closed and Indians were prohibited from owning slaves.[3]

Before the 1860s the British made little effort to enforce these treaties. The Indian Navy had been responsible for controlling the movement of slaves and did little to interfere with it. Although Indian Navy officers were entitled to bounties based on the number of slaves they captured or the tonnage of the vessel, they usually took flight at the sight of a slave dhow. Their reticence was caused by the fact that they

---

[2] Abdul Sheriff, *Slaves, Spices and Ivory in Zanzibar* (London: 1987), pp. 36, 47.
[3] ZNA AA1/3, Hamerton to Aberdeen, 4 October 1845, L.W. Hollingsworth, *Zanzibar Under the Foreign Office, 1890–1913*, (London: 1953), p. 14, ZNA AA1/2, Kirk to Foreign Office, 26 June 1873. Sheriff, *Slaves, Spices, and Ivory*, pp. 235–8, sees this as the great rupture in Zanzibar's economic history, not because the slave-trade was critical to the economy but rather because, by forcing Barghash to accept the treaty, Britain effectively eliminated what little remained of Zanzibari sovereignty. To Sheriff's mind, the treaty of 1873 marked the beginning of the end of Zanzibar's status as a commercial power.

were required to bring each captured slaver to adjudication and while the adjudication was in process the captain of the capturing vessel was no longer considered to be in command of a warship and so lost the extra pay associated with holding a command. Thus the capture and trial of a slave dhow could spell financial disaster for the captain of the capturing vessel. The Indian Navy, therefore, pursued the suppression of the slave-trade lackadaisically.[4]

In the 1860s the anti-slaving duty was handed over to the Cape of Good Hope squadron of the Royal Navy and they went at it hammer and tongs. Unlike their brothers in the Indian Navy, Royal Navy officers had much to gain from capturing slave dhows or any other dhows for that matter. Royal Navy vessels were given a bounty of £5 10s per ton of captured vessel and suffered no loss of pay while adjudicating their captures.[5] In fact, the adjudication process was taken much less seriously in the Royal Navy than in the Indian Navy.

In the rules set out by the Admiralty for officers on the slave patrol it was stated quite clearly that:

> the purpose of taking the captured vessel to the proper Port of Adjudication is not to procure as a matter of form, a decree of condemnation, but to obtain a full and fair trial of the case; at which trial those concerned in the property may have all reasonable facilities to defend their interests.[6]

There was, however, a convenient exception to this apparently hard and fast rule. If a captured vessel was so unseaworthy as to present a threat to the safety of a prize crew, it could be destroyed at sea and adjudicated later.

There were powerful incentives for naval captains to exploit this loophole. Foremost of these was that ships which destroyed their prizes did not have to leave their cruising ground after each capture. Since slaves were smuggled north during the two windows of opportunity provided by the south-west monsoon, i.e. May and June or September, naval officers hoping to repair their fortunes had a limited time to make their captures. If, after their first capture, they dutifully sailed to a port of adjudication, which would mean Bombay, Aden or Zanzibar, they would be forced to fight the monsoon either on their way to the port or on the way back to their cruising ground. The result would be abandoning their chance at any other captures during that particular season.[7]

There were other incentives. The bounty paid on a captured dhow was based on the tonnage. Tonnage was determined by measurements

---

[4] ZNA AA3/20, Rigby to Bombay, 14 May 1861.

[5] ZNA AA1/22, 'Reports from Naval Officers,' No. 686, 1876, and P.H. Colomb, *Slave Catching in the Indian Ocean*, (London: 1873), p. 78.

[6] ZNA 1/7, Admiralty, 'Instructions for Naval Officers employed in the Suppression of the Slave Trade,' October 1869.

[7] W.C. Devereux, *A Cruise in the Gorgon*, (London: 1968 [1869]), p. 360, and Colomb, *Slave Catching*, pp. 185–93.

made by an officer of the capturing ship. If the captured dhow was towed to a port of adjudication, the tonnage figures submitted when the bounty was collected were likely to be scrutinized by someone else, and that someone often had less interest in keeping the bounties high. If dhows were destroyed at sea, a little fudging of the measurements was not likely to be noticed. In one case, a dhow destroyed by a naval vessel as unseaworthy was salvaged and brought to Zanzibar by an Arab crew. When the British Consul John Kirk saw it, he realized that the figures submitted for the bounty had been exaggerated. The officer making the measurements had included the bowsprit in the length of the dhow, thereby substantially increasing the tonnage of the dhow and with it the bounty.[8] In short, officers in the Royal Navy not only had financial incentives to pursue slave ships at sea, they were also in a position to profit from misrepresenting legitimate trading vessels as slavers.

To be fair, many of the dhows, especially *mitepe* with their leaky, sewn hulls, may have genuinely looked unseaworthy to men who lived in the Royal Navy's world of holystone and polished brass. The condition of some of the dhows that sail in East African waters today is very similar to that of the dilapidated condition of the taxis that cruise the streets of East African cities. So some captains may have had legitimate reservations about putting their men on board captured dhows.[9] But, in general, captured dhows were destroyed because it was convenient and because when the case did eventually come to adjudication, few *nakhodas* would come to the court to argue about an already burnt dhow.

The result was a campaign of semi-legal piracy against dhows in East African waters. Warships cruised the coastal waters and would run down any sail they sighted. Most dhows were inspected and released, on one day in 1871 for instance, HMS *Dryad* stopped and searched eight dhows, only one of which was seized and burned.[10] In most cases, the condemned dhows were not carrying hundreds of slaves chained in their holds middle-passage style, but rather they would have one or two slaves on board, or one or two people whose status the officer in charge and his translator could not account for. A list of dhow captures adjudicated at Zanzibar in the first half of 1873 shows that of the ten dhows condemned, only two had more than five slaves on board, and these had nine and six each. Most had only one or two slaves on board when they were captured.[11]

There were two reasons for these small numbers. One was that slave running had become a specialized business. Dhow owners who were serious about slave running would devote whole vessels to the business and keep them close to shore, where they could escape British cruisers. Until 1873, when it was still legal to move slaves within the Sultan's

[8] ZNA AA1/9, Foreign Office to Kirk, 8 August 1872.

[9] One Royal Navy officer even suggested that most dhows were too rickety to be towed much less sailed, G.L. Sullivan, *Dhow Chasing in Zanzibar Waters* (London: 1873), p. 102.

[10] Colomb, *Slave Catching*, p. 224.

[11] ZNA AA1/12, Kirk to Foreign Office, 5 June 1873.

dominions, slaves were carried in large numbers to Lamu, where they were loaded into *mtepe*. The *mtepe* were able to stay very close to shore on account of their shallow draught, but could also carry a pretty substantial load. The slaves would be whisked along the Somali coast and then there would be a quick open-water dash from Ras Hafun to Mukalla or to the southern shore of Oman. If they were surprised by a naval vessel, it was a simple matter to run the dhow on to the beach and chase the slaves ashore. Naval crews were reluctant to pursue escaping slaves and the crews of the slavers on shore, so, while a ship worth a couple of hundred dollars might be lost, the slaves, who were worth quite a bit more, were not.[12]

Thus many of the open-sea captures involved either cases where a *nakhoda* brought his personal slaves with him, or vessels with equipment related to slave running (usually larger than normal water tanks), or, in many cases, it was a case of gross or even wanton misunderstanding. Since most naval officers spoke little Arabic or Swahili, they had to rely on translators to help them sort out who was who on a captured dhow. In one case a dhow was seized and burned in 1869 by a boat from HMS *Nymphe* on the grounds that its papers, which would allow it to legally trade within the Sultan's dominions, had expired. When the dhow was first taken, the *nakhoda* claimed that he had just left Zanzibar and that his pass had been legal when he left. The interpreter claimed that this was a lie, since the pass was fifteen months out of date. Smelling a rat, the capturing officer condemned and burned the dhow. When Consul John Kirk examined the interpreter he realized that the man was not able to read the pass and that it had in fact been valid at the time of the capture. The *Nymphe* was obliged to pay for the destroyed dhow out of its prize fund.[13] In another case, a dhow seized off Pemba was burned because the translator believed that one of the passengers on board had told him that he was being taken to Pemba to be sold. In fact the man was on his way to Pemba with a load of cassava which was to be sold, but the translator's Swahili apparently did not allow him to distinguish between subject and indirect object of a passive verb.[14]

The effects of the anti-slavery campaign on dhow shipping are hard to judge. By 1880, almost the entire slave-trade had been shut down, so dhows had lost one of their traditional cargoes.[15] The transportation of slaves from the mainland to the clove plantations of the islands had been a big business, so the treaty of 1873 and the subsequent crack-down probably took its toll on the local dhow trade. Ironically, the northern slave-trade, about which abolitionists and government types were more concerned, was much less important to the dhow trade than the local

---

[12] Colomb, *Slave Catching*, p. 34 note 2, 194, and ZNA AA1/8, Foreign Office to Kirk, 23 August 1871.

[13] ZNA AA7/3, Proceedings of the Zanzibar Vice Admiralty Court, 5 May 1869.

[14] ZNA AA7/4, Proceedings of the Zanzibar Vice Admiralty Court, 11 January 1872.

[15] See note 16 below.

movement of slaves. To be sure there was a market for slaves in the Gulf. A few were used in agriculture, especially on date plantations, but most were domestic servants and mostly served to bolster the status of their owners. But the actual volume of slaves that moved north each year in the middle of the nineteenth century probably did not exceed a few thousand per year. All sorts of efforts have been made to come up with the type of quantitative analysis of the northern slave trade that has been done with greater success for the Atlantic trade, but no consensus has yet been reached. It is generally agreed, however, that the volume of the northern trade was small compared with the trade to the islands. Thus the loss of the northern slave-trade was probably insignificant compared with the loss of the local slave-trade.[16]

More important than the loss of slaves as a cargo was the general harassment caused by the piratical qualities of the anti-slavery campaign. In 1869 F.R. Webb, an American merchant in Zanzibar, reported that the anti-slavery campaign was

> raising the devil with the trading dows on the coast, and will ruin the trade if they keep it up. Not less than 70 have been destroyed by them in the past year and there is no doubt that a great proportion of them were harmless traders with no slaves on board except their crews.[17]

Not content with harassing legitimate traders, some of the ship's boats that made most of the interceptions seem to have engaged in real piracy. An example of this probably occurred in 1869, when the HMS *Nymphe* captured and burned a dhow which they had purportedly seen throwing water tanks over the side as it was being approached. It also had a layer of palm fronds in the hold. Assuming that the water tanks had been for slaves and that the palm fronds had been intended to make the hold easier to clean after it had been inhabited by seasick slaves, the dhow was condemned by the *Nymphe*'s Captain Meara. When the case was adjudicated the nakhoda said that there had been nothing put over the side and that the palm fronds were to keep the shark oil in the hull from tainting the cargo. Interestingly the *Nymphe*'s translator supported the *nakhoda*'s claims and said that he had not believed at the time that the dhow was a slaver. The *nakhoda* went on to insist that the boarding party that searched his ship had taken most of the crew's personal effects and

[16] R.A. Austen, 'From the Atlantic to the Indian Ocean: European Abolitition, the African Slave Trade, and Asian Economic Structures,' in David Eltis and James Walvin (eds), *The Abolition of the Atlantic Slave Trade*, (Madison: 1981), E.B. Martin and T.C. Ryan, 'A Quantitative Assessment of the Arab Slave Trade of East Africa, 1770–1896,' *Kenya Historical Review*, 5 (1977), pp. 71–91; Sheriff, *Slaves, Spices and Ivory*, pp. 35–41, Paul Lovejoy, *Transitions in Slavery*, (Cambridge: 1983) and, most recently and persuasively, M. Reda Bhacker, *Trade and Empire in Muscat and Zanzibar* (London: 1992), pp. 130–32. Reda Bhacker correctly points out that the slave trade was a much larger and more complex issue than the literature usually makes it out to be. He reminds us that servile labour, originating in many different places (including Slavic Europe, India and Oman), moved in many different directions in the nineteenth century.

[17] PEM, Ropes Papers, F.R. Webb to E.D. Ropes, 13 April 1869.

when they were returned $1,000 had been removed from them. He also said that the boarding party broke into his desk without asking for a key and the Sultan's flag was trampled by the searchers. He was supported in this testimony by several members of his crew.[18]

That this sort of thing went on was confirmed by Devereux of HMS *Gorgon* who wrote of the British sailor:

> Having undergone all the dangers and vicissitudes of boat work, he thinks he should be allowed to keep all loot, whether money or jewelry, &c., collected during the cruise – honestly or dishonestly ... As soon as a prize is taken Jack's first thought is 'loot' ... he sneaks below, breaks open doors and boxes, pounces upon money and jewelry ... The sex to whom he is naturally so gallant, is not only disrespected but roughly handled.[19]

Thus the harassment of legitimate trade was not limited to the unlawful destruction of dhows but also included the theft of goods belonging to the crews and passengers, and this type of behaviour probably encouraged even legitimate traders to try to escape when confronted by a naval patrol.

The harassment did not let up once the slave-trade had been suppressed. In 1883 the American E.D. Ropes Jr wrote to his parents on the subject of the lingering British naval presence in Zanzibar.

> This is a noble work they are doing out here. Three thousand men – ten great men of war iron clad with rifled cannon, yachts, steam-launches, hulks, stations – all work for a year and catch a 7 ton dhow and one little slave! Alla-hum-de-le-la![20]

A year later the American Consul at Zanzibar pronounced the slave-trade to be dead and reported to the State Department that the British had begun to curtail their patrolling.[21] But there were flare-ups of slave running in the late 1880s. In 1888 several slave dhows were captured off Pemba, and some even resisted being boarded.[22]

In the long run the most important effect of the slave suppression campaign on the dhow trade was not the immediate disruption that occurred while the anti-slave patrols did their work. Rather it was that dhows became associated in the minds of the colonial powers with illegal trade rather than with legal trade and hence with disorder rather than order and modernity. Thus the dhow trade entered the colonial period as a legal pariah and was subjected to an intense vigilance to ensure that it would not slip back into its old slave trading ways. But before we begin to look at the creation of these regulations, let us look at how the carving up of the mainland into colonies transformed Zanzibar's trade.

[18] ZNA AA7/3, Proceedings of the Zanzibar Vice Admiralty Court, 6 August 1869.
[19] Devereux, Gorgon, p. 129.
[20] PEM, Ropes Papers, E.D. Ropes Jr to his parents, 1 May 1883.
[21] 'Trade Report on Zanzibar June 1883 to June 1884' quoted in Norman Bennett, *The Zanzibar Letters of Edward D. Ropes Jr., 1882–1892*, (Boston, 1973), p.121.
[22] PEM, Ropes Letters, E.D. Ropes Jr to his father, 11 Nov. 1888.

Dividing up the coast

Although the slave trade had more or less expired by the mid-1880s, it was too useful a cudgel for the emerging colonial powers for them to put the issue to rest. Suppressing the slave-trade was always a handy way of selling military activity in far-off lands to a sceptical public and, when the German bid to take the Sultan's mainland possessions stagnated, it was 'slave-trade suppression' they fell back on.[23]

Since 1884, a German private citizen who directed the *Gesellschaft für Deutsche Kolonisation*, Karl Peters, had been travelling around the hinterland of Zanzibar's coastal possessions signing treaties of protection with anyone he could persuade to put pen to paper. Then, in 1885, shortly after the Berlin Conference, at which the colonial powers had divided Africa among themselves, the Kaiser placed the territories under imperial protection.[24]

With the 1885 recognition of Peters's treaties, the Kaiser's government claimed a German Protectorate over the lands to the west of the Sultan's possessions and not claimed by any other European power.[25] While this sounds innocuous, the Germans maintained that the Sultan's territories consisted only of the custom-houses on the coast, and the towns that surrounded them. Even the territory between them was, according to their interpretation, not under his suzerainty. To exploit this new claim, Peters formed the German East Africa Company and began to install posts in some of the lands they claimed. This immediately caused tensions on the coast to rise, the immediate focus of these tensions often hinged on the question of whether the Company's flag could be flown alongside the Sultan's. In coastal towns people refused to sell land or provisions to the Germans and a party of Zanzibari soldiers travelled to the Kilimanjaro region where they gathered their own set of treaties. This provoked the Germans into sending a naval squadron to Zanzibar. Given twenty-four hours to agree to the Germans' territorial claims, staring down the guns of ships lined up to bombard Zanzibar town and left out to dry by his British allies, Sultan Bargash had no choice but to accept the Germans' terms.[26]

By 1888, the coastal strip that had once been the Sultan's had been divided by the Germans and the British. The Imperial British East Africa Company, whose directors included Sir John Kirk, got what is now the Kenya coast, while the Germans got the present-day Tanzania coast. In the areas under British administration, things went fairly smoothly and trade seems not to have been unduly interfered with. In

---

[23] Hollingsworth, *Foreign Office* (London: 1957), p. 28.

[24] Ibid., p. 17. For a detailed account of the complex series of events that led to the collapse of the Zanzibari state and the German acquisition of the coast and interior, see Norman Bennett, *Arab versus European* (New York: 1986) and Jonathon Glassman, *Feasts and Riot* (Portsmouth, NH: 1995).

[25] Bennett, *Arab versus European*, p. 132.

[26] Hollingsworth, *Foreign Office*, p. 20, and Glassman, *Feasts*, pp. 179–88.

the areas that were under the ostensible control of the Germans things did not go so smoothly on either the political or the economic fronts. In the summer of 1888, there was a big rush to get all the caravans off from the coast early so that they could have their goods from Zanzibar and be on their way before the Germans took over the customs on the coast. As it turned out, the caravan leaders had been wise to get on their way early since the first thing the Germans did was to ban the importation of gunpowder. This made those who had not set out early 'tired', according to E.D. Ropes.[27]

Apart from German bans on some caravan goods, there were other troubles for the world of trade. The transition to German administration was not at all smooth. Of trade conditions in 1888, Ropes had this to say:

> The 'German' business on the Coast has paralyzed business. All this red tape and regulations can have but one end – rows and confiscation … The Coast natives are sulky, no powder is permitted to be sent over nor any other goods & business is at a standstill.[28]

Before long there was more than red tape to worry about. The Germans went about the task of winning the hearts and minds of their new protectees with characteristic subtlety. They brought dogs into mosques, forbade the carrying of weapons in coastal towns and seemingly went out of their way to provoke conflict.[29] The result was armed uprisings in several towns, the most important of these being the one led by Bushiri of Pangani. The fighting resulted in further restriction on trade. The Germans held Bagamoyo and Dar es Salaam but lost control of the rest of the coast. The rebels would not allow goods to be landed or to leave the German custom-houses in Dar and Bagamoyo, and so the trade was reduced by about one-tenth according to Ropes's estimate.[30] It was then that the Germans played their slave-trade card. The German Navy then began a blockade of the coast, ostensibly to root out the slave-trade and further interfering with trade. They were soon joined by the British, who were afraid to let Germans have the whole thing to themselves.[31] The result was a naval blockade that went on for the next two years.[32]

Ships on the blockade stopped large numbers of coastal craft and found little in the way of slaves. One British man-of-war stopped 104 dhows without encountering a single slave. On occasion slaves were seized by the blockaders. One German vessel caught a dhow with 100 slaves on board and then had to decide what to do with them. The

---

[27] E.D. Ropes Jr to his father, 28 August 1888, in Bennett, *Zanzibar Letters*, p. 100.

[28] Ibid.

[29] E.D. Ropes Jr to his father, 23 September 1888, in Bennett, *Zanzibar Letters*, p. 101.

[30] E.D. Ropes Jr to his father, 18 November 1888, in Bennett, *Zanzibar Letters*, p. 107.

[31] Hollingsworth, *Foreign Office*, p. 28.

[32] Glassman, *Feasts & Riot*, sees the uprising on the coast as a much more socially intricate event than either Hollingsworth or Bennett does, but for our purposes it does not matter who was rising against whom or why. What concerns us are the effects of this uprising on trade.

capture of so many slaves, even though this was the ostensible purpose of the blockade, seems to have come as a surprise, and no one had any idea what to do with so many slaves.[33] The blockade seems to have been limited to the stopping and harassment of dhows and the sort of thinly disguised piracy that had been commonplace twenty years earlier was less prevalent. Still, with the fighting interfering with the movement of caravans and the blockade interfering with the movements of coastal dhows, trade was lacklustre.

For this period there are no trade statistics, so it is hard to say how badly the dhow trade was interfered with by the initial division of the coast and the blockade. It is likely that both the long-distance trade and the local dhow trade suffered, but it was probably the local trade that suffered the most. Since Arab dhows were mostly involved in supplying the needs of the coast and the island communities, the temporary demise of the caravan trade was probably not a major blow to them. American merchants in Zanzibar reported that during the blockade and coastal uprising, they had trouble getting rid of their cotton, a caravan trade good, but were doing well in kerosene, which was used on the coast and in the islands.[34] Thus it seems that on the coast there was a continuous demand for imported goods for local consumption throughout the crisis. Indian dhows, which were more reliant on the caravan trade, probably suffered a bit more than their Arab counterparts, although it is clear that major Indian merchants in Zanzibar continued to ship by dhow during the crisis, especially to the Benadir where trade was going on without interference.[35]

The uprising on the coast and the separation of Zanzibar from her coastal territories was detrimental to the entrepôt trade, but for dhows it was only a portent of worse things to come. It is significant that, when confronted by social and political upheaval on the coast, the emerging colonial powers revived their interest in suppressing the almost non-existent slave-trade in an attempt to crack down on dhows. From the inception of the colonial enterprise, dhows and the free movement and trade they allow were identified as a threat to the colonial state. Beginning in 1890 a convergence of events in Europe and in East Africa codified the dhow's pariah status and began the long and never completely successful state-directed process of separating dhows from the emerging colonial economies.

The protectorate

By 1890 the Germans had the situation on the coast more or less under control and were beginning to show a growing interest in Zanzibar itself.

[33] E.D. Ropes Jr to his father, 16 December 1888, in Bennett, *Zanzibar Letters*, p. 110, 108 note 298.

[34] PEM, Ropes Papers, E.D. Ropes Jr to his father, 23 September 1888.

[35] PEM, Ropes Papers, E.D. Ropes Jr to his father, 23 September 1888, and E.D. Ropes Jr to his father, 21 October 1888.

Sultan Ali, after a little arm twisting, decided to go with the devil he knew and Zanzibar became a British Protectorate. Although the original terms of the agreement said that the Sultan's government would retain control of internal affairs, the British were soon in charge of the local administration.[36] This change affected dhows immediately, since Captain Hardinge, a Royal Navy officer, was put in charge of administering the port area.

The Zanzibar port had been a free-for-all until the British took over. There were no port fees, no lighting, no fairways, and no cargo-handling equipment. By 1892 this had all changed. By 1892 the Port Office had buoyed the approaches to the harbour, required all vessels to gain pratique (i.e. to undergo an inspection for the presence of contagious disease) before entering the harbour, imposed order on the anchorage and introduced a system of published fees and tariffs.[37]

The British also made physical improvements to the harbour. A new quay was put in along the waterfront. This allowed lighters and dhows to come alongside at high tide, and meant that goods could be unloaded directly on to the quay instead of over the beach. Most importantly, the Port Office installed several steam cranes on the jetty so that cargo could be handled mechanically. In general, the new cargo-handling equipment was intended for use by the lighters that served the government ships and other steamers rather than dhows. In this case, though, it looks as though dhows may have been able to use the steam cranes. Photographs of the waterfront in this period show dhows in position under the cranes and since dhows had not yet been segregated from the main harbour, it seems likely that dhow owners who could afford the fee were allowed to use the cranes.[38]

In general, these changes were not too important to dhows. The buoying of the channels was a great advantage to steamers; dhow captains already knew how to get in and out of the harbour. None the less, they paid port dues, lighting fees and wharfage fees to help cover the cost of these things, in effect subsidizing their competition.

While the port improvements of 1892 may have brought some advantage to dhows, they brought even greater advantages to their steam-powered competitors. The same year brought the Brussels Treaty into effect and formalized the pariah status of dhows, pushing them even further from the mainstream economy. The Brussels Conference of 1890 was held at the behest of King Leopold, mostly as a last-ditch effort to save his faltering Congo Free State. Since 1888, Cardinal Lavigerie, the Basque founder of the missionary order the White Fathers, had been preaching a crusade against the horrors of slavery in Africa. Relying on anti-slavery propaganda that was twenty to thirty years out of date, he

[36] Hollingsworth, *Foreign Office*, pp. 42–3.
[37] Ibid., p. 67.
[38] ZNA AV7/25 and AV7/42 (photos) and B.S. Hoyle, *The Seaports of East Africa* (Nairobi: 1967), p. 101.

came up with wildly exaggerated figures about the volume of the East African slave-trade. The Brussels Treaty, which emerged from this conference reflected the popular outrage stirred up by Lavigerie, and set the new colonial powers to the task of extending their control over their new possessions in order to control the slave-trade.[39]

The Brussels Treaty called for the colonial powers to extend their imperium and administration in their territories in order to put a stop to the slave-trade. It called for the establishment of interior outposts, flying columns to 'support repressive action', telegraph lines, river steamers, railways, so that porters would no longer be needed, and a ban on the importation of alcohol and firearms. In short, it called on the parties who had signed the Berlin Treaty of 1885 to make colonies of their possessions, all in the name of ending the slave-trade.[40]

While most colonial powers eventually did all of these things, it took a while. Railways, telegraph lines and river steamers take years to construct. There were, however, more easily obtainable goals set out in the treaty. As part of the slave-suppression effort, the treaty called on all the 'civilized' nations with possessions in the western Indian Ocean to undertake a coordinated effort to control and document the dhow trade. Since this was a natural, land-based extension of the anti-slavery patrolling that had been on going for over thirty years at this point, these provisions of the treaty were enacted rather faster than many of the others. The Brussels Treaty is important because it represents the first effort to legally define dhows and the trade they carried as a discrete entity, and because its call for close scrutiny and regulation of dhows was an implicit recognition of their subversive potential.[41] The implementation of the Brussels Treaty was the state's first effort to make the dhow 'legible', to use a term coined by James C. Scott. If one of the threats the dhow posed to the colonial order was its illegibility, by creating a system that documented and described the dhow the Brussels Treaty represented a first step towards making the dhow trade legible.[42]

In the area west of a line between Baluchistan and an imaginary point 20 miles off the eastern coast of Madagascar, the navies of the signatories would have the right of 'visit, search and detention' of ships under 500 tons. While the 500 ton limit almost entirely limited the scope of the Brussels Treaty regulations to dhows, it did not do so entirely, since there were some European vessels operating in the defined area

[39] Robin Hallett, *Africa since 1875* (Ann Arbor: 1974), pp. 438–9.

[40] Admiralty, *Instructions for the Guidance of Captains and Commanding Officers of Her Majesty's Ships of War Employed in the Suppression of the Slave Trade* (London: 1892), Vol 1, pp.104–5.

[41] Both Norman Bennett, *A History of the Arab State of Zanzibar* (London: 1978), p. 160 and Frederick Cooper, *From Slaves to Squatters* (New Haven: 1980), p. 115, mention the Brussels conference but neither seems to be aware of the extent to which the colonial government of Zanzibar followed the stipulations of the treaty that emerged from the conference, nor do they mention the economically interventionist position espoused in the treaty.

[42] James C. Scott, *Seeing Like a State* (New Haven: 1998).

3.1 A Lamu jahazi. *Note the designation 'L.38' on the stern. This is the vessel's registration number, a relic of the Brussels Act of 1890*

which were under 500 tons. Thus to further fine tune the treaty so as to ensure that it interfered only with dhows, most of the rest of the rules were specified to apply only to 'native vessels'.[43]

But what exactly is a native vessel? This was a question that was to nag the authorities well into the 1950s. The Brussels Treaty, took the tautological approach and declared that a native vessel was a vessel that 'presented the outward appearance of native build or rig', or it was a vessel that was 'manned by a crew of whom the captain and the majority of the seaman belong by origin to a country having a sea-coast on the Indian Ocean', either condition satisfying the law. In other words a 'native vessel' was either a native vessel or it was a vessel full of natives.[44]

This ambiguity caused trouble as soon as the treaty went into effect in 1892. The SS *Kilwa*, one of the Zanzibar government's steamers, which was manned by and captained by 'natives', was seized by the HMS *Blanche* while some slaves were travelling as passengers. Ironically, since Captain Hardinge, the Port Officer, was in charge of the government's steamers, he should have been prosecuted and the steamer should have been a prize of the *Blanche*. Instead, it was decided to impound the slaves and not the vessel or Hardinge.[45]

Having defined native vessels, the treaty then called for them to be 'carefully watched' and regulated. First dhows were to be flagged according to where the owner lived or to whom the owner was subject. Owners seeking to get their vessels flagged were required to show that they had not been involved in the slave-trade and had to either own real estate or post a bond against any fines they might incur later on.[46]

When a dhow was registered, the treaty required that the registration papers contain sufficient information to identify the vessel. A uniform system of measuring tonnages was used so that registration certificates issued by the various national authorities would all be using a consistent system. Each dhow should have its name, tonnage and home port written on its stern in Latin letters and its sail should carry its registration number. The registration numbers began with a letter indicating where the vessel was registered, e.g. 'Z' for Zanzibar, 'L' for Lamu, and a number. This system of numbers and letter has survived over 100 years and is still in use today.[47]

Since it was an article of faith among British naval officers that dhow crews were often slaves being transported for sale in distant ports and since it was often difficult for them to distinguish between slaves being transported for sale and crew members, the crews of dhows were to be closely tracked and accounted for.[48]

[43] Admiralty, *Instructions*, p. 115.
[44] Ibid., p. 114.
[45] *The Zanzibar Gazette*, 12 October 1892.
[46] Admiralty, *Instructions*, p. 116.
[47] Ibid., p.116.
[48] See for example Colomb's elaborate description of how slave crews were sent to Bombay and then sold in the Gulf, Colomb, *Slave Catching*, p. 98–9.

Article XXXV of the Brussels Treaty required that each *nakhoda* must keep a 'crew list', which was to be checked by the authorities at the 'moment of departure'. Furthermore, it stated that:

> No negro shall be engaged as a seaman on a vessel, without his having been previously questioned … with a view to establish that he has contracted a free engagement.

Officials examining the crew list were also charged to ensure that the size of the crew was not disproportionate to the size of the vessel. In drawing up the crew list, the port officer was to include a brief description of each crew member, in order to prevent substitutions.[49]

Passengers were also to be documented, but not all passengers, only 'negro' passengers. Before a dhow captain could transport black passengers, each had to be interrogated to ensure that he was travelling of his own free will. Once interrogated, the passengers' names and descriptions were entered on a passenger list. It was illegal for a dhow to pick up or discharge passengers at a port that did not have a 'resident authority belonging to the one of the Signatory Powers'.[50]

All the information gathered in this process was to be transferred to the International Maritime Bureau in Zanzibar, which was responsible for keeping records of all the dhow registrations and transfers of flags in East Africa.[51] And for a few years it seems to have done just that. Records from 1892 up to 1913 are fairly complete. The 'Signatory Powers' actually took the trouble to register thousands of dhows from Mozambique to Somalia and to transfer all this information to a central repository in Zanzibar. They also took the trouble to fill out the passenger lists and crew lists, and even to scrutinize them carefully. A crew list from 1900 includes such thorough descriptions as 'Salim Ali, Swahili, long and thin, ugly face,' and it includes a critical note from a British port official in Zanzibar to his German counterpart in Dar es Salaam complaining that his descriptions were not accurate.[52] Thus it seems that the officials charged with these duties took them seriously, even though they must have been painfully aware that there was no slave trade to suppress. Why did they go to all this trouble?

The most obvious answer is that it gave them more control over their new colonial subjects. The handful of Europeans trying to administer vast new territories needed all the help they could get, and some way of keeping track of these thousands of water-craft must have helped in that effort. Dhows and their crews have been and remain a disruptive and at times subversive force in Zanzibari life, and the new colonial officers must have known this. As early as 1861 the crews of Suri 'pirate' dhows

---

[49] Admiralty, *Instructions*, p.116.

[50] Ibid., p.117.

[51] Ibid., p.114.

[52] The AT series at the ZNA is composed entirely of documents generated by the International Maritime Bureau from 1892 to 1913. For crew and passenger lists see TNA G1/56 n.177 and also G1/57 and G1/58.

had run amok in Zanzibar Town, assaulting employees of the US consulate, barricading the consul in his house and running through the streets calling for the blood of white men.[53] As recently as 1994, dhows were used to bring people from northern Unguja to Zanzibar town for an opposition political rally, after the government had closed the roads from the north to keep them out.[54] The sea is hard to control and so ships and their crews inject a note of anarchy into a polity. This explains at least part of the reason why these officials adhered to at least some of the provisions of the Brussels Act.

The other reason for this seemingly bizarre behaviour is a bit more subtle and for our purposes more important. Throughout the nineteenth century European observers of East Africa in general and Zanzibar in particular commented on the economic potential that was going to waste on account of the misgovernment, sloth and decadence of the Arabs. A reflection of this 'misgovernment' and 'sloth' was that no records were kept by the government. Instead of trying to keep the accounts and records that directly running the custom-house would have required, the Sultans farmed the customs to Indian merchants for a flat fee. Zanzibari dhows were required to carry the Sultan's flag and a pass from the customs master, but there were no central records of these papers and there were no returns kept of the vessels that entered and cleared the various ports in the Sultan's dominions. The custom-house did not keep records of the quantity or value of goods that passed though the port. To the British this was no way to run a government or an economy. So, as soon as they took over they set about remedying this 'flaw' in the Arab administration.

Shortly after the British formally took over the Zanzibari state, an Englishman was engaged to bring order and record keeping to the custom-house. Other departments of government were formed, each with a European director and a budget and records. In the Port Office, returns were kept, bum-boats were registered and, of course, all the dhows were enrolled in the Brussels Act programme. In the town, residents were required to light the area in front of their houses at night and street-cleaning crews were formed.[55] All very orderly and very English.

The British assumed that order and regulation were an essential part of the modern economy that was going to blossom under their rule. As they took more and more of the affairs and economy of Zanzibar under their control, the more they strove for modernity. Given a choice between dhows or steamers, they went with steamers, even though the economic arguments for steamers were often weak. Given a choice between regulation and efficiency, they invariably chose regulation. As we shall see as we move into the twentieth century, this idea that certain technologies or ways of doing things were inherently superior dictated many of the economic choices made by British colonial authorities.

---

[53] ZNA AA2/4, Rigby to Oldfield, 19 March 1861.
[54] *Family Mirror*, August 1994.
[55] Hollingsworth, *Foreign Office*, pp. 60–1.

Usually these assumptions were so ingrained that the people making or debating the decisions did not even articulate their adherence to them. To them it was obvious that, if Zanzibar were going to progress, then the dhows would have to be replaced by steamers, the dozens of informal, undeveloped ports by fewer ports with quays and storage sheds, the seasonality of dhows with the regular schedules of steamers and so on.

And, of course, they were right. Steamers, which allow small crews to carry huge cargoes, are, all things being equal, more efficient than dhows. But all things are rarely equal and in the small-scale economy of the East African coast steamers were too large and costly to operate cost-effectively except on a few major routes. Their need for expensive port facilities, which of course meant as few ports as possible, made them ill suited to a region where much of the economy functioned because producers could count on ships coming to them rather than moving goods and crops overland to a few well-equipped and capital-intensive ports. Much of the economic history of colonial Zanzibar is the story of state-directed efforts to make trade use steamers with their fewer and more 'legible' ports rather than dhows and their many uncontrollable creek ports.

How much these early manifestations of the British desire to modernize affected dhows is difficult to say. Certainly not all the requirements were new. Some dhows had been flagged and carried passes as early as the 1840s, so the need to deal with paperwork was not entirely new. The regulations about crew and passenger lists probably added to the cost of doing business, directly in the form of fees and indirectly in the form of delays and hassles. But these were surmountable difficulties. For dhows the real threat posed by the Brussels Act was that it cast dhows into that part of the economic life of East Africa that was to be left behind by progress. Dhows were part of the old, slave-based, indolent Zanzibar that the new economy was going to sweep aside.

Creating a 'modern' economy

By the time the British took over in Zanzibar, it was clear that Zanzibar's position as a trade entrepôt for the East African coast was in danger. In the late 1880s, the decline in trade could be attributed to the disruption of the caravan trade by war on the coast and in the interior. But the easing of tensions on the coast did not immediately improve trade. Before 1891 the only duties charged at Zanzibar had been a 5 per cent *ad valorem* tax on imports. Once imported to Zanzibar, goods were free to move to the mainland, which was part of the Sultan's dominions, without paying additional duties. In 1891 the Germans began to levy a 5 per cent duty on goods imported to the mainland, whether or not they had paid a duty in Zanzibar.[56]

[56] E.D. Ropes to the State Department, 11 January 1891, in Bennett, *Zanzibar Letters*, pp. 113–15.

3.2 The Zanzibar waterfront in 1994. The seawall was built by the British in the 1890s as part of their effort to facilitate trade

This caused an uproar in Zanzibar. European and American merchants demanded refunds from the Sultan's government since their most-favoured-nation treaty status dictated that they should only be taxed once on their goods destined for the mainland. The American merchant house Ropes Emmerton demanded $44,000 in drawbacks from the custom-house, and other merchants, including British Indian subjects, did likewise. The situation was temporarily resolved in 1892, when Zanzibar was declared a free port and duties were lifted on all imports except alcohol and arms.[57]

The loss in revenues that accompanied the creation of the free port was to be made up by the 25 per cent export tax on cloves. But the clove industry was having problems of its own and so in 1899 the 5 per cent *ad valorem* duty on imports was reintroduced and the free port experiment was over. Merchants were allowed to transship goods without paying duty on them, which helped Zanzibar to cling to what remained of its position as a entrepôt.[58] The transit trade never completely collapsed; it had far too much inertia to simply disappear. Instead its importance slowly diminished over a twenty-year period. In 1893 £228,000 worth of goods were imported from German East Africa, most of which were intended for re-export. In the same year £286,000 worth of goods were re-exported through Zanzibar to German East Africa. That year the total value of the clove crop was

---

[57] Ibid.
[58] Hollingsworth, *Foreign Office*, p. 68 and R.H. Crofton, *Statistics of the Zanzibar Protectorate, 1893–1920* (London: 1921), p. 7.

only £139,000. By 1910 imports from German East Africa had dropped to £155,000 and re-exports to German East Africa had dropped to £217,000. While the value of the transit trade had been dropping the value of Zanzibar's clove exports had been going up and by 1910 had reached £253,000.[59] The dynamic of Zanzibar's emerging official economy was moving away from the transit trade and towards cash-crop production. In Zanzibar this meant cloves and coconuts.

Cloves had been a part of the Zanzibar economic scene since the first half of the nineteenth century, but always as a supplement to the entrepôt trade with the mainland. There were some huge clove estates that belonged to the Sultan and other members of the royal family and smaller holdings that belonged to more humble people who had made a certain amount of money in the caravan trade and then invested that money in clove plantations. Initially most of the clove production had been on Unguja but the hurricane of 1872 destroyed most of the clove trees on Unguja but spared those on Pemba. Pemba's climate turned out be more favourable to clove production than Unguja's and the bulk of clove production shifted to Pemba, which still produces 85 per cent of Zanzibar's cloves. Pemba is blessed with many sheltered bays and coves but they are shallow and difficult of entry, and ocean-going ships rarely called at Pemba. Combined with the desire of the authorities in Zanzibar to retain control over the clove trade, this has meant that cloves were not exported directly from Pemba, but were instead brought to Zanzibar and then exported to the outside world.[60]

At the same time that Zanzibar's economy was shifting to clove production and government revenues were increasingly dependent on clove duties, British officials were in the process of outlawing slavery (as opposed to the long since outlawed slave-trade). By 1897, slavery had been legally abolished, and clove producers were beginning to feel the need for labour. Clove trees need plenty of attention; they require weeding and twice-annual harvesting, all of which must be done by hand. While some of the former slaves were willing to pick cloves during the harvest, there were too few of them to go around and most of them considered weeding to be beneath their dignity.[61] Thus, around the turn of the century, clove planters and colonial officials began a pattern of labour recruitment on the mainland that survived into the postcolonial period.[62]

So where Zanzibar had once been a transshipment point for goods and slave labour from the mainland it was now becoming a transshipment point for cloves and free labour to and from Pemba. As time

[59] Crofton, *Statistics*, pp. 20–21, 27–29.
[60] In 1892 this tradition was reinforced by Gerald Portal's decree that no dhow could sail to a port outside of the Protectorate without being examined in Zanzibar, *Zanzibar Gazette*, 12 October 1892.
[61] For a through discussion of the labour requirements of clove trees and the difficulties caused by the abolition of slavery, see Cooper, *From Slaves to Squatters*.
[62] Clove pickers continued to migrate to Pemba during the harvests until the late 1980s; now they rarely bother and most of the harvest remains on the trees.

went by, the government grew increasingly interested in making the clove industry more productive and progressive. Their first action on this front was to declare, in 1894, the deliberate mixing of low-grade cloves with high-grade cloves or the deliberate wetting of cloves to be a criminal offence.[63] The wetting of cloves was associated with their theft by dhow crews, so the first bit of regulation in the clove industry was directed at dhows. This was the opening thrust in a fifty-year struggle between the government and the shippers and transporters of cloves over the role dhows would play in the transport of cloves.

A related move was to put the government steamers on a regular schedule and to make service to Pemba – in direct competition with dhows – the central purpose of the government steamer service. Beginning in June 1892 there were three steamer trips a month to Pemba by the Sultan's ships *Kilwa* and *Barawa*. At first these steamers went only to the ports of Chake Chake and Wete in central and northern Pemba respectively, but in 1906 a third steamer port was opened on the southern end of the island of Pemba.[64] Then, in 1907, in an attempt to alleviate the labour shortages in Pemba during the clove harvests, the steamer service began to offer free passages to anyone who called himself a clove picker.[65]

Thus by the early years of the twentieth century, Zanzibar's dhow trade had been seriously threatened by the emergence of a new type of economy. This was an economy that had in a relatively short time transformed itself from a trade depot with a sideline in clove production to a clove producer with a sideline as a trade depot. It was also an economy over which a new type of government was trying to exert a new type of control. This new government was equipped with a range of hitherto unknown accounting and record-keeping technologies and was anxious to use them to transform the Zanzibar economy into something more modern and rational.[66] Furthermore, it was clear from the special dhow provisions of the Brussels Act and the speed with which government steamers were employed to serve the clove industry, that dhows were not envisioned as part of this new economy.

Dhows in a changing economy

Not surprisingly, the effects of this economic transformation were more pronounced for the local dhow trade than for the long-distance trade.

[63] Hollingsworth, *Foreign Office*, p. 118.

[64] Mkoani was chosen as the site for the southern port after the Goan clerks stationed at Fufuni, the alternative site, 'were always ill, and one if not two became insane'. ZNA BA18/1, 'Report of the Collector of Pemba,' 1906.

[65] ZNA AB4/1, Lyne, 'The Clove Crop 1908–09,' 16 Sept. 1908.

[66] In Crofton, *Statistics*, p. 5, Crofton describes the purpose of his book, which was the earliest compilation of general statistics about the Zanzibar economy, as an effort to 'present in concise and modern form the principal statistics of Zanzibar'. Statistics were themselves modern and so contributed to the modernization of the Zanzibar economy.

With the loss of much of the transit trade from the coast, there was a decline in the need for coastal dhow traffic. What remained for local dhows was the traffic between Unguja and Pemba and the residual trade between the coast and the islands that remained after the demise of Zanzibar's role as entrepôt to the Atlantic economy. The Pemba trade involved bringing passengers and imported goods to Pemba and returning with cloves. The trade with the mainland involved bringing food, timber and other bulky items available on the mainland to the islands and transporting goods brought by the northern dhows, i.e. dried fish, salt, dates, etc, to the mainland. By 1893 dhow registrations in Zanzibar under the Brussels Act numbered 414 vessels with a combined tonnage of 2,943 tons. These vessels seem to have been about equally divided between British Indian owners and Zanzibari owners, although the average tonnage of the Indian vessels was a bit higher.[67] Over the next twenty years the number of local dhows registered at Zanzibar went into slow but steady decline. By 1907 there were 397 dhows registered in Zanzibar, by 1908 there were 350 and by 1910 the number had dropped to 323.[68]

What seems to have caused this steady erosion was the steamer service to Pemba. There are no statistics available to show where Zanzibar's dhows went until 1913, but it appears that most of the trade between the mainland and Zanzibar moved in dhows owned on the mainland, while Zanzibar dhows controlled the trade between Pemba and Unguja. The 1910 Port and Marine Annual Report says that 'Zanzibar dhows do most of their trading to Pemba,' although no documentation of this is offered.[69] An important part of the Pemba trade was the transportation of passengers, and steamers had some important advantages over dhows from a passenger's point of view. Steamers are bigger and so passengers stay drier and are less likely to get seasick. The time of one's arrival is fairly predictable in a steamer, while in a dhow the vagaries of wind and current can make arrival times hard to predict. Most importantly, dhows sink with disturbing frequency, and dhow sailors, most of whom can swim, are fairly cavalier about sinking. Until the 1940s dhows did not carry even rudimentary life-saving gear, the usual response to shipwreck being to cut the yard away from the mast and use it as an impromptu float.[70] This did not do much to assuage the worries of most landsmen, and people who needed to travel over water preferred a big, dry steamer when they had a choice.

By 1905 the steamers were splitting the passenger trade to Pemba

[67] ZNA BA110/1, Zanzibar Government, *Diplomatic and Consular Reports on Trade and Finance: Zanzibar, Supplementary Report for the Year 1891* (London: 1892), p. 8, and ZNA AT1/5 and AT1/6, Registration Books of the International Maritime Bureau.

[68] ZNA, BA 110/13, Zanzibar Government, *Diplomatic and Consular Report on Trade and Finance: Zanzibar, Report for the Year 1893*, and ZNA BA18/3, 'Port and Marine Annual Report,' 1910.

[69] ZNA 18/3, 'Port and Marine Annual Report,' 1910, p. 220.

[70] ZNA AB45/47, Port Officer to Chief Secretary, 21 October 1947.

about evenly with dhows. In that year 6,757 passengers went to Pemba by steamer while dhows carried 5,519. Three years later, when the port of Mkoani had been opened, the steamers were set on a more regular timetable and free passages were offered to clove pickers, the total number of passengers and the share claimed by the government's ships increased dramatically. In 1908 17,334 passengers travelled to Pemba by steamer, while dhows carried only 4,244 people. Steamers were clearly gaining the upper hand in the growing passenger market.[71]

Despite the popularity of steamers among travellers, the government steamers never covered their own costs. In 1909, a year of heavy passenger traffic to Pemba, the steamer service did not cover even half of its Rs.97,417 operating cost. The steamers were designed to haul both passengers and cargo, but the only cargo that was ever offered to them was government stores. Cloves from Pemba and goods from Zanzibar on their way to Pemba always moved by dhow. Simply put, dhows moved cargo much more cheaply than steamers.[72] The reasons for this have to do with the nature of Pemba's ports, the geography and the costs of cargo handling, all of which will be looked at in more detail in the next chapter. The ability of dhows to move even valuable cargo more cheaply than steamers, especially between Pemba and Unguja, gave local dhows a market niche they were able to defend up to independence. So, while the government's ships were often filled to capacity with passengers, they usually travelled with their cargo holds empty and so could not operate profitably.

The importance of the Pemba trade for dhows increased steadily in the early years of the twentieth century as trade with German East Africa dropped off. In 1911 1,005 dhows from German East Africa arrived in Zanzibar. By 1912 that number had dropped to 681 and in 1913, while the number of German-flagged dhows entering Zanzibar was up slightly to 746, the number of dhows leaving Zanzibar for the German-controlled mainland had dropped to 276. In the same year, the number of dhows leaving Zanzibar for Pemba was 1,956. Thus the Pemba trade, as best one can tell from the limited amount of information available, was becoming the principal activity of Zanzibar's local dhow fleet.[73]

How the long-distance trade adapted to the new economy is much less well documented, but in many ways more interesting. For the most part it seems to have been unaffected by the changes caused by the British attempt to modernize the Zanzibar economy. There are no shipping returns that include dhows until 1911, when 173 Arab dhows and 137 Indian dhows arrived at Zanzibar, so it is not possible to know exactly how the volume of the long-distance trade changed during this period. The closest we can come is to look at the quantities of dried fish

---

[71] ZNA BA18/3, 'Port and Marine Annual Report,' 1910, p. 214.

[72] Ibid., pp.220, 224-5.

[73] ZNA AT1/10, 'Rapport sur les Travaux de 1911' and 'Rapport sur les Travaux de 1912,' and Zanzibar Government, *Blue Book*, 1913.

and ghee brought to Zanzibar during the 1893 to 1910 period. Since these cargoes were usually brought by Arab dhows, their movement should give us some perspective on the volume of the Arab component of the long-distance trade during the period for which there are no statistics.

The value of the dried fish imported to Zanzibar fluctuated between a low of £8,000 in 1900 and a high of £17,000 in 1907 with an average value of £10,500. The years from 1904 to 1907 seem to have been a sort of mini fish boom, when the value of imported dried fish never dropped below £13,000. Ghee values fluctuated between a high of £32,000 in 1899 and a low of £16,000 in 1902 with an average value of £21,800. The volumes of fish and ghee imported during this period were volatile, but had a slight upwards trend.[74] In neither category is there a strong trend towards higher or lower import volumes, nor does there seem to be a strong correlation between the flux in these dhow cargoes and the also variable output of the clove trade or other official-sector economic activity. The flux in the dhow trade represented by the changes in the value of these imports probably reflects subtle variations in the availability or demand for fish or ghee much more than it represents any kind of response to the changing political economy in Zanzibar. In other words, the Arab component of the long-distance trade was, by the 1890s, already sufficiently removed from the main-stream, official economy for the events of the turn of the century to have little effect on them. Their preferred cargoes – fish, cereals, mangrove poles, salt, etc. – were far removed from the critical revenue-generating clove economy, so what few attempts there were to interfere with them were at best desultory. Arab dhows and their cargoes were already marginal enough for them to be mostly unaffected by the new economic policies imposed by the British. Furthermore, the lifting of the coastal blockade and replacement of the anti-slave-trade patrols with anti-slave-trade regulations probably contributed to a revival of the trade between Arabia and East Africa.

Indian dhows are a bit harder to track during this period. Since there was plenty of steamer traffic between Zanzibar and India, it is more difficult to correlate cargoes with dhow activity. The cotton piece-goods trade had been partly recovered by the Indians in the early part of the 1890s when British India furnished over half of the cottons imported to Zanzibar, but it is likely that much of this was transported in the roughly 140 ocean-going steamers that visited Zanzibar each year in the 1890s. Assuming that at least some of these cotton goods were moved by dhow, it is worth noting that India's share of the piece-goods market in Zanzibar dropped from a high of £170,000 in 1896 to £49,000 in 1910. In the pre-First World War years for which there are records, the Indian dhow trade was declining slightly. In 1911, 137 Indian dhows called at Zanzibar while only 105 came in 1913. Those same years also witnessed a decline in the numbers of Arab vessels coming to Zanzibar. In 1911

[74] Crofton, *Statistics*, pp. 20–21.

173 Arab dhows came, while in 1913 that number had dropped to 140.[75]

Although this appears to provide evidence of a decline in the dhow trade, it is hard to blame it on the emerging colonial economy. For one thing there are only three years of statistics available, so the sample is small.[76] And while the decline looks substantial – 20 per cent in the case of the Arab dhow trade and 25 per cent in the case of the Indian dhow trade – it would be hard to argue that this was not simply a normal variation. During the first decade of the twentieth century the dried-fish trade took several 30 and 40 per cent jumps, both up and down, while its overall trend was upwards. So, while it is possible that the long-distance dhow trade was going into a period of decline in the immediate prewar period, and this decline may have been due to the new political situation in Zanzibar, there is no way of being certain of this, especially since it is hard to see how the changes inaugurated by the British would have interfered with the long-distance trade. Thus it seems safe to conclude that the long-distance trade, which had begun the transition to marginality before the local trade, was less affected by the emerging official economy than the local dhow trade. If anything, the 245 Indian and Arab vessels that came to Zanzibar in 1913 probably represent an increase over the 150 to 200 dhows per year that came to Zanzibar in the 1860s and 1970s. The long-distance trade seems to have entered the twentieth century well separated from the official economy and better off for it, in that its very marginality protected it from state interference.

Conclusion

In 1870 Zanzibar was the capital of a commercial system that stretched from the offshore islands to beyond the Central African lakes. Zanzibar had trade links to the North Atlantic, the Mediterranean, the western Indian Ocean and, through Bombay, to Eastern Asia. Dhows were a critical and fully integrated part of this system. They carried trade goods and African produce between Zanzibar and the ports of the East African mainland and moved those same trade goods and African produce within the western Indian Ocean, as well as carrying on a much older trade between Arabia and the East African littoral.

By 1913 Zanzibar's economic and political situation had changed dramatically and the role of dhows had changed with it. Zanzibar was no longer the capital of a commercial empire; it was a clove producer, cut off from its former mainland possessions, and a British Protectorate to boot. Dhows, no longer needed to bridge the gap between the Atlantic

---

[75] Ibid., pp. 24, 32; ZNA AT1/10, 'Rapport sur les Travaux de 1911' and 'Rapport sur les Travaux de 1912;' Zanzibar Government, *Blue Book*, 1913.

[76] Of course, there are records after 1913, but the sharp drop-off in shipping of all kinds is easily attributable to the war.

and Indian Ocean economies, were left with the work of bringing Pemba cloves to Zanzibar, a small coastal trade with the mainland and maintaining the link between East Africa and Arabia. Where once they had been players in the 'trade of Zanzibar', they were now something separate – the 'dhow trade' – a vestige of the old economy.

Even in this new, more limited role, dhows laboured under special disadvantages. They were singled out and severely harassed during the anti-slavery campaigns of the late nineteenth century. As political control of Zanzibar went over to the British, the naval anti-slavery campaign was transformed into a bureaucratic anti-dhow campaign. Dhows were monitored, listed, registered, labelled, flagged, charged fees and relegated to their own corner of the Zanzibar harbour. As the British tried to modernize the Zanzibar economy, dhows were one of the first things they consigned to the past. A regular steamer service was inaugurated. This competed with dhows for passenger traffic, ran at a loss and was subsidized partly with port fees collected from dhows.

Dhows, formerly the heart of Zanzibar's economy, were now on the margins, both economically and conceptually. Dhows had been defined into a different legal category from other sailing craft and were subject to regulations and restrictions that other vessels were not. Years after the slave-trade had ended, they still bore the taint of their involvement in it and virtually all the dhow-specific regulation was ostensibly meant to control slave trading. More important than this conceptual marginality was their more tangible economic marginality.

From the colonial government's perspective, the principal economic activity in the new Zanzibar was to be cash-crop production for export. In this new system, the dhow's only role was bringing cloves from Pemba to Zanzibar town and the government was determined to put an end even to that. Dhows were almost entirely excluded from the new official economy. But there was more to the Zanzibar economy than the official economy. Parts of the older economy survived and even thrived alongside the official economy. Arabian dhows continued to bring goods desired or needed by the coastal population. The distribution of these goods and the collection of goods for the return voyage to Arabia went on much as it always had. The local dhow trade, which had formerly channelled African produce to Indian merchants in Zanzibar, who in turn directed that African produce to the world market, shifted towards carrying cloves from Pemba to Indian merchants, who then sold the cloves on the world market. The old patterns of the precolonial trade system survived as a second, alternative economy to the official economy that was being created by the British.

Four

Cloves, Dhows & Steamers
The Twentieth-century Struggle Between the Official & Unofficial Economies in Zanzibar

The city desk of a newspaper, a rabbit's intestines, or the interior of an aircraft engine may certainly look messy, but each one reflects, sometimes brilliantly, an order related to the function it performs. In such instances the apparent surface disarray obscures a more profound logic.

James C. Scott, *Seeing like a State*

By the 1920s, Zanzibar's economy had been divided between an emerging official sector centred on the clove economy and a second economy directly descended from Zanzibar's nineteenth-century economy in which dhows, both local and long-distance, played a critical role. While the long-distance trade was largely insulated from the official economy by its own economic marginality, the local trade was in direct conflict with the official economy over the carrying trade between Pemba and Zanzibar.

The size of the local dhow fleet had been shrinking in the early part of the twentieth century and the dhows that remained in business increasingly focused on the Pemba trade. Pemba had long been a sort of internal colony of Zanzibar. It produced the bulk of Zanzibar's clove crop, but since all exports from Pemba had to pass through Zanzibar, control of the trade remained in the hands of Zanzibar-based merchants. Similarly, since Pemba lacked port facilities for ocean-going ships and seagoing dhows were not allowed to call at Pemba without first calling at Zanzibar, all the imports consumed by Pembans passed through Zanzibar before being sent north to Pemba. This situation created a market niche in which dhows thrived and the government's ships struggled. This did not sit well with the British. Intent on rationalizing and modernizing the clove industry, they quickly set about trying to dislodge dhows from the Pemba trade. The result was a twenty-year struggle between the government and the official economy they were trying to promote, and the Asian shippers, who were fighting to retain their position in the clove industry and their preferred means of transporting cloves – the dhow.

The problem with dhows

When the British spoke of 'modernizing' or 'rationalizing' the clove industry, they had in mind something not too different from what we now call development. Their goal was to improve the efficiency and productivity of the clove industry and so increase government revenues and the general prosperity of the Protectorate. Colonial modernizers, like their development successors, sought to improve the economies they encountered through legislation, subsidies, education and public-sector investment in infrastructure. Early infrastructure improvements usually involved replacing older forms of transportation with newer ones. On the mainland, for example, the overland trade, which had relied on head-loading by porters, was modernized by building railways which terminated in modern ports like Mombasa and Dar es Salaam.

When the British began the process of modernizing the clove industry their opening move was legislative. In 1893 they passed the Adulteration of Produce Decree, which made it illegal to mix foreign matter with cloves to wet them in order to increase their weight. The idea here (and with later Adulteration of Produce Decrees of which there were several) was to ensure that no adulterated cloves made it into the international clove market, where they might harm Zanzibar's reputation for high-quality cloves. This was followed by subsidies to the industry in the form of free transport of clove pickers to Pemba, a system of bounties paid to clove growers and an agricultural research station.[1]

Despite these early interventions, the financial situation of clove growers remained precarious. Most clove growers were deeply in debt to the Asian merchants, who loaned them money and sold them goods on credit and then took their annual clove production as repayment or, more often, partial repayment for the year's loans and advances. Thus most clove plantations, though nominally owned and managed by Arabs, were mortgaged to Asians.[2]

The ongoing instability of the clove industry worried the British and so triggered a series of commissions and reports on the clove trade that began in the early 1920s. The first of these, the 1923 Commission on Agriculture, narrowed the problems of the clove industry down to four categories. These were credit, communications and transport, 'hygiene of plantations and labour,' and education.[3] Foremost among these problems was credit, by which they meant the indebtedness of the Arab plantation owners to Asian merchants. The financial weakness of the producer compared with the middleman meant, they argued, that the clove tax – 25 per cent *ad valorem* – was not passed on to the middleman and hence to the consumer but

---

[1] See Chapter 3 above.

[2] For a more detailed account of the nature and extent of this indebtedness, see M. Lofchie, *Zanzibar, Background to Revolution* (Princeton, NJ: 1965) and Frederick Cooper, *From Slaves to Squatters* (New Haven: 1980), pp. 139–145.

[3] ZNA BA3/11, Zanzibar Government, *Report of the Commission on Agriculture, 1923*, p. 3.

swallowed by the producer. Thus '[t]he remedy is to make the grower independent of the middleman'.[4]

As for the problem of transport, they pointed out that most of the clove carriage trade was controlled by dhows. They allowed that there were good reasons for this:

> The western coast is deeply indented with creeks navigable by dhows. No attempt is made to move by the Government steamers produce other than is offered at the three ports of Weti, Chake Chake and Mkoani and in the course of regular sailings. These sailings usually take place once a week but are not always regular. The cargo space offered by these sailings during the clove season is wholly inadequate.[5]

While it was understandable, given these conditions that shippers preferred dhows to the steamer service, there were also problems with dhows.

> The inter-island carriage of produce by dhows is far from satisfactory. These vessels leak. They afford little or no protection against sea and weather. Their capacity is extremely limited. Cloves are stolen or adulterated on route.[6]

In order to rectify this situation they suggested that the main outlets for cloves in Pemba be Wete in the north, Chake Chake in the middle and Mkoani in the south. Since the cost of building a road system that connected these three areas of Pemba to each other was financially out of the question, the Commission suggested that instead road systems that connected each area to its designated port be built. In the ports themselves they thought that godowns and customs sheds should be built, so that cloves could be examined and stored while they awaited the steamers.[7]

The two steamers, the *Khalifa* and the *Cupid* at 230 and 200 tons dead-weight cargo capacity, respectively, were, they thought, up to the job of bringing in most of the Pemba clove crop, provided that each ship made seven monthly journeys to Pemba during the clove season. Furthermore, '[i]n order ... to eliminate the dhow', they suggested that the remote creek ports used by dhows should be served by a lighter and tug service. They thought that these lighters could bring produce from the creek ports and then load it directly on to steamers or, if it proved possible, carry it straight to Zanzibar in the lighter.[8]

Almost as an afterthought they pointed out that 'Dhows returning from Zanzibar to Pemba carry merchandise for use on the plantations; and if the dhow is to be driven out of the trade it will be necessary to make provision for this service.' They made no concrete suggestions as to how this might be accomplished.[9]

The 1923 Commission on Agriculture report set out the basic objections

[4] Ibid., p. 4.
[5] Ibid., p. 14.
[6] Ibid.
[7] Ibid., pp. 13–14.
[8] Ibid., p. 15.
[9] Ibid.

the government had to dhows in the clove trade; these would remain the core of the government's argument for the next fifteen years. Three years later another report gave a slightly more nuanced explanation of the government's objections to dhows and drew a more explicit link between dhow transport of cloves and the undesirable control Indian middlemen exercised over the clove trade. The report stated that:

> The position of the middleman in Pemba is further strengthened by the control which he exercises over the transport organization linking that island with the export market in Zanzibar. That control may be partial as far as inland transport is concerned, but in the case of many large districts, where sea communication with Zanzibar is carried out entirely by dhow, it is complete. And the Indian, who is the only available carrier, controls the supply of bags necessary for packing ... the Pemba dealer, in relation to the clove industry is virtually in the position of a toll gatherer.[10]

In addition to highlighting the link between the Indian middleman and the dhow, the 1926 report also went into greater detail on the subject of clove losses and adulteration during shipment. The report estimated that about 10 per cent of the cloves shipped by dhow were stolen *en route*. *En route* to Zanzibar the dhows stopped at various points in the maze of islands that hem in Pemba's western coast. Here they were met by canoes or smaller dhows, which bought a portion of their cargo. The missing weight was made up by wetting the cloves or by mixing earth with the cloves. So, in addition to having part of the cargo go missing, those cloves that arrived in Zanzibar were adulterated and so of lower value on the world market. On steamers the rate of loss was only 4 per cent, and this was attributed not to theft by the crewmen, but to shrinkage (cloves lose weight in storage as they dry) and to 'manoeuvring' by the Indian middlemen who shipped by steamer.[11]

The author conceded that dhow transport was nominally cheaper at 7 annas a bag compared with 12 annas per bag for the steamer service, but actually more expensive 'taking into consideration the condition in which the cloves arrive at their destination and ignoring all together the consideration of deliberate thefts in transit'.[12]

The authors of the 1926 report were more circumspect than their 1923 predecessors in their recommendations. They still wanted to expand the steamer service, begin a lighter service to a few of the more important outports, close some of the less important outports and to build godowns in all the ports. The 1926 report also concedes that the total elimination of dhows would probably be impossible and might not be desirable, since the 'dhow fleet represents an important part of our business organization'. The

[10] ZNA BA4/5, 'Memorandum on Certain Aspects of the Zanzibar Clove Industry' (London: 1926), p. 17.
[11] Ibid., pp. 18, 53. A former clove merchant confirmed that cloves were indeed stolen and adulterated by dhow crews, but he said that the steamer crews did much the same thing. Interview with Sherali Haji Rashid, 16 August 1994.
[12] ZNA BA4/5, 'Memorandum' pp.17–18.

author did suggest that perhaps it would be wise to license only the most seaworthy of the dhows to carry cloves. Despite the more moderate recommendations of the 1926 report, a year later it was the 'established policy of Government to divert the sea-carriage of the Pemba clove output from the dhow fleet to the Government Steamers'.[13]

By 1927, the government of Zanzibar had decided that dhow transport was one of the problems facing the clove industry. It is noteworthy that, while there was some discussion of the possibility of improving the existing dhow transport network, the overwhelming response of the colonial administration was to replace the 'traditional' dhows with 'modern' steamers and all the infrastructure that steamers required. This response was dictated less by the actual facts of the situation than by the government's anti-Indian sentiments and an unarticulated belief in the superiority of the 'modern' over the 'traditional'. The colonial state looked at the clove industry in Pemba and saw disorder and backwardness. What they failed to notice was that dhows suited the economic scale and geography of Pemba's clove industry better than steamers ever could.

Pemba's clove trade from a sailor's perspective

The geography of the island of Pemba and the nature of the clove trade itself made the dhow uniquely suited to the work of removing Pemba's cloves to Zanzibar where they met the world market. When the colonial regime attempted to drive dhows out of the Pemba trade they failed to take into account how thoroughly the clove trade was structured around dhow transport. Their attempt to simply add steamers to the equation without fundamentally changing the economic geography of Pemba and the social networks that linked dhow owners and clove shippers was doomed from the start. In order to understand how deeply embedded dhows were in the structures of the clove trade, we need to take an extended look at the geography of Pemba, the seasonality of the clove business and the social networks linking clove merchants and dhow owners.

Pemba, unlike its sister island Unguja, is quite hilly. The hills are not particularly high, the highest point on the island being only about 400 feet, but they are steep and closely spaced. As a result the island feels far more mountainous than it really is and land transport is quite difficult compared with the much more level Unguja. Roads came much later to Pemba than to Unguja and even today the road system does little more than link the three main regions of the island.

Whatever Pemba lacks in internal transport it makes up in its water-transport possibilities. Pemba is about 40 miles long and about 12 miles wide. Pemba's eastern coast is moderately indented and unlike the eastern coast of Unguja, which is exposed to the full force of the Indian Ocean,

---

[13] Ibid., pp. 19–20, ZNA AB45/51a, Comptroller of Customs to the Chief Secretary, 30 March 1927.

4.1 Cloves drying on mats in Pemba. Cloves were a cargo carried by local dhows.
The mats were made in Oman and brought south by long-distance trading dhows

outlying islands protect much of Pemba's eastern shore. The western coast is deeply and frequently indented and lavishly endowed with fringe islands. As a result, no place on Pemba is more than 4 miles from the sea, and in most places some inlet or creek is quite close by.

The creeks and inlets not only provide shelter for dhows, but some of the creek heads are as much as a half mile to a mile from the sea, which allowed dhows to come to the cloves instead of vice versa. While dhow transport was easily available in most areas, land transport was difficult and expensive. Cloves were moved overland by donkey cart or pack donkey at an average cost of Rs.8 per ton per mile. By way of comparison, the same ton of cloves could be moved a much flatter mile on Unguja for Rs.1. Thus, on Pemba clove shippers did whatever they could to minimize the distance their produce moved overland.[14]

A prospective clove shipper did not have to look far to find a waiting dhow port. From Msuka on the north coast and all down the west coast to Kengeja on its south coast, Pemba was rife with dhow ports. A 1927 list of the ports on Pemba used only to export cloves (there were a few others used primarily for mangrove poles) shows eleven ports, or approximately one port for every 4 miles of the island's length. Of these eleven ports, the two most important in terms of volume were Wete and Chake Chake (see Map 1.3, p. 11), which were served by both dhows and steamers. The third most active port on this list was Jambangome, which was served only by dhows.

---

[14] ZNA BA4/5, 'Memorandum,' p. 17

4.2   Abandoned CGA lighters in Wete, Pemba, 1994

Jambangome's dhow fleet carried away an average of 51,229 frasilas (one frasila = 35 lbs.) of cloves per year in the 1920s. Pemba's third steamer port, Mkoani, ranked only seventh in volume, behind Jambangome, Kengeja, Kisiwani and Fufuni, all of which were dhow-only creek ports. Mkoani, despite regular calls by the government's ships, was the least significant port in the district of which it was the administrative centre, shipping only 20,000 frasilas annually compared with 50,000 for Jambangome and 35,000 for Kengeja.[15]

In Pemba's northern and central districts the clove trade was more centralized. In the north the steamer port of Wete an annual average of 96,000 frasilas of cloves left from Wete while the four outports of Msuka, Mtambwe, Junguni and Kipangani together claimed about 50,000 frasilas. In Chake Chake district in the middle of the island, 93,000 frasilas a year left from Chake Chake itself, and the one dhow-only port in the district, Kisiwani, exported roughly 29,000 frasilas a year.[16]

But, even in the two districts in which there was some centralization of the clove shipping business, steamers had a hard time attracting much of the cargo. In Mkoani district, where dhows were in virtually total control, a mere 8.8 per cent of the annual clove crop was shipped by steamer and only 1.4 per cent of the northbound traffic was carried by steamer. In Chake Chake, even with its highly centralized shipping trade, only 6.9 per cent of the clove crop moved by steamer while 3.9 per cent of the northward cargo

[15] ZNA AB45/51a, Senior Custom Officer to Chief Secretary, 12 March 1927.
[16] Ibid.

arrived by steamer. In Wete, which was the stronghold of the steamer service, 21.5 per cent of the clove crop was carried by steamers. Although steamers were doing an acceptable job of attracting Wete's clove crop, they were still failing to capture much of the 'up traffic', of which they carried a paltry 2.8 per cent. For Pemba as a whole, steamers carried 14.8 per cent of the clove crop and 2.8 per cent of the up traffic was carried by steamers. So, even in the more centralized districts, where much of the clove crop was shipped from ports accessible to steamers, clove shippers still chose dhows over steamers.[17]

Since even cloves which were shipped from steamer ports were usually transported by dhow, the reasons for the dominance of the dhow in the Pemba clove trade are not just geographical, they also have to do with the economics of cargo handling, the business practices of the Asian merchants who shipped most of the cloves and the physical peculiarities of the ports. The shippers' preference for traditional rather than modern technology was not atavistic; it was economically rational. But at each Pemba port the rationale for choosing dhows over steamers was different. The conditions that made dhows cheaper to use were different at each port, so no single policy or infrastructure change the colonial administration might make could undo the tangled web of economic, geographical and social forces that made shippers favour dhows. Let us, then, consider the three regions of Pemba separately with an eye to the advantages dhows enjoyed over steamers in each.

In the southern district of Mkoani the average plantation was relatively small and instead of being dominated by one big town as the other two districts are, Mkoani district had four towns which served as ports for the clove trade. The biggest of these was Jambangome, which was situated on a fork of a creek north of the town of Mkoani, the two arms of which penetrated a kilometre or two into the surrounding clove-growing area.[18] Jambangome, which is now abandoned and listed on maps as a ruin, was a thriving town with several mosques and a large population of the dreaded Indian 'middlemen'.

The other three towns, Kengeja, Fufuni and Mkoani, were spread out at intervals along the coast south and east from Jambangome. Kengeja, the easternmost of these ports, was the second most important after Jambangome. It and Fufuni drained a huge clove-producing area on the eastern side of the central chain of mountains. Kengeja, like Jambangome, was on a spit of land that separated two mangrove creeks, which meant that cloves could easily be brought by canoe from a large area to the dhows waiting at Kengeja. Fufuni, on the south coast, was accessible by water only by way of a small creek that led to the sea, and consequently was of lesser significance than Kengeja and Jambangome.

Mkoani town was not situated on a creek, so everything that came to

[17] ZNA AB44/65, Secretary Manager of the CGA to Treasurer, Board of Management, 13 May 1936.
[18] ZNA AB45/51a, Comptroller of Customs to Chief Secretary, 30 March 1927.

Mkoani for shipment came overland. Mkoani's main attraction was that it is the first town on the coast that is not hemmed in by the reefs and islands that cluster around Pemba's south coast and the water remains fairly deep right up to the shore. Thus the authorities chose Mkoani as the steamer port for southern Pemba, not because it had a history as a collection point for cloves but because it was easily accessible to steamers. In 1927 it had a shed and a couple of lighters, which had to be beached to be unloaded – there was no jetty. The steamer stopped for only an hour or so, enough time to unload its passengers, when it called, so even if there were cloves waiting in the shed there was rarely time to load them. And, if the tide was out and the lighters were trapped on the shore, there was not even the possibility of handling cargo. Passengers who came ashore in small boats could land no matter what the tide was doing, so Mkoani was able to function as a passenger port, but as clove port it did very little business.[19] At Mkoani, steamer transportation was disastrously inefficient.

Mkoani suffered from disadvantages that the other two steamer ports did not. Being the southernmost steamer port, it was closer to Zanzibar than Chake Chake and Wete. The four dhow ports in the region that competed for the clove trade were thus about 20 miles closer to Zanzibar than dhows leaving from the Chake Chake region and almost 30 miles closer than dhows leaving from some of the more northerly ports. Mkoani district dhows thus had a comparative advantage over dhows in the other two districts, which partly explains the degree to which dhows controlled Mkoani's clove trade.

Mkoani's other disadvantage as a steamer port was that the town of Mkoani did not dominate its region the way that Chake Chake and Wete did. As we have seen, it was chosen as a steamer port mostly because it was easily accessible from the sea. The Indian merchants who controlled the trade lived in other towns – Jambangome and Kengeja, for instance – and so preferred to ship from their own ports and by dhow. So, in the late 1920s, when the British began their campaign to get dhows out of the clove trade, Mkoani district was dominated by dhows to a degree not seen in the other two districts.[20]

Just to the north of Mkoani District is Chake Chake district. Chake Chake town had for most of the twentieth century been the administrative centre of Pemba, although at times it has shared this distinction with Wete town. It lies at the head of a long creek, which runs so far inland that Chake Chake town sits at what is nearly Pemba's narrowest point. The areas north and south of this creek are heavily planted with clove trees and, unlike Mkoani, Chake Chake town was a major collection point for cloves. Chake Chake had a sizeable population and even had a small 'stone town' like

[19] ZNA AB45/51a, 'Memorandum by Resident on Pemba Shipping Facilities,' 8 March 1927, ZNA AB44/66, Resident Engineer, 'Report on Landing Facilities at Pemba Ports,' 8 October 1926. This was still true in 1951: ZNA AB44/65, Barber, DC Pemba to Port Officer, 27 June 1951.

[20] ZNA AB45/51, Port Officer to Chief Secretary, 21 March 1927, and ZNA AB45/58a, Port Officer to Chief Secretary, 25 February 1929.

4.3 The old quay at Chake Chake, Pemba, 1994. Mangroves and silt have rendered the creek inaccessible to boats bigger than canoes. The creek began to silt up in the 1940s, possibly because wartime pressure to produce food caused soil erosion. In the 1930s dhows could get up the creek at high tide and this is where Chake Chake clove merchants loaded their cargoes for Zanzibar

Zanzibar town. And, unlike Mkoani, 75 per cent of the cloves shipped from Chake Chake district left from Chake Chake town.[21]

From an economic standpoint, Chake Chake would seem to have been an ideal place for a steamer port to thrive. But, despite the concentration of so many cloves in one place, dhows carried 73 per cent of Chake Chake's clove trade and 84 per cent of its imports. In this case, the dominance of the dhow owes much to soil erosion. The long creek that puts Chake Chake into the heart of the clove country and still allows it access to the sea is shallow and has been getting steadily shallower over time. In the 1920s the creek had silted up substantially and canoes were used to move cloves down the creek to dhows waiting in deeper water at Wesha, although some smaller dhows continued to make it all the way to Chake Chake steps. During the Second World War there was an effort to bring more land under cultivation which increased the erosion rate and caused further silting in the Chake Chake creek and the encroachment of mangroves into the channel in the creek. By the early 1950s the situation was so bad that the

[21] ZNA AB45/51a, Senior Customs Officer to Chief Secretary, 12 March 1927.

Agriculture Department initiated an expensive mangrove removal programme to try to revive Chake Chake creek. This was not successful and the creek is now a tidal flat and mangrove swamp. When I was there in 1994, there were small *Avicennia* mangroves growing next to the jetty and the only boats that could come into the head of the creek were canoes.[22]

Not surprisingly, steamers cannot reach Chake Chake town. In order to bring Chake Chake into the steamer system, the government made a new port at Wesha, about 4 miles down the creek from Chake Chake. At Wesha there was a small mole and a large shed served by a lighter and a launch. The original plans had called for a full-size pier at Wesha, but the £16,000 price tag for this had been prohibitive and the government settled for a small mole. The mole was so small that it was useless except at half or full tide. The new port at Wesha was connected to Chake Chake by a 4 mile road that cost £26,000 to build and crossed the three different arms of the creek.[23]

By 1927 it was clear to people in the Customs Department that Wesha was 'a white elephant'.[24] The reasons for this failure are illustrative of one of the great advantages dhows enjoyed over steamers, both at Chake Chake and at other ports served by both steamers and dhows. One of the principal costs of shipping a bulk cargo is that of cargo handling. This is doubly true when the distance the cargo is moved once loaded is short. In the case of Chake Chake cargo-handling costs were of paramount importance in the merchants' decision to ship by dhow. If a Chake Chake merchant were to decide to ship by steamer, he would be faced with a tremendous amount of cargo handling, which would add to his shipping costs. Beginning from the godowns in his shop, he would first have to pay to have his cloves removed from the godown and loaded on to a truck. Then he would have to pay for the truck to go to Wesha, where he would again pay for the goods to be unloaded from the truck. With luck he might unload his truck directly into a lighter, but in all likelihood he would have to move his cloves into the shed, where they would await the next steamer. Then when the steamer came, if low tides did not force a cargo 'shut-out', he would pay to have his cloves removed from the shed and loaded into a lighter.[25] The lighter would then go out to the waiting steamer and the cloves would be shifted on board the steamer. Once in the port of Zanzibar things were a bit more simple. There, the steamers could come alongside to handle their cargo, and there were even steam cranes with which to work the cargo. This is a lot of cargo handling for a relatively short distance covered.

If, on the other hand, our merchant chose to ship by dhow, the amount

---

[22] ZNA BA 30/22, Pemba Monthly Report, March 1943, ZNA AU 1/340, District Agricultural Officer to Forestry Officer, 11 November 1950, and ZNA AKP39/5, 'Report of the Chake Chake Town Board Concerning the Reopening of Wesha Port,' n.d. [1959].

[23] ZNA AB45/51a, 'Memorandum by Resident on Pemba Shipping Facilities,' 8 March 1923, and ZNA AB44/65, Resident Engineer, Zanzibar Harbour Works, 'Proposed Landing Facilities in Wesha Pemba,' 8 November 1922.

[24] ZNA AB45/51a, Senior Customs Officer to Chief Secretary, 12 March 1927.

[25] Cargo 'shut outs' occurred when the steamer schedule called for the port to be visited at low tide when all the lighters were stranded on the beach.

of cargo handling would be greatly reduced. Dhow freight charges, which were nominally higher than steamer freights, included the costs of moving the cloves from the shipper's godown in Chake Chake to his godown in Zanzibar. The dhow would be brought up to the jetty in Chake Chake and then its crew would bring the cloves from the shipper's godowns to the dhow. The dhow would then sail to Zanzibar, where the crew would unload it and carry the cloves to the shipper's Zanzibar godowns. It was a door-to-door service. And as often as not the Chake Chake shipper owned his own dhows, which further contributed to keeping his costs down.[26]

So, despite the centralization of the clove trade in Chake Chake and the half-hearted investment by the government in creating a steamer port at Wesha, Chake Chake shippers remained resolutely wedded to their dhows. Further north in Wete district, steamers played a significant role in the clove trade. Wete district, like Mkoani, had numerous outports but the volume of traffic through these ports was rather small. Sixty-eight per cent of the clove traffic passed through Wete town and Wete was the commercial capital of the district.[27] Wete is, like Chake Chake, at the head of a creek. Unlike Chake Chake, the Wete creek, though tricky to get into, is fairly deep and steamers can enter it at all tides. In 1927 the pier allowed the two lighters at Wete to float alongside at all tides, provided they were empty. Full they could only float at full tide. Soil erosion seems to have played a role at Wete also. In the 1950s the District Officer in Wete complained that mangroves were encroaching on the port, and today the lighters at Wete will float neither empty nor full at low tide.[28]

As a steamer port Wete had advantages that neither Mkoani nor Chake Chake could boast. It was far enough from Zanzibar for the amount of time a load of cloves would spend in transit on a dhow to be part of a shipper's calculation. Wete district had a larger proportion of big clove plantations, and for the bigger growers the storage facilities at Wete port (only available to cloves awaiting shipment by steamer) offered a place to protect a large harvest from the elements.[29]

Wete was also the headquarters of the Clove Growers' Association (CGA) in Pemba. The CGA was an organization created by the government with the intention of helping the clove growers get out from under the thumbs of the middlemen. It bought cloves directly from the producers and did so at a 'fair' price, offered storage for cloves so that producers could keep them off the market when prices were low at the end of the harvest and in keeping with the government policy of favouring steamers over dhows, all CGA cloves were moved by steamer. The presence of the CGA in Wete thus contributed to the modest use of the steamers in Wete.[30]

[26] ZNA AB45/58a, Comptroller of Customs to Chief Secretary, 18 April 1931.
[27] ZNA AB45/51a, Senior Customs Officer to Chief Secretary, 12 March 1927.
[28] ZNA BA37/8, Bish and Partners, *Pemba Harbour Project: Pre-Investment Study,* June 1977, ZNA AB45/51a, 'Memorandum by Resident on Pemba Shipping Facilities,' 8 March 1927, ZNA AU1/340, District Agricultural Officer to DC, Pemba, 7 April 1953.
[29] ZNA AB45/51a, Comptroller of Customs to Chief Secretary, 30 March 1927.
[30] ZNA BA30/19, District Commissioner, 'Annual Report from Pemba 1934.'

4.4 A dhow loading timber at Wete, Pemba, 1994

Geography and cargo-handling costs were probably the main reason for the dominance of dhows in the clove trade, but the seasonality of the clove business was also a factor. Cloves are harvested twice a year. Since there was a limited amount of storage space in Pemba, getting the harvested cloves out of Pemba and on their way to the world market was a matter of some urgency. Access to dependable transport during the harvest was critical to clove shippers, and dhows owned by friends, family members or co-religionists were more likely to be reliable than the impersonal bureaucracy of the steamer service. The seasonality of the clove business also meant that between the periods of intense activity were slack times, and dhows were better suited to accommodating inactivity than steamers.

While there was always at least a trickle of cloves leaving Pemba the monthly variation in exports was huge. In April 1936 a mere 4,544 frasilas of cloves left Pemba and through the summer the monthly exports limped along below 10,000 frasilas. Then in September the pace picked up dramatically and 79,000 frasilas were exported. The next month saw 93,000 frasilas leave the island. In the next two months the numbers began to decline and then there was another smaller export burst in the months of January and February.[31]

It is significant that the steamers claimed a larger share of the privately shipped cloves during the less busy months and a significantly smaller share

---

[31] ZNA BA30/12, Monthly District Reports from Pemba, 1936.

during those months when things got busy. Thus we find that in April of 1936, the quietest month of that year steamers carried 43 per cent of the privately shipped clove crop. In the busiest month of that year steamers claimed only 5 per cent of the privately shipped cloves. This pattern held for the entire year of 1936 and, although similar data are not available for other years, it is likely that this pattern holds true for other years as well.[32]

What this suggests is that, when there was time to do so, at least some merchants found it made sense to ship cloves by steamer. But, when things got busy, they almost universally abandoned steamers for dhows. There are several reasons for this. For one thing, the steamers in most years did not really have the capacity to handle the entire clove crop. Whether this was theoretically possible was debated at length between the Port Office and Customs Office in the late 1920s. Judging from this debate it seems that the steamers might have been able to handle a significant portion of the clove crop had they devoted themselves entirely to carrying cloves to from Pemba.[33] The steamers had other duties, including maintaining the buoys and lights, carrying government stores and passengers, making the occasional run to the mainland, and now and then being commandeered by the Resident for official travel. Given these other duties and the other sorts of delays and breakdowns that complex mechanical and administrative systems are prone to, it is certain that the steamers were not up to the task of moving the entire clove crop, especially in the busiest months. Further complicating matters was the practice of holding space on the steamers for CGA cloves. Private shippers in Pemba simply could not rely on the government ships when they most urgently needed to move their cloves.

What Pemba shippers could rely on at the busy times of the year were the personal relationships they had with dhow owners. Some Pemba shippers owned their own dhows and carried their own produce as well as that of others. In Chake Chake in 1941 three local merchants owned their own dhows and only one of these, Taherali Nurbhai, did not regularly carry produce for another Chake merchant. Significantly the other two resident dhow owners did not just let out space in their vessels to just anybody, but to a specific person. Abdulkarim Siwji, for example, carried his own produce and that of Devchand Premji.

Shippers who did not own dhows usually relied on a Zanzibar-based merchant who owned a dhow or dhows to get his produce from Pemba to Zanzibar. Thus the Zanzibar-based Dwarkadas Morarji had his dhow number 30 earmarked for the use of I.G. Rawal, for whom that dhow made an annual average of fifty voyages. I.G. Rawal also shipped on another Morarji dhow, number 18, which also carried the produce of two other merchants. Janmohamed Lalji, a Zanzibar resident who owned four dhows, seems to have done business with two families who lived in Pemba. His dhow number 70 served the needs of Rajabali Hirji and Walji Hirji. His dhows 37, 39 and 4 were devoted to Janmohamed Datoo, H.J. Datoo and

[32] Ibid.
[33] ZNA AB45/51a, Comptroller of Customs to Chief Secretary, 30 March 1927.

Gulamhussein Datoo. In some cases the shipper relied on relatives to handle their shipping; dhow number 27, which belonged to Haridas Amra, made fifty voyages a year to Chake Chake on behalf of Gadhvi & Co., a firm owned by his son-in-law. I stumbled on this relationship while interviewing Vijay Gadhvi, Amra's grandson.[34] It is highly likely that some of the other relationships I have mentioned involved more than just business ties.

These relationships, wherein the shipper not only had a dhow owner he regularly worked with but a specific dhow or dhows at his disposal, served to reassure the shipper that during the busy part of the year his cloves would not get left behind. Further strengthening these ties was the fact that none of the Zanzibar-based dhow owners were transport specialists. For them dhows were part of a diversified business, which usually involved the importation of consumer goods and the exporting of cloves and other local produce. Thus the dhows used to transport a client's cloves were also used to bring consumer goods, which had been imported by the dhow owner, to Pemba for the client's shop. These types of relationships were not likely to be replaced by the bureaucratic world of the steamer service, with its rational but impersonal published fares, rigid schedule and cargo shut-outs. For shippers, the convenience, security and trust involved in shipping their cloves with a trusted business associate or even a relative helped to ensure that the steamers ran at only partial capacity while the dhows stayed busy.

The other side of seasonality was idleness. Between the two busy periods were times when neither dhows nor the steamer service could hope to run at full capacity, since there was little in the way of cargo to carry to Zanzibar from Pemba except cloves. Dhows still had some work in that they still carried most of the northbound cargo to Pemba, but they could also be laid up quite easily and their crews sent off to shift for themselves. Steamers, on the other hand, were expensive to run when not operating at full capacity. The Marine Service still had to pay its employees and all the capital tied up in ships, lighters, cargo-handling gear and storage facilities was sitting idly by. Even if dhows ran at only partial capacity during the lulls, 'their maintenance charges are small and their dependence on shore facilities negligible'.[35]

When the government decided to modernize the clove trade by forcing dhows out of the trade, they were embarking on a formidable task. For steamers to replace dhows the whole clove industry would have to have been transformed. The economic geography of Pemba would have to have been re-shaped, with roads, harbour projects and storage facilities, and the long-standing personal relationships between shippers and dhow owners would have to have been overcome. Some of these changes, specifically those that involved infrastructure, could have been brought about by a hearty dose of capital investment, but it is not clear that this would have been cost-effective. Pemba did not produce enough cloves to justify the level of investment needed to fully mechanize clove transportation. Pemba is a

[34] Interview with Vijay Gadhvi, 27 August 1994.
[35] ZNA AB45/51a, Comptroller of Customs to Chief Secretary, 30 March 1927.

small and very hilly place and clove production was only economic there because of the ability of dhows to come to the clove crop. To local observers this was perfectly obvious. To the state the baroque and highly locally specific conditions that allowed dhows to do their work at a lower cost than steamers were not as obvious and so they stuck by their apparently logical position that steam transport was cheaper than sail. Personal preferences and business relationships are much harder to overcome, but even shippers with strong ties to the dhow world would probably have eventually come around if the government had succeeded in making steamer transport cheaper than dhows. This, as we shall see, they never did, and dhows held their own against state-sponsored modernity until the 1964 revolution.

Opening salvoes in the bid to squeeze out dhows

The initial efforts to increase the quantity of cloves moving by steamer rather than dhow concentrated on improving the steamer service and on legal requirements that cloves that came to Zanzibar from Pemba be dry and unadulterated. As we saw in the previous chapter, these pre-First World War efforts had little effect on the use of dhows in the clove trade. After the war, there was a more concerted effort to improve the ports, in both Zanzibar and Pemba. A great deal of money was spent on making the Protectorate's ports more steamer-accessible and efficient. These improvements either ignored the requirements of dhows or, in the case of the Zanzibar port, actually cut dhows off from what little mechanical cargo-handling equipment was available.[36]

In the early part of the 1920s the government initiated two harbour works programmes. One, the creation of Wesha port, was relatively small-scale. The other, the new Zanzibar port, was substantial. When finished, both were smaller and less accommodating than when initially conceived, and neither fulfilled the modernizing purpose for which it was intended.

As we saw in the previous chapter, one of the first acts of the Protectorate government was to build a quay on the northern side of Ras Shangani, the westernmost part of Zanzibar town. Prior to the construction of the quay, cargo was handled over the beach. The new quay, built in 1892, let lighters and smaller dhows come alongside at high tide. It had a few steam cranes and was the terminus of a narrow-gauge railway that went about 6 miles up the coast to Bububu. Because ocean-going ships could not come alongside this quay, cloves from Pemba that came by steamer were subject to lighterage twice – once when they arrived from Pemba and again when they were shipped to their final destinations. This level of cargo handling naturally added to the overall cost of steamer transport. So in the early 1920s the Protectorate government decided to build a new, more modern port.

---

[36] Interestingly, this little drama has entirely escaped notice in the literature on colonial Zanzibar.

This new port was built at the northern end of what was then a peninsula in the Malindi neighbourhood of Zanzibar. It was originally intended to be a deep-water port, i.e. a port that would have allowed ocean-going vessels to come alongside and load or unload cargo directly on to the pier. When the port was opened in 1929, enough dredging to let the government ships come alongside had been done, but this provided only an 18 foot draft and even this depth was only achieved at the far end of the pier. The result was that while the government's relatively small ships could come alongside, ocean-going ships could not. Thus, while the cost of bringing cloves from Pemba by steamer had been reduced by the cost of one lighterage operation, lighterage from the wharf to the ocean-going ships remained part of the cost of exporting cloves from Pemba. The dredging needed to let ocean-going ships come alongside was not done until the 1980s, when the whole harbour was improved.[37]

In addition to offering steamers a comparative advantage in the Pemba clove trade by eliminating one lighterage operation, the new harbour segregated dhows into a special dhow basin with its own wharf and a special dhow shed for goods landed at the dhow wharf. While it might at first glance seem odd that the same people who were bent on driving dhows out of the Pemba trade would be so solicitous as to build them a special harbour, a closer look reveals that the new dhow basin was part of an effort to control and hinder dhows – all part of the modernizing process (Map 4.1).

Before the new port was built, dhows had the whole waterfront over which to move their cargo. Since the sea wall, which served as a quay, was some 950 feet long, it meant that dhows had a big area to pick from when they were looking for a spot to land their cargo, and the customs and port officers who were trying to impose order on the place had a large area to oversee. In the new port the dhow basin was more compact and, since it was shaped like an 'L' with a kink in the bottom, could be observed from two sides. So the new basin meant that much greater supervision could be exercised over dhows.

This increased supervision was probably less significant than the segregation that the new structure imposed on dhows. The dhow basin was on the northeast side of the main wharf, and well separated from the west-facing berths where the government steamers and the lighters that served the ocean-going ships handled their cargo. In itself this was probably only of psychological importance and part of the ongoing process of separating the world of the dhow from the more 'modern' world of steamships. But there was a side-effect that had somewhat more significance and this was that what mechanical cargo-handling equipment there was in Zanzibar port was on the steamer wharf. At the old Customs quay, there had been a couple of steam cranes and these appear to have been accessible to dhows.[38] In the new port the steam cranes were all on the steamer wharf and dhows

[37] ZNA BA37/8, Bish, *Pemba Harbour Project*, and B.S. Hoyle, *The Seaports of East Africa* (Nairobi: 1967), pp. 104–5.
[38] ZNA AV7/25, Photograph.

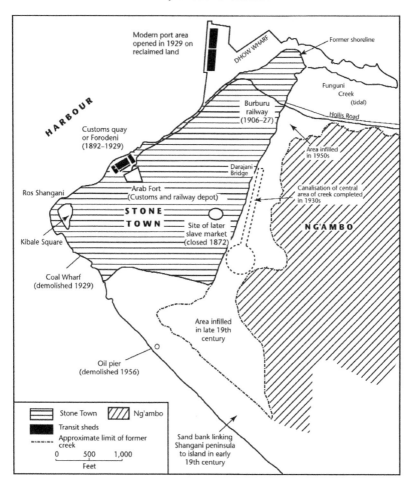

Map 4.1 *Zanzibar port*
(*Based on Hoyle:* Seaports, *p. 99*)

had to make do entirely with human labour to handle their cargoes. Thus the creation of the new port, while advantageous to steamers, was probably detrimental to dhows though certainly not grievously so. What is most significant about the new harbour is not the relative advantage it gave to steamers, rather it is what the final form of the project tells us about British ideas about the direction Zanzibar's economy was going to take and the sorts of steps they were or were not willing to take to push the economy in that direction.

As part of a steady process of separating dhows from the official economy, the separate dhow basin in the new harbour works was of a piece with the larger process. The new harbour rendered in concrete form – literally – the government's ideas about which was the modern part of the economy and which was the archaic part of the economy. Dhows, denied access to the 'main wharf', cut off from the cranes and given their own segregated cargo sheds, had been relegated to the past.

The new harbour reflects another aspect of the government's attitude towards infrastructure development – its proclivity for half-measures. The original intention in building the new harbour was to have a three-berth deep-water port. This was never realized (Zanzibar as of the 1980s has become a deep water port, but with only two berths). Thus despite all the money that was put into the harbour works, lighterage was not eliminated and steamers remained a relatively inefficient way of getting cloves from Pemba to the world market.[39]

The Wesha project, which was undertaken at about the same time the harbour works began, followed a similar but much smaller scale pattern. Originally intended to be jetty accessible to lighters at all tides, the final product was a tiny mole, which ensured that Wesha would be a failure as a steamer port. By 1929 both Wesha and the new Zanzibar harbour were open. Neither had a tremendous effect on anything except the Treasury.[40]

While the government was spending all this money in pursuit of a clove-transport system based on three steamer ports in Pemba and one modern port in Zanzibar, at least one member of Zanzibar's Indian community was rising to protest. In 1923 when the Wesha project was finished and the Zanzibar port scheme was going full tilt, Yusufali Esmailjee Jivanjee,[41] a member of the Protectorate Council, published a rebuttal to the 1923 Commission on Agriculture report which had first set out the government's plan for reforming the clove-transport system. Jivanjee took issue with

---

[39] Hoyle, *Seaports*, p. 104.

[40] ZNA AB44/66, Director of Public Works and Engineering to Chief Secretary, 19 December 1934.

[41] Yusufali Esmailjee Jivanjee, *Memorandum on the Report of the Commission on Agriculture 1923* (Poona: 1924). Though I cannot confirm my theory, I believe that the author is a Jivanjee of Karimjee Jivanjee fame. Karimjee Jivanjee was and remains one of the most important corporations in East Africa. Originally based in Zanzibar, Karimjee Jivanjee was once a major clove-exporting firm as well as representing several shipping and insurance firms in East Africa. Today it is still in the import–export business and owns some large tea estates in Tanzania. So, in writing this diatribe, Yusufali Jivanjee is probably writing from the point of view of a prominent clove exporter.

almost every point raised in the 1923 report and with the entire harbour scheme.

Jivanjee was outraged by the whole programme and wrote with the muted anger that Chambers of Commerce reserve for their responses to proposals from Greenpeace. Of the plan to ship all Pemba cloves through the three steamer ports, and the roads that this would require, he pointed out that the roads alone would cost £80,000 and that this price did not include the cost of the piers and customs sheds which would also be needed. He claimed he was not the only one disturbed by the Pemba roads and ports scheme. He wrote: 'The execution of this scheme which is proceeding for some time now, has been the subject of ceaseless adverse comment from unofficial quarters.'[42]

Jivanjee also questioned the usefulness of the Zanzibar port improvements. He wondered whether it made sense to invest so much money in a port that was not consistently busy.

> The capabilities of the projected wharf, costing as it will do a large sum of money for a small port like Zanzibar, to serve economically even one large liner are problematical. The very slow progress the works are making and the amount of money already spent on them, lend strength to the conclusion that scheme as well as its execution are in keeping with the usual haphazard methods of Government in its commercial undertakings.[43]

Jivanjee was not content with merely criticizing the government's port improvement scheme: he was an active defender of dhows. '[T]he whole of the African coast', he wrote, 'is served by dhows ... it is unthinkable that such a useful local dhow industry should have been thought of being driven out of the trade.' He also suggested that the entire 'modernization' programme was intended 'merely to buy foreign made craft [a reference to the government's steamers and some expensive dredging equipment purchased for the harbour works]'. He conceded that the steamers had their uses in that they were good at hauling passengers, but he wanted to see the steamer service run entirely on 'commercial lines' and not used to shuttle around government officials.[44]

As far as I know, Jivanjee's pamphlet was the only open opposition to the government's clove-transport scheme. What is so interesting about Jivanjee's argument is that it shows that the Indian business community was fully aware of the economic irrationality of the British modernization scheme. Jivanjee's position on the usefulness of dhows was a reasoned one; it had nothing to do with a conservative desire to cling to tradition. Jivanjee's objections aroused little interest in offical circles. This is a bit surprising since, in other circumstances, especially those involving Arab and African members of the Protectorate Council, the British were surprisingly responsive to the complaints of Council members. As the programme was implemented and the struggle over how cloves were going to be transported

---

[42] Jivanjee, *Memorandum*.
[43] Ibid.
[44] Ibid.

continued, the reactions of the clove shippers moved out of the arena of written protest and into the realm of practical response. No matter what carrots or sticks were offered, they shipped almost entirely by dhow.

Fare reductions and other subsidies

By 1929, Wesha was open and already faltering, the Zanzibar harbour improvements had been completed and dhows still dominated trade in cloves and everything else between Pemba and Zanzibar. So the government took new steps to attract cloves to the steamer service. To this end they began to run the steamer service at an ever-increasing loss and they tried to make the cost of dhow shipment higher by cracking down on adulterated or wet cloves.

The freight fares collected by the steamer service had always been less than adequate to cover operating expenses. In 1927 the cost of the Pemba service was Rs.197,147 while the revenue from the Pemba service had been only Rs.138,929, of which freight charges were only Rs.31,341. Most other years for which there are similar data also followed this pattern.[45] Thus it is not surprising that in 1929 we find the Port Office asking for permission to raise fares for freight carried by the steamer service. In 1929 the fare for a bag of cloves from Pemba to Zanzibar was 15 cents (Rs.) from either Mkoani or Wete and 12½ cents from Wesha, which in view of its troubles got an extra subsidy. Dhow freight was 36 to 50 cents per bag depending on the port, so the Port Officer thought it would be acceptable to raise the freight to 20 cents a bag. For other commodities the fares were so low that 'no private steam ship company could carry at such low rates': bags moved at 30 cents, bales 84 cents and cases 120 cents, 'bag rates being kept low because so many dhow owners own shops in Zanzibar and Pemba'.[46] The Port Officer was denied his request on the grounds that low freights helped the Pemba producer and helped steamers 'compete with the dhows for the carriage of produce so as to ensure better condition'.[47]

In 1933 the Port Office tried a different approach and offered to lower fares by 10 per cent on everything except cloves, the idea being that if the steamer service could attract a larger share of the goods shipped to Pemba the books might look a little better. His suggestion was accepted this time and the reduced fares were implemented in January 1934.[48]

At the same time that all this was going on, the Agriculture Department was stepping up its efforts at inspecting produce brought down from Pemba. The idea here was that by seizing produce that was either wet or adulterated

[45] ZNA AB45/581, 'Statement of Revenue and Expenditure of Government Steamers for the Years 1925, 1926, and 1927, indicating the value of the various services undertaken.'

[46] ZNA AB45/58a, Port Officer to Chief Secretary, 7 February 1929, and ZNA AB45/58, Port Officer to Chief Secretary, 19 February 1929.

[47] ZNA 45/58a. Chief Secretary to the Resident, 3 March 1931.

[48] ZNA AB45/58a, Port Officer to Chief Secretary, 23 November 1933, and ZNA AB45/58a, extract from Zanzibar Government, *Annual Report of the Port and Marine Department*, 1933.

the cost of shipping by dhow could be increased to the advantage of the steamer service and the clove industry in general.[49] In 1934 a new Adulteration of Produce Decree came into effect (there had been at least two precursors to this decree, neither of which seem to have had much effect on the quality of Zanzibar's cloves). The intent of this new version of the Adulteration of Produce Decree was that cloves should be inspected in Pemba before they were shipped. To this end an inspector was sent to Pemba in 1935 who was able to examine a small percentage of the crop at Chake Chake. By 1936 there were produce inspectors in each of the three Pemba steamer ports and dhows were expected to call there for inspection before going to Zanzibar. Thus dhows from the outports were required to pass through one of the three main ports before going to Zanzibar. Still the majority of the crop was not inspected, since most of the dhows arrived at the officially recognized ports fully loaded. Short of unloading all the dhows, it was virtually impossible to inspect these vessels, so they were given a pass indicating that their cargoes had not been examined.[50]

The Adulteration of Produce Decree did little to control the quality of cloves arriving in Zanzibar, but it did require all dhows to pass through one of three steamer ports and to go through one more bureaucratic step per voyage. Like so many of the steps taken by the government to assist the clove industry, the implementation of the Adulteration of Produce decree was a half-measure. If the Agriculture Department had been willing to put inspectors in some of the bigger dhow ports where cloves could have been inspected before they were shipped, the decree might have had a salutary effect on the clove industry and might have encouraged some shippers to switch to the steamer service to protect the quality of their cloves.

In the end neither of these initiatives, neither the fare subsidies nor the inspection procedures, had the opportunity to run its full course. Before either measure could really exert its full force, the clove crisis of 1937 came along and brought the steamer and dhow conflict to a head.

The clove crisis

Conflict between Zanzibar's Indian clove merchants and the Zanzibar government had been simmering since the 1920s. It should be remembered that the government's attempt to squeeze dhows out of the clove business was rooted in its desire to aid Arab clove planters by eliminating the role of the Indian middlemen who financed the clove industry. Thus at the same time that they launched the first wave of port improvements and other

---

[49] The Adulteration of Produce Decree was consciously being used as a weapon in the war against the dhow. In 1927 an official in Pemba suggested that the Decree be 'so enforced in Zanzibar as to make shipments by dhow commercially unprofitable'. The same official conceded that this level of enforcement was not likely to be achieved 'at the moment'. ZNA AB45/51a, Asst. District Commissioner, Chake Chake to District Commissioner, Pemba, 21 March 1927.

[50] ZNA AB4/628, Director of Agriculture to Chief Secretary, 11 June 1938.

efforts to attract cloves away from dhows and into the holds of the government ships, the government was taking other, broader steps to aid the planters and hinder the middlemen.

In 1927 the government created the CGA with the intention of providing low-interest harvesting loans, and storage space for cloves and setting a minimum price for cloves. Initially membership was high since the CGA distributed the bonuses the government offered to growers. When the bonus programme was cancelled in 1928, membership dropped. In 1934 the government set about a wholesale reform of the clove industry (the Adulteration of Produce Act was a part of this effort) and made the CGA an official part of the government, with authority to license clove dealers, keep records of dealers' activity and inspect produce. Additional legislation placed a temporary moratorium on debts and prevented the alienation of land. This was a major blow to the Indian community and the Indian National Association protested in the Legislative Council.[51]

In 1937 the government made the CGA the sole legal buyer for cloves, authorized the CGA to export cloves and cut the number of export permits they issued. This was the final straw for the Indian community and they launched a boycott of the clove industry. The boycott was not limited to Zanzibar. The Indian National Congress, India's dominant political party, also launched a boycott. This was a far more serious matter than the internal boycott since India consumed two fifths of Zanzibar's clove production. By 1938 the boycott was having an effect and the Zanzibar government was under pressure from London to patch things up with the Indian community. So an agreement was reached that allowed Indians to buy cloves and ship cloves, but required exporters to purchase half of their cloves from the CGA.

For the dhow world 1937 and 1938 were rough years. The CGA, which was part of the government's 'rationalization' scheme, supported the government's ideas about the undesirability of dhows and shipped only by steamer. So, in 1937, the entire clove crop was shipped by steamer. It was a big year for the steamers. The government ships carried 161,000 bags of cloves, up from 31,000 in 1936. Dhows were allowed to carry stems and copra only once the steamers became too busy to accommodate these less important cargoes.[52]

The effect of this policy on the number of dhows registered in Zanzibar was dramatic. At the beginning of 1937 120 dhows were registered at Zanzibar to British subjects (mostly Indians) and 55 were registered to Zanzibaris. By 1938, the number of British vessels had dropped to 78 and the Zanzibari to 31. While the number of Zanzibari vessels registered at Zanzibar eventually recovered and their tonnage eventually far exceeded their 1937

[51] For more on the origins of the clove crisis see Lofchie, *Background*, J.R. Mlahagwa and A.J. Temu, 'The Decline of the Landlords,' in Abdul Sheriff and Ed Ferguson (eds), *Zanzibar Under Colonial Rule* (London: 1991), and Timothy Welliver, 'The Clove Factor in Colonial Zanzibar, 1890–1950,' unpublished PhD thesis, Northwestern University, 1990.

[52] ZNA BA36/5, Zanzibar Government, *Report on the Port and Marine Department*, 1937, p. 11, and ZNA AB4/54, Port Officer to Chief Secretary, 18 May 1938.

tonnage, the British category never fully recovered in either numbers or tonnage. The financial stress of a year without cloves to haul and the more general effects of merchants boycotting the industry on which their wealth was based seems to have dealt the dhow business a permanent blow.[53]

But, contrary to the assertions of Sheriff and Martin, who both state that 1936 was the last year that dhows were allowed to move cloves between Pemba and Zanzibar, dhows were back on the job in 1938 and remained in control of the Pemba trade until the Revolution.[54] The agreement reached between the Indian community and the government in 1938 included the proviso that:

> Cloves may be transported from Pemba to Zanzibar by dhow or by government steamer. All dhows used for such transport shall conform to regulations to be drawn up by Government and will be subject to inspection … in order to ensure that they are suitable for the carriage of cloves. Cloves transported by dhow will be subject to quality inspection at Wete or Chake Chake or Mkoani and again in Zanzibar.[55]

In the same year the government drew up regulations, the Clove (Dhow Transport) Rules, 1938, which set the standard to which dhows must adhere if they wished to carry cloves. In order to be endorsed as an official clove-carrying dhow, a vessel needed a covering to keep spray out of the hold, dunnage to keep the cargo out of the bilge and a 'suitable bailing apparatus'. In addition the vessel must, when carrying cloves carry no other cargo and only carry as many bags as its endorsement allowed. It was estimated that achieving these standards would cost the average dhow about £10.[56]

In practice these standards could be easily achieved since, when the time came to enforce the new rules, the thatch that virtually all dhows carried anyway was judged to be a sufficient cover, mangrove poles sufficed as dunnage and a couple of buckets were deemed a 'suitable bailing apparatus'.[57] Thus, in terms of equipment, dhows conceded little in the agreement. Where they did make concessions was in agreeing that each cargo of cloves would be inspected at one of the three official ports in Pemba. This led the outports to atrophy gradually. Ports like Jambangome were abandoned and others, such as Kengeja, Mtambwe and Fufuni, declined in importance. Despite these concessions, dhows were back in the clove trade again and from 1938 until the Revolution the government tolerated and on occasion encouraged their presence.[58]

[53] Interview with Sherali Haji Rashid, 16 August 1994, and ZNA BA36/5 and BA36/6, Zanzibar Government, *Report on the Port and Marine Department*, 1937 and 1938.
[54] Abdul Sheriff, 'The Peasantry Under Imperialism, 1873–1963,' in Abdul Sheriff and Ed Ferguson, *Zanzibar Under Colonial Rule* (London, 1991), p.123–4, and E.B. and C. Martin, *Cargos of the East* (London: 1978), pp. 137–8.
[55] ZNA AB4/53, 'Paragraph 8 of Heads of Agreement,' quoted in Port Officer to Chief Secretary, 9 May 1938.
[56] ZNA AB4/53, Senior Customs Officer to Chief Secretary, 31 May 1938 and ZNA AB4/53, 'The Clove Decree, 1938 – The Clove (Dhow Transport) Rules, 1938.'
[57] ZNA AB4/53, Senior Customs Officer to Chief Secretary, 31 May 1938.
[58] The clove crisis figures prominently in the literature on colonial Zanzibar, but the transportation component of the crisis is never mentioned. Furthermore, some (mostly of

The era of accommodation

The clove crisis of 1937 seems to have purged the government of much of its bile and from 1938 on relations between the government and the dhows on the Pemba route were remarkably cordial. In May of 1938, at about the same time that dhows were being allowed back into the clove trade, there was some talk of trying to lower the steamer freights to retain some of the clove-carriage business that the steamers had captured in 1937, but prior experience indicated that it was unlikely that lowering freights would have any effect other than driving the steamer service deeper into the red. So the idea was scrapped, and the steamer service went back to being the official carrier for the CGA and scraping up what ever else it could.[59]

During the war there was a dhow renaissance. Shortages of fuel and tyres and the commandeering of one of the government ships by the Royal Navy for wartime duty, combined with a severe cash and manpower shortage that meant that most routine maintenance of roads, bridges and ports was put on hold, helped dhows to reassert themselves. Before the war dhows controlled most of the private shipping between Pemba and Zanzibar, but during the war the government was forced to rely on dhows as well. Thus we find that in 1942 the CGA, the great bastion of the steamer service, was forced to ship its cloves by dhow and this seems to have gone on until at least 1944. In addition to local dhows hauling cloves for the CGA, there seems to have been sufficient need for shipping for Muscati dhows to come up to Pemba in fairly large numbers. In 1942, local merchants formed the Pemba Shippers Association, a cartel that set prices for dhow transport between Pemba and Zanzibar. This seems to have been an entirely Indian association in that their notices were all published in Gujarati with English translation. So, by the late 1940s, the situation was entirely reversed. The CGA may have been able to control producer prices, but it is clear who controlled the transport of cloves. Ten years after the government made its crowning effort to get Indians and their dhows out of the clove business, the Pemba Shippers Association was able to dictate prices to the CGA. Government-subsidized modernity proved less efficient than tradition.[60]

The government's effort to force dhows out of the clove trade had transformed the clove industry. Many of the dhow ports in Pemba withered in the late 1930s, the numbers of dhows registered to Indians never fully

[58] (cont.) the Marxist persuasion) seem to interpret the resolution of the crisis as a victory for the CGA and the government, which overlooks the continuing importance of Asian clove shippers during the 1940s, 1950s and 1960s. See Norman Bennett, *A History of the Arab State of Zanzibar* (London: 1978), pp. 213–15, Sheriff, 'Peasantry Under Imperialism,' p. 133, and Lofchie, *Background*, pp. 124–6. Sheriff takes at face value the CGA's assertion that the outcome of the crisis was a victory for them, without exploring the real limitations placed on the CGA by the private clove shippers' control of the transport system.

[59] ZNA AB4/54, Acting Port Officer to Chief Secretary, 18 May 1938.

[60] ZNA AP37/134, 'Wete CGA Godown: Statement of purchases, deposits, and shipping for the month ending 31 August 1942,' ZNA AP37/134, 'CGA statement of produce operation of Wete Godown for the month March 1944,' and ZNA AP2/81, Illeg to General Manager, CGA, 6 August 1952.

recovered and dhows were forced to clear Pemba through the same three officially recognized ports that the steamers used. But dhow owners quickly adapted to the new conditions. As a result the clove industry continued to rely on dhow transport and the official clove economy continued to be propped up by its unofficial shadow. Dhows and their Asian owners continued to dominate the clove transport business until 1964, when the Revolutionary Government finally cut them out of the trade by simply banning the use of dhows.

The conflict between clove shippers and the colonial state was the most clear-cut confrontation between the dirigist economic policies favoured by the state and the free-market inclinations of the informal sector. Dhows played a critical role in this victory. By providing cheap access to the many creeks and inlets of Pemba, by being well suited to the seasonal nature of the clove trade and because they were controlled by the people who needed them, dhows fitted the clove trade perfectly. In the end dhows helped the clove merchants retain control of the clove business, to the advantage of the clove industry and Zanzibar in general. By staving off the government's efforts at modernization, Zanzibar's merchant class was using its control over a bottleneck in the Protectorate's economy to subvert the colonial project.[61]

[61] Zanzibar's clove merchants played a role in Zanzibar's economy oddly similar to that of the Kenyan dock workers whose story Frederick Cooper told in *On the African Waterfront* (New Haven: 1987). In each case a transportation bottleneck gave the people who controlled it extraordinary leverage over the colonial states that depended on the passage of exportable goods through that bottleneck.

Five

Mangrove Poles
& the Long-distance Dhow Trade
in the Colonial Era

Arabia is a treeless land and any wood is at a premium there. The cheapest wood, and the strongest for many uses, has always been the mangrove pole.

Allan Villiers, *Sons of Sinbad*

The informal, dhow-driven economy that so successfully resisted British efforts to force dhows out of the clove industry was also present on a regional level. Throughout the colonial era, seagoing dhows came to East Africa from the Red Sea, Somalia, southern Arabia, the Persian Gulf, and western India, much as they had during the nineteenth century, bringing with them a range of cargoes little changed from the nineteenth century. What had changed were the cargoes these ships took home with them. Ivory, slaves and spices, the glamour cargoes of the preceding century, were mostly unavailable to dhows during the colonial period. So, by the middle decades of the twentieth century, mangrove wood had become the single most important cargo carried to Arabia by long-distance dhows. The colonial-era mangrove trade is intriguing. Just as the clove-carriage trade represents an adaptation of the nineteenth-century coastal trade between the mainland and Zanzibar, the mangrove trade was part of Zanzibar's nineteenth-century trading economy that survived, with minor modifications, until independence. The continuing demand for mangrove wood in the Persian Gulf ensured that Zanzibar remained part of a western Indian Ocean trade system more than a century after the global capitalist economy had sunk its hooks into the island. During the twentieth century Zanzibar participated in both the global economy and in a regional western Indian Ocean economy and mangrove wood, more than any other commodity, let Zanzibar keep a foot in the regional economy.

The mangrove trade linked the texture of daily life on the East African coast to life in the Gulf and southern Arabia. East African labourers migrated and toiled to feed Arabia's demand for timber. Businessmen invested and schemed at both ends of the monsoon system. In the Gulf, fishermen caught shark and other fish, often from flimsy craft little different from rafts, to exchange for mangrove wood. And over everybody's heads, rich, poor and in between, from Zanzibar to Aden to Kuwait and beyond, was a roof supported by East African mangrove rafters.

In addition to ensuring that Zanzibar kept its hand in the trade of the western Indian Ocean, the mangrove trade served as an international shadow economy. It was an export trade, attached to a remarkably well-developed and complex system of production, that was almost entirely outside colonial control. Neither the advent of colonial governments in East Africa nor the transformations those governments wrought on their subjects' economies nor the new political borders they imposed had any great effect on the mangrove trade. Throughout the colonial era, labour, capital, cargoes, ships and sailors engaged in the mangrove trade ebbed and flowed across the waters of the western Indian Ocean, moving to the rhythm of the monsoon and beyond the bureaucrats' reach.

Another important aspect of the mangrove trade is the way in which the long-distance trade in poles tied in with a local trade in poles and other mangrove products. The same cutters who migrated to swamps each year to cut poles for the Arabian pole trade also cut poles to supply Zanzibar town. Likewise, some Arab dhows made two trips to the swamps each year, once for poles to be sold locally and once to gather their return cargo. This integration of the regional economy into the local economy is indicative of the degree to which this regional economy affected life in East Africa.

Why did this sector of the economy retain so much of its autonomy? For one thing access to the mangrove swamps was virtually impossible to control. There were economically important mangrove swamps in Kenya, Tanganyika and Zanzibar. Each swamp was riddled with inlets, creeks and channels. Easily accessible from the sea, the swamps were hard to reach overland – so much so that in some cases colonial officials were not even aware that their districts had economically significant mangrove resources. Because there were mangroves to be had in each of the three East African polities, any government attempt at regulation that was actively enforced would simply drive buyers to the other two colonies. And, finally, the amounts of money involved seemed small to colonial officials – too small to worry about – though they must have seemed bigger to cutters who sailed for several weeks just to reach the swamps.

The mangrove pole

Mangrove trees grow along tropical shorelines in the mud that is deposited where creeks or rivers debouch into the sea. East Africa's mangrove swamps vary from tiny clusters of trees to the vast mangrove forests of the Rufiji delta. Several species of mangrove, of which the *Rhizophora* (Swahili *mkoko* or *mkandaa*) is the most important, are shade tolerant. As the young trees try to break through the forest canopy they grow rapidly and directly upwards, producing long straight trunks that make excellent poles. Ideally these are cut when they have reached 18 feet and have a butt diameter between 4 and 8 inches.

These poles, called *boriti* or *mambore* in Swahili, were valued for use as rafters. Not only did their shape make them ideally suited to the work of holding up mud roofs and ceilings, but they are also resistant to the depredations of termites. Mangrove poles had dozens of uses beyond holding up roofs. They were used to make scaffolding and for the construction of date-drying sheds and other sorts of temporary shelters. They were used for punting poles, to build boats and to make ox carts. The fruit of one type of mangrove is a natural top and is used as a children's toy. The same fruit yields a medicine that soothes the stomach. Some varieties of the tree yield not big rafter-size poles but thin flexible withes called *fito*. *Fito* are used by the thousand to build the traditional Swahili mud house and also do duty as a fencing material.

The tannins which make the bigger varieties *Rhizophora* and *Bruguiera* resist termites also make the bark of these two species of mangrove valuable. In East Africa mangrove bark is used to tan and stain leather and to dye some basketwork. Especially associated with mangrove bark tanning is the reddish leather that is used to make *makobazi*, a popular style of sandal associated with Lamu and Bajuns. This bark has also attracted the interest of the industrial economies of the West. From the turn of the century until the late 1930s there was an off-and-on trade in mangrove bark. For the most part this was compatible with the pole trade, since the bark had to be stripped off poles anyway, and the species which were most sought after for poles were also the most sought after for bark. In the 1940s the price of bark went up dramatically, and a frenzy of bark stripping presented a significant challenge to the pole trade. We shall look at the ecological effects of bark stripping and how bark stripping affected the pole trade later in this chapter.

The nineteenth-century mangrove trade

As we saw in Chapter Two, the pole trade was an important part of Zanzibar's nineteenth-century dhow economy. Mangrove poles constituted a third of Zanzibar's exports to Arabia. None the less, the nineteenth century offers only scattered references to the mangrove trade. American merchantmen passing through Zanzibar in the 1840s carried mangrove poles to Aden and Muscat. The volumes involved were relatively small. In 1844, for instance, the Salem barque *Cherokee* loaded 772 rafters (about 38 *korjah* or score) at Zanzibar for Aden. This is roughly a tenth of what a fully loaded *boom* or *bagala* would have carried in the 1930s. The Salem vessels used American cotton goods to trade for cargoes in Arabia, and mangrove poles would seem to have been little more than a way of filling in some of the empty spaces created when trade goods were landed at Zanzibar. None the less, this does provide evidence that *boriti* were readily available in Zanzibar, and that the demand for them in Arabia was obvious enough for the Americans, who were newcomers at this point, to notice and pick up on it.[1]

When Richard Burton visited East Africa in the late 1850s he reported that

> The only timber now used in commerce is the … mangrove, which supplies the well-known bordi or 'Zanzibar rafters' …The rafter trade is conducted by Arab dows: the crews fell the trees, after paying 2 or 3 dollars in cloth by way of ada or present to the diwan, who permits them to hire labourers. The korjah or score cut and trimmed red mangrove rafters formerly cost at Zanzibar 1 dollar; the price has now risen to 2 and 3 dollars. This timber finds its way to Aden and the woodless lands of Eastern and Western Arabia; at Jedah they have been known to fetch a dollar each.[2]

While Burton made no effort to determine how large the *boriti* trade was, the second British Consul in Zanzibar reported that in 1859 6,000 'rafters' worth 1200 Maria Theresa dollars (MT$) were exported from Zanzibar to Cutch, while another 12,000 worth MT$ 38,000 were sent to Arabia.[3] A quick look at those numbers would suggest that the poles going to Arabia were radically more expensive than those that were sent to Cutch. The standard unit of measure for mangrove poles is the *korjah*, which consists of twenty poles. For some reason, poles that were sent to India were usually counted individually while poles going to Arabia were usually counted by the *korjah*. If you assume that Rigby, the consul in question, mistakenly recorded 12,000 poles when he should have said 12,000 *korjahs* (240,000 poles), the value of the poles bound for Arabia comes into line with those headed for Cutch. This would make the Cutch poles worth 0.2 MT$ each and the Arabia poles worth 0.15 MT$ each. This would be remarkably consistent with twentieth-century practice, wherein a smaller number of higher-value poles were sent to India while much larger numbers of cheaper poles went to Arabia. Even more interesting is the fact that one hundred years later the volume of poles leaving Zanzibar for Arabia was virtually unchanged at 265,000 poles.

In the later part of the nineteenth century there is photographic evidence for the mangrove trade. There is a photograph at the Peabody Essex Museum that dates from *c.* 1885 which shows an *mtepe dau* beached at Zanzibar. Piled on the beach and jutting out of the hold of the *mtepe* are large *boriti*. The beach in question is most probably Funguni, which in the twentieth century was where poles from the mainland were stacked and stored. The *mtepe* played an important role in the collection of mangrove poles for sale in Zanzibar as late as the 1930s, and it is interesting that it seems to have played the same role in the 1880s.[4]

---

[1] Peabody Essex Museum, Michael Sheppard Papers, Box 2, Folder 9, Voyage of the *Cherokee*, 1843–4.

[2] Richard Burton, *The Lake Regions of Central Africa* (New York: 1961 [1860]), Vol. 2, p. 415.

[3] ZNA AA2/4, Rigby to Russell, 16 May 1860.

[4] The photograph is in the E.D. Ropes Album at the Peabody Essex Museum. E.D. Ropes, who lived in Zanzibar from 1882 to 1892, appears in several of the photographs in the album, so it seems probable that the photograph was taken during his stay in Zanzibar.

It is not clear whether the poles exported from Zanzibar were mostly cut on the mainland and brought to Zanzibar, or if a percentage of them came from the swamps on Pemba and Zanzibar. Burton says that *boriti* are 'felled by slaves on the mainland and are brought over by Arabs and other vessels'.[5] What is most noteworthy about the nineteenth-century references to the mangrove trade, hazy as they are, is that nothing seems to be glaringly different from the colonial-era mangrove trade. Indeed, the similarities and continuities are more pronounced than any differences. If there is an important difference, it is that in the nineteenth-century mangrove poles were just one of a range of options available to dhow captains seeking a cargo to carry home to Arabia.

The twentieth century

One hundred years later, dhow captains had fewer options and mangrove poles had become the staple of their trade.[6] Slaves were no longer available. Ivory was highly regulated and valuable enough that most shippers preferred the security of knowing their ivory was safely on board a steam ship rather than risking it in dhow. Cloves were sometimes available, especially during shipping shortages during the war, but again most shippers preferred the tight, dry hold of a steamer to the wet, dunnageless hold of a dhow.[7] This left dhows with mangrove poles and cereals. Perhaps because the mangrove trade was so much more important during the twentieth century, it is also much better documented.

For the first sixty years of the twentieth century the mangrove trade followed this basic outline: Arab dhows came to Zanzibar on the north-east monsoon, where they sold their cargoes. Obligated by the wind to remain in East Africa for four to five months they would travel to the mainland, usually the Rufiji delta, to get a cargo of poles. They would return to Zanzibar to sell their poles on the local market or, having collected their papers and cleared customs in Zanzibar, they would carry their poles back to Arabia. Most of the information below about supply and demand is probably as true of the nineteenth century as it is of the twentieth, but there is no way of knowing for sure.

[5] Richard Burton, *Zanzibar: City, Island, and Coast* (New York: 1967 [1872]), vol. 1, pp. 240–1.

[6] ZNA AK18/13, DC, Urban to Senior Commissioner, 23 April 1960, and ZNA AK18/13, Comptroller of Customs to Senior Commissioner, 22 June 1960. See also Allan Villiers, *Sons of Sinbad* (New York: 1969) pp. 300–303, who describes the intense competition in 1939 between dhows to be the first back to the Gulf in order sell their mangrove poles before the market is saturated.

[7] Interview with Mohammed Hussein, 17 Aug. 1994. A.P. Hirji, the firm for which Mohammed Hussein works, bought two dhows during the Second World War to export cloves to India. This was a reaction to the shortage of shipping during the war.

The demand

As we have seen, mangrove wood was used for a variety of purposes ranging from rafters to scaffolding to fuel. For the export trade, the most important of these was their use as rafters. A pole destined to be used as a rafter is called a *boriti* and has a 4 to 8 inch butt diameter, tapering in the course of its 16 to 18 foot length.

It is worth looking at how exactly *boriti* were used in the construction of houses in the Gulf, since it was the survival of this building technique into the 1960s that provided most of the demand for poles in the Persian Gulf. The poles were used to support the flat, mud roofs of Arab houses. They were placed from wall to wall at a 6 to 9 inch spacing. Over this was placed a layer of woven mats and then a layer of split bamboo. On top of all this went a 'twelve to eighteen inch layer of mud, puddled and pressed and rolled until it is firm and impervious to the elements. A well constructed roof of this type may last over a century, but a poorly constructed roof is liable to collapse during winter rains.' This building technique was in use long after concrete and reinforced steel became available in the Gulf, since concrete roofs tended to crack in the extreme heat of the summer and so required more maintenance than a mud roof. It took until the mid-1950s for the Kuwait Department of Public Works to devise a concrete roof superior to a mud roof. And even then it took a decade or so for the new technique to become widespread. Thus there was steady demand for poles in the Gulf and southern Arabia for new construction and for the restoration of roofs that did not survive the winter rain.[8]

Demand for poles was not limited to rafters. The Middle East has been timber-poor for centuries and has imported wood from East Africa since at least the time of the *Periplus*. Thus there were numerous other uses to which a relatively cheap and durable wood like mangrove wood might be put. One of these was scaffolding. This probably helped to sustain the demand for poles into the 1960s, since even once houses began to be built from concrete, the scaffolding used in their construction was made from mangrove poles. One still sees mangrove-pole scaffolding in use in Tanzania. Other Middle Eastern uses for mangroves included punting poles, the construction of temporary date-drying sheds, the construction of poorer-class housing in Iran and Iraq, dhow building, and firewood. So there were uses for mangrove products that were not as susceptible to replacement by cement and re-bar as the *boriti* rafters.

Mangrove wood was also used for fuel in the Gulf. Rawlins reports that Lamu exported 50,000 to 60,000 billets (4 foot sections of mangrove poles) each year in the late 1950 and guessed that the Rufiji sent 100,000 billets to the Gulf annually. Charcoal made from mangrove wood was also exported to the Gulf. As late as 1968 Fakrudin Gulamhusein produced

---

[8] ZNA AP10/21, S.P. Rawlins, 'The East African Mangrove Trade,' 10 August 1957. The information in this paragraph and the following paragraph on how poles were used in the Gulf comes from this report.

2,000 tons of mangrove charcoal per annum for export at Shela and another similar business was in operation north of Mombasa.[9]

In addition to the Arabian demand there was also a large local demand for mangrove poles. Mangrove poles were used in the construction of the stone houses of Zanzibar town and in the building of the more widespread mud and thatch houses. In 1942 it was estimated that an 'average native house' used sixty *boriti* as well as hundreds of smaller types of poles (most of these would be *fito*, which are small and flexible enough to be woven into the framework created with large poles to make walls – over a thousand *fito* could go into an average house).[10] The colonial economy also found uses for mangrove wood. Mangrove poles did duty as temporary railway sleepers and pit props. Temporary housing built with mangrove wood helped to shelter KAR troops during the Second World War. In 1942 1,320,034 poles were cut in Kenya – a million more than the year before – and the increase was attributed to military demand.[11]

Transport

The demand for East African mangrove poles in the Gulf and southern Arabia created an opportunity for seagoing dhows. Steamer traffic between East Africa and the Gulf was almost non-existent, and poles were so cheap that it was hard to transport them profitably by steamer. So the transport of poles between East Africa and the Gulf was virtually monopolized by dhows. There was more steamer traffic between Aden and East Africa, but I have seen little evidence that the steamers carried poles. Shihr and Mukhalla, the main ports on the southern Arabian coast east of Aden, were dominated by dhows.[12]

Seagoing dhows from Arabia also dominated the local pole-carrying trade in East Africa. The local trade was well suited to the needs of dhows waiting for the winds to change. During the time they were stuck in East Africa, they could carry two cargoes of Rufiji poles to Zanzibar, selling one for local consumption and then taking the other as a return cargo. By the late 1950s many seasonal dhows carried auxiliary engines, which made it possible for them to make as many as three trips to the delta.[13]

[9] E.B. Martin and C. Martin, *Cargoes of the East* (London: 1978), p. 91 and interview with Sherali Haji Rashid, 16 October 1994.

[10] ZNA AB4/151, DC, Zanzibar and Senior Agricultural Officer, 'Report on Mangrove Areas: Chwaka Peninsular [*sic*],' 19 September 1942.

[11] Rawlins, 'Mangrove Trade,' p. 23.

[12] By way of example see the Zanzibar Government, *Blue Books*, for 1931, 1932 and 1933, which are fairly representaive years. In 1931 three steamers cleared Zanzibar for Aden with a collective tonnage of 2,195, and two steamers cleared Zanzibar for the Gulf at a collective tonnage of 6,213. In the same year 228 dhows cleared for Arabian ports at a tonnage of 1,5432. The next year one steamer cleared for Aden and none for the Gulf, in 1933 Aden and the Gulf each got one steamer from Zanzibar. Steamers were present but they in no way dominated the trade.

[13] ZNA AK4/35, 'Minutes of the Meeting of Simbauranga Mangrove Pole Shippers Held at the DC(U)'s Office,' 30 May 1960.

5.1 The creek port at Tumbe in Pemba. This was once a busy port frequented by Arab dhows in Pemba to buy mangrove poles

5.2 Kichenge creek at Micheweni in Pemba at low tide. This is the largest mangrove swamp in Pemba, and was the main source of poles for export on Pemba

There were other options closer to Zanzibar. Kichenge creek in Pemba and Chwaka Bay on the island of Unguja were both visited by dhows seeking cargoes, although these cargoes were generally intended for use in the local market rather than for export. Poles could also be obtained near Kilwa, Mikindani and Tanga on the mainland. Kenya, the area around Lamu in particular, also produced large numbers of poles.

Production

Mangrove poles exported from Zanzibar came from two types of sources: big swamps and little swamps. The Rufiji delta was the biggest of the big swamps and supplied most of the export-grade poles that passed through Zanzibar. For most of the twentieth century the Rufiji was subject to at least limited regulation and control. The smaller swamps were remote enough to be mostly outside the control of the state and small enough not to be of interest to the official economy. The Rufiji and the other smaller sources of mangrove poles each had distinctive patterns of production. For most of the colonial period the Rufiji was leased to various businessmen, who were supposed to organize cutting and 'rationalize' production. While this never happened, the attempt affected the way in which poles were obtained. In the smaller swamps a different and in many ways more interesting pattern obtained, and this pattern, which was apparently less influenced by the official economy, may be more representative of the way in which poles were obtained in the nineteenth century. Proceeding with this assumption, let us look first at the small-swamp production pattern.

The Bajuni and the mangrove trade

The Arab dhow sailors were not interested in actually wading into the swamps and cutting the poles themselves and anyone who has spent much time around mangrove swamps can easily sympathize with their reluctance. While mangrove swamps are not the insect-infested nightmares that one might expect a tropical swamp to be, their pleasures are best savoured from a boat or from one of the channels or *vipenyo* where the tide scours out the mud, leaving a nice layer of firm sand to stand on. To stray off the sand and into the muck in which the economically valuable species of mangrove grow is to be immobilized by 10 inches to a foot of sucking ooze. Wrestling 18 foot *boriti* out of the swamp and into a boat is very hard work, and requires boats capable of getting into the shallow waters of the swamps.

Happily for the Arab dhow sailors, there were people who specialized in this type of work. At the same time of the year that the Arabs were getting ready to sail from their home ports, mangrove cutters from Lamu were also sailing south to mangrove swamps in Tanganyika and Zanzibar. Once there they went to work cutting mangrove poles for both the local and export trades.

In the Lamu archipelago there are about 80,000 acres of mangrove swamp, and not much else of economic importance.[14] Lamu lacks a wealthy hinterland and it did not support the type of plantation agriculture that Zanzibar and Pemba did. Thus the Bajuni have looked to the sea for a living. They built dhows, they fished, they worked in the coasting trade, and they cut mangrove poles.[15] Some combined the coasting trade with mangrove cutting and became seasonally itinerant mangrove cutters, called Wagunya by Zanzibaris.[16] The best description of how the Arab dhows acquired their cargoes from the Bajuni comes from a report filed by the District Officer in Wete on the island of Pemba in 1933.[17]

Most of northern Pemba is fringed by mangroves. The largest of northern Pemba's swamps is Kichenge Creek, at the head of which is the town of Michweni. In 1933 the creek at Michweni had roughly three square miles of mangroves and had been worked for as far back as local memory stretched. One Bajuni who had settled at the nearby port of Tumbe said that his great-great-Grandfather had been a pole cutter at Michweni. At this time the area was still productive (it was overcut later) and the regular cutting had created a series of *vipenyo* – channels in the swamps that allow canoes to wend their way into the swamps.

The Arabs would bring their seagoing dhows up from Zanzibar and anchor at Tumbe, a small creek port about 3 miles from the mangrove swamps at Kichenge. They would remain there, usually being disruptive, while they accumulated a cargo to take back to Zanzibar with them. Meanwhile, local cutters and Bajuni from Lamu would be running back and forth between Tumbe and Kichenge bringing poles for sale. In 1933 there was a colony of Bajuni who had settled around Kichenge creek but only thirty to forty of them were actively engaged in pole cutting, the others directing their energies towards fishing. These local cutters seem to have been engaged in cutting for the local market, since the District Officer tells us 'in the supply of foreign vessels they are cut out by the better equipped and more practised visitors from Lamu'. Thus it would seem that the local cutters were Bajuni who had settled near areas that produced mangrove poles, and it was these settlers who were being outcompeted by the migrants.[18]

---

[14] Rawlins, 'Mangrove Trade', p. 35.

[15] The best description of the life and domestic economy of Lamu comes from A.H.J. Prins, *Sailing from Lamu* (Assen: 1965).

[16] Rawlins, 'Mangrove Trade,' p. 21. This term is considered highly offensive by the Bajuni, who take it as a derogatory word for Bajuni in general. In Zanzibar it is used to describe either seasonal migrants or settlers from Lamu and is specifically associated with mangrove cutters.

[17] ZNA AB4/151, DO, Wete to Provincial Commissioner, 6 Oct. 1933. This is a very interesting and thorough report. Its author was either an anthropologist *manqué*, or was looking for promotion. He made maps and charts and even took photographs. His report is the source of all information in this section unless otherwise noted.

[18] ZNA AB4/151, 'Mangrove Woodland: Collection of Information,' 10 June 1933, enclosed in Director of Agriculture to Provincial Commissioner, 17 June 1933. This document suggests that any place that had consistently been yielding poles would have a resident colony of Wagunya.

What made the migrants 'better equipped' was probably their ships. According to the Wete District Officer, the Bajuni came to Pemba in *mitepe* and used those same vessels to work the swamps. In 1933, J. Clive, the District Commissioner of Lamu, wrote a description of the *mtepe* and pointed out that '[t]hese mtepe are used almost entirely for the boriti trade, and the average capacity is 1,000 korjahs…'[19] Doubtless part of their appeal to the Bajuni was that they have a very shallow draught for their size. A 168 ton *mtepe*, for example, captured by the Royal Navy in 1877, had a length of 97 feet but drew only 6 feet of water.[20] Such a vessel can carry lots of cargo in very shallow water and so makes an ideal boat for working in the shallow water around mangrove swamps.

Since the entrance to Kichenge creek was quite shallow, even the shallow bottoms of the *mitepe* could only get in on a high tide and the bigger Arab dhows were completely excluded. The Wete District Officer's report tells us that the creek was accessible only to 'vessels of the usual *mtepe* draught and build'. Thus, even if the Arab dhow crew had been inclined to work in the swamp, they could not get there and had to rely on the Bajuni to supply them with poles. Poles acquired at Kichenge were usually taken back to Zanzibar and sold into the local market, although at least on one occasion six dhows left directly, which was illegal, from Tumbe for Muscat.[21] It should be noted that the Bajuni did not limit their activities to supplying the Arab dhows but also carried 'large quantities of poles to Zanzibar themselves'.

Swamps like Kichenge were virtually uncontrollable. The Wete District Officer wrote in 1933, 'I wish to stress the utter impracticability of exercising any control over Kichenge Creek itself owing to its remoteness from communications of all sorts.' Furthermore, in Zanzibar permits to cut could be obtained free.[22] Thus small swamps like Kichenge were completely outside the control of the official economy. The Arab buyers as well as the Bajuni cutters came from outside the Zanzibar Protectorate and operated in an area so remote that there was little possibility that the state would be able to control their activities. The only intrusion by the state was the permit system, but since these were issued for free they had little effect on the cutting.

Poles from Kichenge and other small swamps constituted a relatively small proportion of the poles which were exported from Zanzibar, but the small swamps played an important role in preserving the informality of the mangrove trade. As we shall see below, their presence served to limit state control of the Rufiji Delta. When royalties and regulation became too

---

[19] Quoted in Martin and Martin, *Cargoes*, p. 94. His assertion that an *mtepe* could carry 1,000 scores of poles is difficult to believe.

[20] ZNA AA1/22, 'Certificate of Measurement for Dhow name unknown,' 1 February 1877. The captured *mtepe* had a length of 97 ft, breadth of 24 ft, girth of 40 ft and depth of 9.5 ft. I am assuming that it would have had at least 3 ft or so of freeboard and so a draft of about 6 ft.

[21] ZNA AB45/44, Provincial Commissioner to Chief Secretary, 19 July 1933.

[22] ZNA AB4/151, Provincial Commissioner to Chief Secretary, 9 May 1933.

oppressive in the Rufiji, pole buyers could simply shift their business to small swamps like Kichenge.[23]

The Rufiji delta

The Rufiji delta was the principal source of the mangrove poles that were transshipped through Zanzibar, in the twentieth century. Unlike the smaller swamps on Zanzibar, the Rufiji delta was big enough to attract the attention of the colonial government. Both the Germans and the British in their time tried to bring the Rufiji's mangrove trade into the official economy and neither was terribly successful.

Under the Germans the mangroves in the delta were considered state property, but 10,000 hectares in the delta were leased to Denhart & Co in 1904.[24] Denhart & Co. paid the government a royalty of between Rps. 10 and 4 per *korjah* depending on the butt diameter of the poles.[25] This trade brought the government Rps. 30,000 per annum, but once the war started trade shifted away from the Rufiji.[26] It is hard to say how successful the Germans were at bringing the delta under their control, but whatever success they achieved was wiped out during the war.

After the war the British decided to follow the German example and in 1921 the Rufiji was leased to the Rufiji River Trading Co., owned by a Captain Ingles, who agreed to pay a royalty of 6 to 8 shillings per *korjah* of poles depending on the size of the poles. Furthermore he agreed to pay a minimum of 12,000 shillings in royalties and more if his cutting exceeded the guaranteed minimum.[27] From the start the Forest Department and Ingles seemed to have different ideas of what the concessionaire was to do with concession. The Department sought to make things as modern, efficient and rational as possible. They envisioned the concessionaire investing money in jetties and storage sheds, and expected that poles would be stockpiled before the arrival of the dhows so that the dhows would not have to wait for poles or organize their own labour to cut the poles.[28] In short, they hoped to draw the Rufiji mangrove trade into the official sector and to profit from that transition.

Ingles, on the other hand, saw himself as a monopolist and had no money to invest in infrastructure anyway. He seems to have felt that the purpose of the concession was to allow him to parasitize the informal sector. Shortly after he obtained his concession, he complained that the government

[23] Ibid.

[24] TNA 2796/2, 'Notes on Mangrove Bark Industry Collected from German Records,' n.d.

[25] TNA 2742, Kaiserliches Bezirksamt to Denhart & Co., n.d., and TNA 2742, Administrator's Office, Wilhelmstal to Political Officer, Tanga, 8 February 1917.

[26] TNA 2742, Chief Secretary to Conservator of Forests, 18 April 1921, and TNA 21120 Vol.1, Symes to Fowle, Resident Bushire, 21 March 1933.

[27] TNA 2739/1, Ingles and Kerr to Conservator of Forests, 10 Feburary 1922, and TNA 2739/1, Governor of Tanganyika Territory to Secretary of State for the Colonies, 22 May 1922.

[28] TNA 2739/1/– Vol II, Conservator of Forests to Chief Secretary, 20 December 1926.

had allowed a dhow to come and organize their own labourers to cut poles in an adjacent swamp. The dhow captain paid only 'the Royalty and actual cost of cutting. Whereas should he have come to us, we should have charged him over and above the amount of our profit and overhead charges.'[29] The government informed him that it was not their intention to give him a monopoly but rather that by having poles ready cut and stockpiled and by investing in infrastructure that he should be able to attract trade and make a profit. None the less, Ingles was soon given control of the entire Rufiji delta, still not a monopoly since there were swamps all up and down the coast, but close to it, since most of the export poles came from his lease.[30]

From then on, the relations between the Tanganyika government and Ingles went downhill. Ingles spent the next fifteen years asking the government to reduce their royalties while he consistently raised his prices. The volume of *boriti* being exported from the Rufiji dropped off, as did the royalties coming to the government. Ingles never made any investments in infrastructure and as early as 1924 he went into arrears on his minimum royalties payments. The government kept renewing his lease in the hope that he would be able to pay off his debt. By 1933 the Rufiji River Trading Co. was in debt to the government to the tune of Shs.20,506, and *boriti* exports had dropped from a 1923 high of 125,000 to 33,000 poles. The Forestry Department, apparently unaware of the extent of Ingles's bungling, began to wonder whether the trade was dropping off due to a change in building techniques in the Gulf.[31]

What seems to have been happening is that dhow captains had finally had enough of Ingles and, in keeping with their usual adaptability, were taking their business elsewhere. In 1933, the same year the Rufiji trade bottomed out, Zanzibar exported 28,560 locally produced poles, a fifteen-fold increase over the year before.[32] The availability of other sources of poles meant that, when prices got too high on the Rufiji, trade went elsewhere.

Soon after this Ingles died and the concession was taken over by the Liverpool Uganda Co. and then in 1941 by a Greek named Ghaui. Ghaui had been in the trade for a long time in Kilwa, and unlike Ingles he was a man of substance.[33] His principal advantage seems to have been that he was a major dhow owner, with close to thirty vessels, ranging from tiny swamp boats to large 40-ton coasters.[34] The Ghaui family seems to have retained control of the Rufiji concessions until at least the mid-1950s.[35] While the Ghauis ran the delta profitably, getting contracts to supply

[29] TNA 2739/1, Ingles to Chief Secretary, 9 August 1922.

[30] TNA 2739/1, Chief Secretary to Ingles, 30 September 1922.

[31] TNA 21120 Vol. I, Conservator of Forests to Chief Secretary, 3 March 1934, and TNA 21120 Vol. I, Pedlar to Assistant Chief Secretary, 23 March 1934.

[32] Zanzibar Government, *Blue Book*, 1933.

[33] TNA 61/3/XVI /D, Annual Report of the Rufiji District 1941, p. 14, and TNA 21120 Vol I, Conservator of Forests to Chief Secretary, 7 June 1935.

[34] TNA 27412 Vol. II, 'List of dhows belonging to the estate of M.Ghaui deceased and now sold to Mr. Hanna Ghaui', n.d.

[35] TNA 11310 Vol. II, Conservator of Forests to Member for Agriculture and Natural Resources, 12 March 1954.

mangrove poles for railway sleepers during the Second World War and paying their bills, they never 'rationalized' the export trade. Ghaui seems to have used his dhows and employees to supply Dar-es-Salaam. Monsoon dhows still had to organize their own cutting and labour.[36] Like his Asian counterparts in the clove trade, Ghaui realized that the mangrove trade was ill suited to modernization; he stuck with the dhow and prospered.

On the official level the Rufiji was part of the formal economy. There were royalties collected, concessions granted, Forest Guards and even a white Forestry Officer stationed in the delta. In the swamps, however, things were a bit more casual.

Our best window on activities in the delta comes from a British seaman named Alan Villiers who shipped out on a Kuwaiti *boom* in 1938. He spent the entire monsoon season with the *Triumph of Righteousness* as the dhow was named. This included a one-month stint in the Rufiji, and his account of what happened in the delta is at odds with any idea that the Rufiji end of the mangrove export trade was under colonial control.[37] Let us then look in some detail at Villiers's trip to the Rufiji.

Two weeks after selling their cargo in Zanzibar, Villiers and the *Triumph* set out for the Rufiji. With them was a Suri, assigned to them by the dhow's agent in Zanzibar, who acted as their pilot and general fixer. The dhow first called at Salale, where the Forestry Officer lived. They told the Forestry Officer what their mangrove-pole needs were and he assigned them to an area he thought would provide for their needs.

The dhows then began to recruit labourers to do the actual cutting. Since all the dhows showed up in the delta at the same time there was intense competition for labour. Recruiting a crew could take two weeks, since 'the Swahili had no liking for the back-breaking, wretched work. For this no one could blame them.'[38] Once recruited the labourers lived on board and ate food provided by the dhow.

During the day the cutters would cut and stack poles at various points in the area designated by the Forestry Officer. Now and then the Forest Guards would come by, count the poles in each stack and put a hammer mark on the poles and in theory no pole was to be loaded until it had been counted and so marked. The dhow crews then went around collecting the poles in their ships' boats and loading them in their dhows. The Forestry Officer made periodic visits and seemed quite intent on keeping everything above-board.

At night a slightly different system was in effect. By night poles were brought from remote stockpiles and stowed in the dhows under a layer of poles with the official hammer mark. Local village headmen, who organized surreptitious cutting and stacking, provided these poles. The end result was that each dhow left with roughly twice as many poles in its hold as were on its papers. The *Triumph* had papers for 150 *korjahs* of poles and paid royalties

[36] ZNA BC16/2, Tanganyika Government, *Annual Report of the Forest Dept.*, 1947, and interview with Sherali Haji Rashid, 16 August 1994.
[37] The whole of the following account is from Villiers, *Sons of Sinbad*, pp. 220 48.
[38] Ibid., p. 243,

on that number, but took 300. Villiers claims that everybody, including the Forest Guards, was in on this except the British Forestry Officer.

The only role the Liverpool Uganda Co., the concessionaire at the time, played in all this was to collect the royalty. When Villiers's dhow was ready to sail, the second in command made a two-day journey by canoe to deliver the royalty for 150 korjas to the company's agent. The dhow crews felt little guilt about this. Villiers was told that if the poles were ready and they did not have to hire their own labour, they might feel differently about the royalties. 'So far as they could see the company's agent existed to take their cash and for no other reason. They made it a point of honor to see that he got as little as possible.'[39] It would be interesting to know if, after Villiers's account of the Rufiji was published in 1940, there was a clamp-down in the swamps. His book was popular enough to go through several printings, and it seems likely that somebody in the Tanganyika government read it. If there were repercussions from this, there was no evidence in the archives.

In the delta, colonial attempts at controlling and modernizing the *boriti* trade did affect the way business was done, but neither the state nor the concessionaire seems to have had much control over how the work was done, what quantities of poles were taken or how much was paid for the poles. The British had hoped that the trade would be rationalized – that the concessionaires would employ year-round labour to cut and stockpile poles, so that dhows could simply arrive, buy poles and be on their way. This never happened. The concessionaires did little for the export trade except to skim off a royalty and the mangrove trade remained part of the informal rather than the formal economy.

The bark mania

In the early twentieth century, East African mangroves were of little interest to the world economy. But in the late 1930s the demand for mangrove bark, used in industrial leather tanning, increased and East Africans responded by increasing their production. By the mid-1940s there was a boom in the bark trade and Zanzibar exported record amounts of bark. This brought the world economy into competition with the western Indian Ocean regional economy for mangrove resources and the labour needed to do the harvesting. By employing labour that would otherwise have been engaged in cutting poles, the bark trade caused a minor dip in the number of poles exported. More importantly, the bark boom encouraged people to overwork swamps that were not under government supervision or private control. As a result the mangrove swamps in the Zanzibar Protectorate were decimated and by 1950 Zanzibar swamps were producing neither poles nor bark. The industrial economies of the West had taken a sporadic interest in mangrove bark in the early parts of the twentieth century. In 1904 for instance, the German Imperial Forestry Department in German East Africa

[39] Ibid., p. 247.

sold 83 tons of mangrove bark at a profit of Rps.3,500. By 1911 the world market had gone into decline and production of bark in German East Africa had gone down correspondingly.[40]

In the mid-1930s the bark market slumped along with the rest of the world economy. In Tanganyika the royalties charged to bark cutters were lowered in response to the flaccid demand, and at least one European with a bark-cutting concession was released from his contract because he was making no money.[41] Up to this point the world economy's interest in mangrove bark was so desultory as to have no effect on the regional economy's trade in poles. But, as the 1930s drew to a close, the bark trade began to pick up and the world economy began to affect the pole trade.

As the demand for bark slowly increased in years immediately before the Second World War, Zanzibar became an increasingly important source. Compared with Lamu and the Rufiji delta, Zanzibar was unregulated. So, as demand went up, Zanzibar, which had formerly served mostly as a minor supplement to the Rufiji, suddenly became the leading source of mangrove bark in East Africa.

This would seem to be at odds with my earlier statement that, while the Rufiji was regulated in theory, in practice regulations had little to do with who cut how much and where they cut it. But that was poles and this is bark. In the Rufiji concession, and in other mangrove concessions, bark stripping for export was entirely organized and monopolized by the concessionaire. While the concessionaires were usually satisfied to let other people cut poles in their concessions for a fee, bark they kept to themselves.[42] That they would do so makes sense since the potential for waste in bark stripping is high. Only the *Rhizophora* and *Bruguiera* varieties yield bark with a high enough tannin content to be marketable and only trees with at least an 8-inch butt diameter have the 38 per cent tannin content that industrial buyers want. For a mangrove tree to reach barkable size takes fifty years, or about twice as long as it takes to reach pole size.[43] Concessionaires, who had paid a fixed fee for a specific amount of swamp, were anxious to get as much bark out of their swamps as possible and so required their bark collectors to fell trees and strip the entire tree of bark and usually tried to sell the wood as well. Freelancers found this to be a waste of time and went from standing tree to standing tree stripping off the bark as high as they could reach. The girdled trees soon died. This second method was wasteful in that the timber and often as much as half the bark was lost. So while concessionaires on the mainland were not overly concerned about how poles were taken from their land, they monitored and controlled the bark operations.

---

[40] TNA 2796/2, 'Notes on Mangrove Bark Industry Collected from German Records,' n.d. [1920?].

[41] TNA 13508, Conservator of Forests to Chief Secretary, 19 September 1934.

[42] TNA 13508, Conservator of Forests to Chief Secretary, 17 September 1934 and TNA 13508, Conservator of Forests to Chief Secretary, 28 November 1938.

[43] A.L. Griffith, *Reconnaissance Report on the Forest Problems of the Zanzibar Protectorate* (Zanzibar, 1949), p. 10.

5.3 Bags of mangrove bark in Pemba, 1994

5.4 A pit used for tanning leather with mangrove bark

On Zanzibar there were no concessions, no monopolies and, as a practical matter, no supervision of the swamps. So, when the bark boom struck, it did so with a vengeance. The first intimations that Zanzibar was becoming a major source of mangrove bark come not from Zanzibar itself, but from Tanganyika. In 1937 the Tanganyika government politely suggested that Zanzibar ought to rein in its bark cutters since uncontrolled bark stripping was undercutting Tanganyika's controlled and taxed bark trade. The Zanzibar government considered regulating the bark business but concluded that their bark trade was too marginal to regulate.[44] By 1939 the Zanzibar government sounded a bit more cautious. The District Commissioner, Pemba, announced that, although 'the swamps are inexhaustible', barkable trees might well be unavailable in three to ten years.[45] Still the government did nothing to regulate bark stripping.

In 1939, the first year in which mangrove bark appears in Zanzibar trade records, Zanzibar exported 1,742 tons of mangrove bark. Assuming that this bark was harvested from trees stripped in their entirety, 1,742 tons probably represented about 70,000 dead trees. If on the other hand the trees were only partly stripped, the tree kill would be doubled.[46] Either way this is a lot of trees considering that Pemba and Unguja boast only 40,000 acres of mangrove swamp. By way of comparison, the largest number of poles ever exported from Zanzibar was 28,500 in 1933. Kenya, which has 85,000 acres of swamps in Lamu alone, exported only 60 tons of bark in 1938.[47]

Unlike Tanganyika, where mangrove concessionaires made an effort to organize and control bark stripping, Zanzibar was a free-for-all. One of the bark pioneers was Sherali Rashid. He moved to Wete from Zanzibar town in 1938 and opened a shop. Wete was the closest big town to the mangrove swamps on Pemba. Rashid eventually concentrated on clove shipping, but during his first years in Pemba mangrove bark looked like the ticket to prosperity. His letterhead shows that his cable address was 'mangrove'. In Pemba, bark passed through many hands before it got to Zanzibar and the world market. Merchants like Rashid bought the bark out of their shops and did nothing to control or organize the collection beyond providing advances to the middlemen from whom they bought the bark.[48]

Saidi Korogo of Micheweni was one of these middlemen. He bought bark and later poles from groups of freelance cutting crews, to whom he would advance money. These freelance cutters used canoes, *vidau* and *mashuas* to harvest bark from the swamp at Kichenge creek. They sold their bark to Saidi Korogo, who shipped it to Wete by dhow, where Rashid or

---

[44] ZNA AB4/151, Sayers, Dar-es-Salaam to McElderry, 4 January 1937, and ZNA AB4/151, McElderry to Sayers, 27 January 1937.

[45] ZNA AB4/151, District Commissioner Pemba to Provincial Commissioner, n.d. [1939?].

[46] Griffith, *Reconnaissance*, p. 10. Griffith, a forestry consultant of some sort, estimated that a full size 8" tree would yield 50 lbs of dried bark if fully stripped. Thus, 1,740 tons (short tons?) times 2000 lbs = 3,480,000 lbs/50lbs per tree = 69,600 trees. If the trees were only half stripped, then the figure looks more like 140,000 trees.

[47] Kenya Government, *Blue Book*, 1938.

[48] Interview with Sherali Haji Rashid, 16 August 1994.

some other merchant bought it and shipped it to Zanzibar, where someone else bought it and shipped it to the USA. The cutters had no incentive to strip bark in the approved whole-tree manner and of instead went from tree to tree stripping in the fastest and easiest way possible.[49] The initial efforts to cash in on the bark trade were a little too enthusiastic. Much of the bark exported in 1939 turned out to be below standard and Zanzibar's reputation suffered. But by 1943 things were looking up again and in 1946 an all-time record was set – Zanzibar exported 11,698 tons of bark. Even conservatively assuming that the bark strippers were taking all the bark from the trees this represented the demise of 467,920 trees. Zanzibar's swamps have never fully recovered from this.

The next year Zanzibar's bark exports were down to 4,823 tons. In 1948 bark exports were down to 2,295 tons and the next year bark stripping was banned. By 1949 a system for the management of cutting was in place and the process of creating forest reserves wherever there were mangrove swamps was under way. But all this was too late and too little. By the time the controls on mangrove cutting and bark stripping were in place, Pemba had no poles over 5 or 6 inches in diameter.[50] A study done in 1961, using aerial photographs made in 1953, describes Chwaka Bay, Unguja's biggest swamp, as 'devastated' and totally lacking 'pure stands of either *Rhizophora* or *Bruguiera*'. While a recent survey of Pemba's mangrove swamps maintains that the swamps are in good condition and even expanding,[51] it is clear that they have been changed. An 8-inch mangrove tree has become a rare and exceptional thing and people whose whole lives have involved the swamps maintain that the size of the trees has diminished noticeably since the prewar period.[52]

What were the implications of all this for the long-distance dhow trade? The most obvious effect was that, when Zanzibar banned the export of domestic mangrove poles and bark in 1948, the range of options for dhow captains seeking a cargo of poles for export was narrower than it had been in, say, 1933. In 1933, when dhow captains thought they were getting a raw deal from the Rufiji Delta Trading Company, they could take their business to Zanzibar. In Zanzibar the swamps were small, but unregulated and there was no royalty. By the early 1950s that option was gone. The loss was not devastating, but it added to the increasing precariousness of the long-distance trade's position. At the same time that seagoing dhows were becoming more reliant on mangrove poles, the variety of sources where poles could be obtained was becoming increasingly restricted.

The other way in which the bark boom must have affected the seagoing dhow trade was by tying up labour that might have otherwise been engaged in cutting poles. Here we are on speculative ground. It is not possible to

---

[49] Interview with Saidi Korogo, 4 October 1994.

[50] Griffith, *Reconnaisance*, p. 20.

[51] J.P. Shunula, 'A Survey on the Distribution and Status of Mangrove Forests in Zanzibar, Tanzania,' November–December 1989, Commission for Lands and Environments, Zanzibar.

[52] Interview with Saidi Korogo, 4 October 1994.

prove that more poles would have reached Arabia in the 1940s than actually did if there had been no bark boom. But one gets the feeling that everyone who had a free moment in the mid-1940s spent it stripping mangrove bark. If nothing else, bark stripping as an option for pole cutters probably drove up their wages. In 1945 the Annual Report for Pemba complained that the bark boom was in some ways a problem since it required 'the employment of large numbers of natives at times when they should have been planting their own food crops ... The rate of remuneration for bark collection was good at about average Shgs. 3–4/– a day.'[53] Presumably people were not willing to cut mangrove poles for less than they could get for bark stripping, and this must have increased the cost of mangrove poles. Despite the growing concentration on one cargo, and the narrowing of the supply of that cargo, the heyday of the dhow trade was yet to come. In the 1950s the long-distance dhow trade went into an unprecedented boom as oil money and high clove prices stoked up the economy in the Gulf and Zanzibar.

The final days

In the 1950s Zanzibar's economy flourished. In the official economy, clove prices were high and foreign trade was reaching hitherto unprecedented levels. The informal economy also prospered. The growing postwar global economy had a huge thirst for oil from the Gulf, which created a steady and growing demand for mangrove poles. Zanzibar's swamps were closed to cutting for export in 1949, but the transit trade boomed. Dhows came to Zanzibar in large numbers in the 1950s, bringing the same cargoes they had always brought and taking away mangrove poles in quantities never seen before. In 1953, 530 dhows cleared Zanzibar for Arabia and they carried 164,000 poles. Zanzibar exports of mangrove poles peaked in 1959 at 255,000, but dhows clearing for Arabia had dropped to 192.[54] A new pattern had begun to emerge. Poles were still being brought from the mainland by dhow, but more and more their cargoes were being purchased by Zanzibar dhow agents, who then shipped the poles to Arabia in steamers.

By the late 1950s, colonial officials in Zanzibar began to notice that the long distance dhow trade was dropping off.[55] This was a subject of moderate concern to them since a significant proportion of Zanzibar's foreign trade was carried by dhows and there was quite a local industry built up around handling the business needs of dhows during their stay in East Africa. While the dhow crews were considered an unruly lot whose presence contributed

---

[53] ZNA BA30/23, Pemba District Annual Report for 1945.

[54] ZNA BA1/42, Zanzibar Government, *Annual Trade Report*, 1953, ZNA BA1/53, Zanzibar Government, *Annual Trade Report*, 1959, ZNA BA36/19, Zanzibar Government, *Annual Report of the Port and Marine*, 1953, ZNA BA36/24, Zanzibar Government, *Annual Report of the Port and Marine Department*, 1959.

[55] This was also a concern in Kenya. The 1957 Rawlins report was the result of official concern about the decline of the Lamu mangrove trade.

to unrest, petty theft and often violence, they also spent a lot of money. By one estimate they put out close to Shgs. 200,000/– during the course of the season, not including the value of their cargo.[56]

A series of meetings were held asking dhow agents and captains what could be done to keep the trade going. The captains argued that they would like to see a ban on steamer exports of poles, since the large volumes the steamers could handle and their ability to arrive at times not dictated by the monsoon were making it unprofitable to carry mangrove poles. Since mangrove poles were their usual return cargo this was going to put them out of business. They also noted that in Kenya steamers were only permitted to carry poles if there was not sufficient dhow space and that in India certain cargoes were legally considered exclusively dhow cargoes.[57] Despite several meetings over several years at which most of the same points were brought up the government took no steps to protect the dhows from competition from steamers.

It is not clear how serious a threat steamers really were to the dhows that carried mangrove poles. No one I talked to remembered that steamers had carried poles to Arabia, even people whose fathers had, according to government documents, been shipping poles by steamer.[58] In 1961 a government official noted that, compared with dhows, steamers were not a particularly economic way of shipping poles.[59] And, even if steamers had taken a significant part of the Zanzibar–Arabia trade, the dhows would still have controlled the business of getting the poles to Zanzibar. But before this challenge to the dhow-borne trade could be played out, the long-distance dhow trade came to an abrupt end.

The numbers of dhows arriving at Zanzibar from the north peaked in 1953 (actually there had been 565 Arab dhows in 1946 but this was more postwar boom than oil boom) and steadily dwindled to 147 by 1963.[60] This diminution was also due to the oil boom. As jobs in the oilfields became available in greater numbers, bobbing around for a month in a dhow filled with dried shark began to look less appealing. The oilfields paid better, were safer and were closer to home.[61] The oil boom, after initially increasing the demand for poles, eventually brought about a level of prosperity that allowed most people to build with concrete, thereby lowering the demand for poles.[62] By 1963 the number of poles leaving Zanzibar had

[56] ZNA AK4/35, 'Minutes of the Meeting of Shippers of Simbauranga Mangrove Poles Held at DC(U)'s office,' 30 May 1960.

[57] ZNA AK18/13, District Commisioner (Urban) to Senior Commissioner, 23 April 1960, and ZNA AK4/35, Senior District Commissioner to Senior Commissioner, 15 April 1961.

[58] Interview with H. Baharun, 17 October 1994.

[59] ZNA AK18/13, 'Minutes of the Dhow Agents Meeting held in the DC(U)'s office,' 29 Nov. 1961.

[60] ZNA BA36/25, Zanzibar Government, *Annual Report of the Port and Marine Department*, July 1962 to 30 June 1963.

[61] ZNA AK18/13, District Commissioner (Urban) to Senior Commissioner, 30 November 1960.

[62] ZNA AK18/13, Comptroller of Customs to Senior Commissioner, 22 June 1960, and ZNA AP10/21, Rawlins, 'Mangrove Trade,' pp. 6, 19.

dropped again to 142,000, down by over 100,000 from 1959.[63]

By themselves this combination of economic forces would probably have put a stop to the trade eventually. But instead of dying a lingering death the long-distance trade was brought to an abrupt halt by the Zanzibar Revolution. As early as 1960 Zanzibar's politics were beginning to make Arab dhow owners nervous. The District Commissioner for Zanzibar town in 1960 noted that 'they [dhow captains] now find it a bit hot here with the changes of political wind and are beginning to dislike coming here'.[64] By 1964 the political winds had definitely shifted and revolutionary Zanzibar was not a good place to be an Arab. Most of the dhows avoided Zanzibar in 1964 and by 1965 there was a law forbidding any vessel that had called at an Arabian port in the preceding year to enter Zanzibar.[65] This eliminated all Arab vessels and most of the Indian vessels. Furthermore most of the dhow agents and other business contacts the northern dhows were accustomed to dealing with had either perished or fled or were lying low. The odd Persian or Somali dhow continued to show up in Zanzibar until the 1970s, but the long-distance mangrove trade was finished. To be sure the local dhows still carry poles to meet the needs of Zanzibar town, and as late as the 1980s smugglers carrying Tanzanian ivory to North Yemen would bury their ivory under a cargo of poles.[66] But the mangrove trade was no longer a major part of Zanzibar's economy.

Conclusion

Instead of dying at the beginning of the colonial period when the East African economy was being readjusted to suit the needs of its new rulers, the mangrove-pole trade and the long-distance dhow trade survived the transition from precolonial to colonial economy with its feathers ruffled, but still in good condition. If we take Rigby's figures for 1859 as representative for the nineteenth century as a whole (a tenuous assumption to be sure), then the volume of *boriti* passing through Zanzibar was about the same in 1859 as in 1959. The latter was an outstanding year for the Zanzibar pole trade, and there is no telling how representative or accurate Rigby's numbers are, but the similarity of these two figures, separated as they are by one hundred years, suggests that at least the order of magnitude of the trade remained the same for a century. Furthermore, the poles were transported in more or less the same way and were probably collected in much the same way at both ends of a one hundred year period. Ironically, instead of being harmed by the arrival of the British, the trade ended just as Zanzibar and other East African countries became independent. In

---

[63] ZNA BA1/57, Zanzibar Government, *Annual Trade Report*, 1963.

[64] ZNA AK18/13, District Commissioner (Urban) to Senior Commissioner, 30 November 1960.

[65] ZNA AK18/13, 'Mkutano Hususi Unaoohusu Majahazi ya Musim', 6 June 1965. This document also notes that in 1964 only twenty-three seasonal dhows came to Zanzibar and none of these were Arab.

[66] Interview with a person who wished to remain anonymous.

Kenya, a few poles were still being exported as late as 1972, so it seems probable that, if the Revolution had not suddenly cut Zanzibar off from the Arab world, an attenuated trade would have struggled on for another decade or so.[67]

What is apparent is that the mangrove trade resisted, adapted to or simply endured all the challenges it met during the colonial period. When the business that leased the Rufiji swamps gave them trouble, the dhow captains went elsewhere. When conditions there were endurable dhows went to the Rufiji, but paid royalties and followed the rules only to the extent that they saw fit. When the world economy took a sudden interest in mangrove bark, the pole traders endured. By its very survival, the mangrove trade kept the seagoing-dhow trade alive and kept Zanzibar tied into a regional, western Indian Ocean economy which predated the arrival of the British by centuries.[68]

While the advent of colonialism was undoubtedly a force for change in East Africa and the Middle East, this older trade pattern continued to affect the texture of people's lives until the combined effects of oil and the 1964 Revolution put an end to it. The daily lives of the Bajuni, whose migrations shadowed those of the Arab dhows, the mangrove dealers in Zanzibar and the Gulf, the sailors, shipowners, shipwrights and tradesmen at both ends of this regional economy were more deeply affected by this trade than the low monetary value assigned to the trade by colonial officialdom would suggest. This regional economy may have been marginal. But the mangrove trade was neither irrational nor backward. At all levels of the economy people were willing to adopt new technology when it made sense. Mangrove dealers in Zanzibar were in regular contact with the Gulf by telegraph to track prices, dhows were fitted with auxiliary engines when they became affordable, dealers even experimented with shipping poles by steamer until they found it to be more expensive than using dhows. Dhow captains did not ply their trade out of a romantic attachment to the past or some kind of innate conservatism. They did their work because it was economically rational. People in the Gulf wanted timber, there was timber in East Africa and dhows were the most efficient means of moving that timber. When people in the Gulf started to want concrete and re-bar iron more than mangrove poles, the trade ended and with it went the regional economy that linked Zanzibar to the Gulf and Arabia.

As was the case with the clove-carriage trade, modern forms of transportation and business organization did not replace the dhows and the informal organization of the mangrove trade. Despite colonial efforts to

---

[67] ZNA BB19/21, Government of Kenya, *Forest Department Annual Report*, 1972. In 1972 Kenya exported 197,908 poles, probably mostly to Iran, Iraq and Yemen.

[68] The literature on colonial Zanzibar is strangely silent on the issue of the mangrove trade and the role it played in the long-distance dhow trade. While mangrove poles get the occasional paragraph, Abdul Sheriff, 'The Peasantry Under Imperialism,' in Abdul Sheriff and Ed Ferguson, *Zanzibar Under Colonial Rule* (London: 1991), pp. 125–6 and Frederick Cooper, *From Slaves to Squatters* (New Haven: 1980), pp. 262, 266–7, they are presented in terms of local production increasing or decreasing, with no reference to the larger regional economy.

rationalize production in the Rufiji and to control cutting and ownership of mangrove swamps in Zanzibar, and the increasing availability of steamships on the route between Arabia and East Africa, the basic structures of the mangrove trade remained unchanged. The mangrove trade successfully kept modernity at bay, using its own labour supply, capital, technology and transportation, all of which moved easily across colonial borders, to subvert colonial attempts at control and rationalization. When at last the mangrove trade died, it did so because the fundamental structures of the western Indian Ocean economy had been transformed by oil money. It was not that more modern transport or better capitalization or a more efficient labour supply modernized the existing trade; it was instead a total, abrupt upsetting of the monsoon economy. The Persian Gulf, which was on a relatively equal footing with India and East Africa until the early 1960s, suddenly became one of the richest places on the planet, not through modernization and rationalization but rather through an oil-driven *deus ex machina*. Gulf oil pulled the rug from under the monsoon economy, and that was the end of the mangrove trade.

In the mangrove trade, as with the clove-carriage trade, piecemeal modernization was unsuccessful. One could not simply insert rationalized production or modern shipping while letting the rest of the trade alone. As a result, the mangrove trade and its handmaiden the long-distance dhow trade survived until the mid-1960s as part of a larger, integrated, regional, monsoon economy.

Postscript

In 1997, I met a Zanzibari businessman in Aden. His family had lived in Shangani, the part of the Zanzibar stone town I had stayed in in 1994, and had moved to the Hadhramaut in 1980s. He was in his thirties, educated in Britain, and was running a major construction firm in Aden. When I met him, he was wearing a polo shirt and jeans and was seated in an office that would fit anyone's standard of the modern, wired office. Fax machines, computers and all the trappings of modern business culture were there. We got to talking and it came out, purely by accident, that his brother still lived in Zanzibar. What did the brother do? Import–export, like everybody else. What did he import? Biscuits, paint, soap. What did he export? Mangrove wood.

It turns out that there is still a small market for *boriti* in Iran. My host in Aden took orders by fax from the Gulf. He would fax them to his brother in Zanzibar, who would arrange for *boriti* to be loaded and shipped by motor dhow to the Gulf. Money would then be wired from the Gulf to Aden and biscuits, paints and soap would be dispatched to Zanzibar. What is so interesting about this is that despite the use of fax machines and wire transfers of money in this commercial system, when it comes time to ship the *boriti* they still use dhows. Even now in a world dominated by containerized shipping, the dhow has its place.[69]

[69] Interview with Abdul Shamak, 18 June 1997, Aden.

Six

From Definitions to Deference
An Overview of the Dhow Economy in Colonial Zanzibar

Cloves and mangrove wood were the backbones of the local and monsoon dhow trades, respectively. Both industries affected the lives and livelihoods of people from the swamps and clove groves of Pemba to the ports of Zanzibar, Muscat and Bombay. But the economic relevance of the dhow economy extended far beyond these two commodities and into the mainstream of Zanzibari life in particular and East African life in general. Even as Zanzibar became more deeply integrated into the British Empire and the global economy, dhows saw to it that Zanzibar retained a role in the regional economy and that the rhythms of the monsoon still had their say in Zanzibar's economic and social life.

However, the colonial state was never entirely comfortable with the dhow economy. The state saw in dhows first a threat to the economic order and then just as it became more comfortable with the dhow's economic role, the state began to see the dhow as a threat to security. In this chapter we shall trace the changing nature of the relationship between the colonial state and dhow economy and see what that economy meant to Zanzibar.

If the Zanzibar government sought in the 1930s to drive dhows out of the clove trade and to control and direct the cutting of mangrove wood, it also sought broader measures to control the dhow economy. A major part of this effort at control involved defining what a dhow is, and in so doing creating a discrete entity called the 'dhow trade'. If the anti-slave-trade initiative of the late nineteenth century began the process of separating dhows from the official economy, the efforts at contriving a legal definition of the dhow in the 1930s put the finishing touches to the creation of a discrete, definable dhow trade.

Defining the dhow

In the general coasting trade the lines between the official sector and the unofficial sector were not clearly defined. Instead of being wholly controlled by one or the other sector, the coastal trade in general merchandise was hotly contested between privately owned steamship companies, dhows and an intermediate type of vessel called a schooner. The upshot of this competition was that it forced the colonial governments of Zanzibar, Kenya and Tanganyika to define in the law-books the differences between these types of vessels.

In general the colonialists' ideas about the inherent difference between things 'modern' and things 'native', and hence destined for replacement by the modern, remained unarticulated. But the need to create legal definitions for 'native vessels', especially the unsuccessful attempt to create a definition that would exclude schooners, forced them to articulate some of these ideas. So, in studying this trade and the legal and commercial conflict surrounding it, we have the opportunity of seeing how the informal sector fared in competition with private-sector steamships and of watching an intriguing debate within the colonial state about what exactly a dhow is.

In Chapter Three we saw that the first attempts to differentiate between dhows and other types of vessels resulted from the effort to suppress the slave-trade. Naval officers had such great latitude to interfere with ships they suspected of involvement in the slave-trade that no European country wanted its own shipping handled in so high-handed a manner. To protect European shipping from the sorts of outrages that were regularly visited on dhows, the right of search and seizure was limited to vessels under 500 tons. This was a crude way of differentiating between vessels owned by Europeans, which were usually bigger than 500 tons, and indigenous shipping, which was usually under 500 tons. A slightly more rigorous definition was included in the Brussels Treaty of 1892, which basically declared that a native vessel was either a vessel commanded and manned by 'natives' or a vessel which had the appearance of a native vessel. This tautological definition was in effect until 1921 when the treaty was abrogated.[1] Thus all the slave-trade suppression rules of the Brussels treaty, which had singled out dhows for special scrutiny in the form of crew lists, passenger lists, etc., remained in effect for the first thirty years of the colonial period.

At the same time vessels in the legal category 'dhow' also came to enjoy some advantages. Since dhows were less reliant on wharfs, cranes, lighters and all the other infrastructure associated with ports, they were consistently charged lower port fees than other vessels. And this small advantage was eventually noticed by Constantin Nicolas, who imported a small schooner from Greece. His schooner fitted the legal definition of a dhow, but plainly was not what the authorities had in mind when they set out that definition. To understand the uproar that Nicolas and his schooner caused, we need first to look at the way in which dhows were legally defined in the early twentieth century, the advantages that vessels so defined enjoyed and the

---

[1] ZNA AB44/3, Judge of HBM's Court, Zanzibar to Sinclair Resident Zanzibar, 27 October 1921.

circumstances under which those advantages might outweigh the disadvantages.

Although the Brussels Treaty ceased to be in effect in 1921, most of its provisions seem to have remained in effect. The Zanzibar Ports Rules of 1927, the first update of the Ports Rules after the abrogation of the Brussels Treaty, called for dhows to carry passenger lists and crew lists and stipulated that 'no native shall be allowed to engage as a seaman on a native vessel unless and until the Port Officer shall have been satisfied that such engagement is a voluntary one', that dhows were not to leave port except during daylight, that passengers were to be collected only in ports recognized by the decree and that the rules were not to apply to the government steamers.[2] In short, all of the old anti-slave-trade rules remained in the law-books nearly forty years after they were first devised and long after the slave-trade had disappeared.

At the same time that the authorities reconfirmed the old anti-slave-trade rules, they retained the Brussels Treaty version of the definition of a dhow. About this, though, there was some debate. Following Tanganyika's lead it appears that someone in the Zanzibar government wanted to define dhows only as vessels manned or owned by natives of the Indian Ocean rim.[3] The Comptroller of Customs's comment on this idea was that:

> This interpretation may be satisfactory in view of local conditions, but it is not strictly correct. A dhow would not cease to be a 'Native Vessel' even if it were commanded by a Greek and manned by Fijians.[4]

This view won out and the 1927 Port Rules for Zanzibar included 'the outward appearance of native build, or rig' as part of the definition of a dhow, without specifying what the characteristics of this style might be.[5] The Comptroller of Customs's support of this policy and its retention in the Port Rules are telling. To his mind there was an inherent difference between the 'native vessel' and other craft. That this difference was not just the result of the ethnicity of the owner or crew implies that an identifiable, physical difference existed that separated the dhow from the non-dhow. And this difference was so obvious to him that he saw no need to explain what it was. As we saw earlier, there is no clear-cut difference between a dhow and any other sailing craft. But this colonial officer was expressing an idea about the existence of a discrete entity called the 'dhow', an idea that was so widely accepted in his time, and indeed in ours, that he felt no need to explain how that category might be defined. And it is clear that, if there was some debate within the administration as to whether the rig and appearance ought to figure in the legal definition of a dhow, there was no debate as to whether such a conceptual category actually existed.

[2] ZNA AB44/4, The Zanzibar Ports Decree, 18 August 1927.
[3] ZNA AB44/4, Comptroller of Customs to Attorney General, 2 March 1927 and TNA 19039, General Manager, Ports and Railroads to Chief Secretary, 29 December 1932.
[4] ZNA AB44/4, Comptroller of Customs to Attorney General, 2 March 1927.
[5] ZNA AB44/4, The Zanzibar Ports Decree, 18 August 1927.

In Tanganyika the legal definition of a dhow had been pared down to the point where a native vessel was:

> a vessel other than a small coaster or fishing boat which is either owned by a native or fitted out or commanded by a native or of which more than half of the crew are natives of the countries bordering on the Indian Ocean, the Red Sea, the Persian Gulf, or the Gulf of Oman.[6]

This was a more inclusive definition, but it too made some revealing assumptions. Excluding 'small coasters' assumed that there was some clear-cut difference between a European-built or style coastal craft and native vessels, even though the two often performed the same economic functions. Still this definition left the door open for some vessels to claim 'native vessel' status, even though, in the minds of concerned officials, they were not dhows.

Constantin Nicolas, the man who caused all the fuss, was a naturalized British subject of Greek origin. He had lived in South Africa and after the First World War came to Tanganyika to work on the salvaging of the *Königsberg*, a German cruiser that sank in the Rufiji delta. Once he had salvaged as much of the *Königsberg* as possible, he decided to look into the possibility of entering the local coasting trade. To that end he went to the Marine Department and the Customs Department in Dar-es-Salaam and posed them a question. He asked whether a wooden sailing ship of less than 50 tons with a small engine in it would qualify as a 'native vessel'. He was told that it would. He then sought financing from a Greek lawyer, George Houry, in Dar-es-Salaam, who put up the start-up money in his wife's name. In 1932 the vessel arrived from Greece and was named after Vera Houry, who was George's wife. *Vera* was a wood-hulled schooner-rigged ship of 41 registered tons. In addition to her sails she carried a 60 horse-power auxiliary engine. Today a medium-sized outboard engine might exceed 60 horsepower, so *Vera* probably moved by sail rather than power most of the time. Her crew consisted of Nicolas as master, two Greeks, and ten 'natives'. And Nicolas registered her as a native vessel.[7]

As soon as the *Vera* went to work, everybody from the administrations in Dar-es-Salaam and Zanzibar to the major steamship companies went into a panic. The two governments started to question whether their legal definitions of 'native vessels' were adequate and the conference lines, as these company cartels were known, started to bully their customers in order to prevent them shipping by the *Vera*.

In Tanganyika the first concern was that everybody and anybody would decide to register as 'native vessels'. The General Manager of the Ports and Railways in Tanganyika immediately decided that there was a danger that every locally owned tugboat, lighter and steamer would now expect to be allowed to register as a 'native vessel' and he suggested that mechanical propulsion be forbidden for 'native vessels'.[8]

---

[6] TNA 19039, General Manager, Ports and Railroads to Chief Secretary, 29 December 1932.

[7] TNA 19039, 'Memorandum from George Houry,' 4 September 1933.

[8] TNA 19039, General Manager, Ports and Railways to Chief Secretary, 29 December 1932.

Soon the issue was taken up at a higher level. The Tanganyika government approached Zanzibar and Kenya and suggested that they come up with a uniform set of rules about what constituted a 'native vessel', since all three colonies had slightly different rules. (Kenya's were closer to the Zanzibar/Brussels Treaty approach than to Tanganyika's.) Tanganyika proposed that all three of their definitions should be modified so as to exclude mechanical propulsion. This would limit native vessel status to 'only those types of vessels which were originally intended to be brought within the Native Vessels Ordinance'.[9]

As always, how the 'intended' beneficiaries of this regulation were different from the *Vera* was not spelt out. The authors of both this legislation and the commentary on it seem to have been simultaneously convinced that *Vera* was not a native vessel and unable to say why, except in the easily identifiable case of her engine. Ironically, though, a ban on mechanical propulsion in native vessels never made it to the books, and so the presence of an engine in what was otherwise a dhow did not fundamentally change the identity of that vessel in the minds of the law writers. When the Zanzibar Port Officer was asked his opinion on the question of mechanical propulsion, he said that 'the introduction of an auxiliary engine in a native vessel is, in our opinion, worthy of encouragement.' At the same time he saw the *Vera* as something other than a native vessel and worried that 'the introduction of a large number of such vessels would have a definitely adverse effect on the trade now enjoyed by local native vessels.'[10] Something more fundamental, more essential than her engine set *Vera* apart from native vessels. *Vera* was modern. She had been recently built in Europe, was fore-and-aft-rigged, and was probably fairly up to date in her fittings.[11] Dhows, in comparison, even if they had been recently built, were 'ancient' and 'traditional' and hence different from the *Vera*.

As the Zanzibar government debated Tanganyika's proposed definition, the debaters made some revelatory comments. The most interesting of these was made by the Port Officer, who was responding to a suggestion that they do away with all the convoluted definitions of a native vessel and simply use the word 'dhow' in the regulations that were supposed to apply to dhows. The Port Officer responded, in effect, that this would not work since there was no such thing as a 'dhow' in that sense. He asserted that 'dhow' was just a variant spelling of *dau*, which referred to small double-ended boats. Since the 'majority of locally built craft have square sterns [as opposed to the pointed stern of a *dau*] and are know as "jehazi"', he preferred to stick with 'native vessel'. Furthermore,

> The expression 'native vessel' as now applied to vessels visiting the Port of Zanzibar comprises the following types of craft: dau, jehazi, baggala,

[9] ZNA AB45/120, Acting Chief Secretary, Tanganyika to Chief Secretary, Zanzibar, 19 December 1933.

[10] ZNA AB45/120, Port Officer and Attorney General to Chief Secretary, 31 January 1934.

[11] I have not been able to locate a picture of the original *Vera*. The hulk of a small steel-hulled ship named *Vera* lies beached in Dar-es-Salaam harbour. I assume that since the original *Vera* was wood hulled that this represents a later acquisition by Nicolas and Houry.

bedeni, qwesia, pattamar, batlili, ganja, jalbuti, kachi, grab, ukararu, mtepe, and I dare say a number of others the names of which are not familiar to me.[12]

This is the closest any Zanzibar government type ever came to admitting on paper that the 'native vessel' was an artificial category stuffed full of a variety of styles of ship, each somehow distinctive in its own way. What, for instance, did an *mtepe*, built of mangrove wood, held together with lashings, double-ended and square-rigged with a vertical mast, have in common with a teak-planked, lateen-rigged with a forward-raking mast, square-sterned, nailed-hulled, high-pooped *bagala*? Nothing really, except the presumption that both were economically marginal relics of a traditional economy. And this is why *Vera* was such fly in the ointment. Her owners intended to use her not for traditional cargoes, but to compete for any and all cargoes, even those that the steamship companies considered to be theirs by right. To be sure, dhows had always carried both traditional cargoes and those associated with modernity – rose-water and car tyres both had their place – but *Vera* got more attention since she transgressed more than just the cargo boundary.

It seems, then, that what defined 'native vessels' was partly their appearance; they should have a touch of the exotic East to them – the Piraeus was not exotic enough – and they should also fit the economically marginal role that the government expected of them. They should do traditional, native work and not modern things, like competing with the steamer service for coastal cargo in Tanganyika or cloves in Zanzibar.

If in Zanzibar the local dhow fleet was in competition with a government-run steamer service with the law behind it, in Tanganyika sailing craft competed against private steamship services with significant economic clout. And, if the Tanganyika government saw *Vera* as a threat to a concept, the steamship companies saw her as a very real economic threat, and they took swift action to ensure that *Vera* remained in the economically marginal sector they left to dhows.

To understand how the steamship companies did this, it is necessary to make a brief digression. From the late nineteenth century until the 1950s, the major steamship companies participated in a cartel that ostensibly prevented them from engaging in destructive competition with each other. The conference lines, as they were called, divided up the routes among themselves and set standard freight charges. Then, to ensure customer loyalty, they offered a rebate of 10 per cent of all freight charges to any customers who only shipped with companies that participated in the conference. The rebates were paid out with a six-month delay, so that a shipper who abandoned the conference lines for non-conference competition could only do so at the sacrifice of rebates he expected in the future. This did a good job of keeping shippers loyal and gave the conference lines a great deal of leverage over their customers.

---

[12] ZNA AB45/120, Port Officer to Attorney General, 28 November 1934.

As soon as the *Vera* was registered, the conference lines put out the word that anybody who shipped with *Vera* would lose their rebate. Daya Waljee, a Dar es Salaam merchant, was informed in April of 1933 that his firm was on the 'stop list' and, if he wanted it removed, he would have to 'give an undertaking that you will confine your future coastwise shipments to the Steamship Lines detailed in the Deferred Commission circular'.[13] This approach quickly limited the cargoes available to *Vera*. In some areas, most notably the Rufiji, *Vera* could take cargo only if there was no conference ship available and the shipper had given the conference lines advanced notice. The result was to limit *Vera* to carrying 'native produce, chiefly rice, copra and maize from and to Rufiji, Dar es Salaam, and Mombasa belonging to local merchants not doing the export business to Europe'.[14] The conference lines also pressured Tanganyika to legislate the *Vera* out of the native-vessel category, precipitating much of the legislative debate we saw above.

In the end, the Tanganyika government came up with an interesting way of dealing with the challenge *Vera* presented to their ideas about modernity and tradition. *Vera* was allowed to keep her native-vessel status, but new laws were added that created a special class of dhow cargo. Dhow cargo could be handled over the dhow wharf at Shgs.1/20 per ton as opposed to the main wharf at a fee of Shgs.3/– per ton. Any vessel under 50 tons, regardless of how it was propelled, could carry dhow cargo at the lower wharfage rate. In the category called 'dhow cargo' was an interesting array of goods ranging from important exports, such as cotton, to odd imports, such as bicycles and camping equipment. In general, though, it stuck closely to the sorts of traditional cargoes expected of dhows – fish, *boriti*, tea, sugar, coconuts, hides. Missing from the list were coffee and sisal, two of Tanganyika's main exports and so international trade goods presumably unsuited to dhows.[15] This new rule killed two birds with one stone. On the one hand, it put the *Vera* into a defined position. As long as *Vera* behaved like a dhow and carried dhow cargoes she would pay dhow wharfage dues. If she wanted to participate in the international side of Tanganyika's economy – the modern side – she would have to pay modern wharfage fees. In addition to putting *Vera* into an understandable economic category, the new rules dealt with something else that was bothering the Port Office in Dar es Salaam. Apparently *Vera* was not the only native vessel with a foot in both the modern and traditional worlds. It seems that some imported cargoes destined for Tanganyika were being transshipped from steamships in Zanzibar and put on board dhows so as to avoid the higher wharfage charges for steamers in Tanganyika. The

---

[13] TNA 19039, East African Steamship Conference to Daya Waljee and Co., 20 April 1933.
[14] TNA 19039, 'Memorandum by George Houry,' 4 September 1933, and TNA 25407, Nicolas and Co. to General Manager, Railways and Ports, 7 December 1937.
[15] TNA 19039, 'The Ports (Wharfage Dues) Rules, 1934', TNA 19039, General Manager, Railways and Ports, to Chief Secretary, 25 May 1933, and TNA 25407 Nicolas and Co. to General Manager, Railways and Ports, 7 December 1937.

new rules put an end to this practice, forcing dhows to behave like dhows again.[16]

Thus the furore over the *Vera* forced the government to partially redefine the nature of a native vessel. The rules about the origins of the crew were retained, and the *Vera* continued be manned mostly by 'native' sailors. But in forcing their craft into the native vessel category Nicolas and Houry contributed to the marginalization of the dhow. Once the cargo rules were established, dhows were limited to carrying for the 'country trade' and forced to specialize in 'certain cheap commodities which could not bear an economic shipping freight [on a steamer]'.[17] Just as the Zanzibar government used subsidies and regulations to try to control the clove-carriage trade, the Tanganyika government used the law to ensure that the high-value cargoes of the local coasting trade went to privately owned steamships. If dhows were a marginal part of the coastal trade, their marginality was as much a product of legislation as it was of any inefficiency or other shortcomings. And that legislation was itself the product of colonial ideas about the backward qualities of dhows and lobbying on the part of steamship companies that had an interest in pushing dhows out of the more profitable parts of the carriage trade.

The *Vera* thrived, despite having been regulated into a marginal position. Nicolas charged the same freights as dhows, and included any cargo handling in the freight charges. He was able to attract business since his schooner was better decked than most of the *jahazis* that provided coastal services, so cargos stayed drier, and because even a small engine provided a margin of safety not available in a pure sailing craft. Thus *Vera* attracted the custom of shippers who might otherwise have paid more to ship by steamer. It is also likely that *Vera* took some business that might otherwise have gone to *jahazis*. And in many ways the *Vera* behaved like a *jahazi*. Like the *jahazis*, the *Vera* was affected by the monsoons in that she sailed less frequently during the south-west monsoon and charged rates that were 30 per cent higher during the four months when the seas were rougher and the wind strongest.[18]

At first Nicolas apparently made most of his money by carrying cotton, the one internationally traded commodity that was considered a dhow cargo. In 1935, a revised list of dhow cargoes eliminated cotton and forced native vessels to carry local produce, since this would be the 'most valuable (to the territory) activity' in which they could be employed. Even after his ship was totally cut out of the carriage of internationally traded goods, Nicolas's schooner did well.

The *Vera* did so well that Houry and Nicolas began to expand their fleet.

---

[16] TNA 19309 Vol. II, General Manager, Railways and Ports to Attorney General, 15 September 1934. In 1994 a similar scam kept the Zanzibar dhow harbour busy. Import duties were lower in Zanzibar than in Dar es Salaam, but goods could be shipped from Zanzibar to Dar es Salaam duty-free since this is considered internal trade. Thus it is common for goods destined for Dar to break bulk in Zanzibar and cross the channel in dhow or motor schooners.

[17] TNA 25407, Smith Mackenzie & Co. to Chief Secretary, 9 November 1937.

[18] TNA 25407, Nicolas and Co. to General Manager, Railways and Ports, 7 December 1937.

By 1937 they were about to add a fourth vessel to their fleet. This latest vessel, the *Lindi* caused a stir even before she arrived in Tanganyika. *Lindi* was a steel-hulled schooner with a 70 horsepower engine, bought with the definition of a 'native vessel' in mind, i.e. she was 50 tons so as to be in compliance with the rules about maximum tonnage.[19] Part of the problem was that her steel hull seemed at odds with 'native vessel' registration, but the main problem was economic. *Lindi* was to be used to open up a regular, three times a month service between Dar-es-Salaam and Lindi. The conference lines argued that no real dhow would keep a regular schedule and that by having a regular schedule the *Lindi* could only be intended to take business from the steamships. This was a particular affront since the conference lines claimed to have done much to open Lindi port. Smith Mackenzie, the main representative of the conference lines, even threatened to withdraw steamer service from Lindi and in so doing to kill the port.[20]

In government circles both the *Lindi* and the conference lines' threat to withdraw steamer service if the schooners were not suppressed caused a certain amount of consternation. The government estimated that the *Lindi* would carry about 4,000 tons of cargo a year that would otherwise have been moved by steamer. This represented a loss in wharfage fees to the government and, since schooners did not need lighterage or stevedore services, the Tanganyika Landing and Shipping Co. could expect a loss of Shgs.31,000/–.[21] In addition there was the threat of a boycott by the steamship companies.

By early 1938 the government had concluded that the threat to withdraw steamer services was a bluff, and the conference lines had begun to weep crocodile tears about the damage the schooners were doing to 'real dhows'.[22] But the government seems to have had little sympathy for the conference lines this time, and the *Lindi* was allowed to operate as a native vessel. The conference lines carried on a campaign of rebate withholding and blacklisting of customers who shipped with dhows or by schooner and continued to do this even after the wartime shipping shortages limited the services they could offer. This caused real problems in some areas where food arrived mostly by sea. In Lindi, Kilwa and Mikindani, there were food shortages even after the conference lines decided to allow specially approved packages to be sent by non-conference vessels. And in the end 'dhows had saved the situation for Lindi' by bringing food when steamer space was in short supply.[23]

The arrival of schooners in Tanganyika and the conference lines' efforts to suppress them show some remarkable parallels with the Zanzibar government's effort to drive dhows out of the clove trade. In both cases native vessels were seen to be intruding on a modern sector of the economy.

[19] Ibid.
[20] TNA 25407, Smith Mackenzie & Co. to Chief Secretary, 9 November 1937.
[21] TNA 25407 [Illegible] to Financial Secretary, 30 December 1937.
[22] TNA 25407, Financial Secretary to Chief Secretary, 13 January 1938.
[23] TNA 25407 Vol. II, Provincial Secretary, Southern Province to Chief Secretary, 1 May 1941 and enclosed excerpt from *Tanganyika Standard*, 'Deplorable Coastal Services' (n.d.).

Vera did so first by blurring the line between the traditional and the modern and then by competing for high-value cargo that the steamers considered theirs. *Lindi* did so by trying to establish a regularly scheduled service; something associated with the 'modern' as opposed to the 'traditional.' Zanzibar clove shippers provoked a similar response by continuing to rely on dhows, instead of going along with the government's efforts to rationalize the clove industry by modernizing the transport system. And in both cases the tensions over these issues came to a head in the late 1930s and then abated during the war. In the case of the clove business wartime shipping shortages forced even the most avid proponents of steamships to rely on dhows. In Tanganyika, the same types of shipping shortages made coastal transport increasingly reliant on dhows and schooners. In both cases this seems to have made the government more reliant on native vessels – dhow, schooner or what have you – and this forced the governments to be more accommodating. After the war, there was still conflict but it tended to be of a different kind. At the same time as the government stopped looking at dhows as a threat to the modernity of the colonial economy, they began to perceive dhows as a threat to the internal security of the Protectorate. Before the war dhows were seen as economically subversive. By the time the war was over, the colonial state saw dhows as economically useful, but subversive of the social order.

The stresses of war

The Second World War placed a variety of stresses on the colonial economies of the western Indian Ocean, and many of these strains proved to be opportunities for the dhow economy.[24] Foremost among these strains was a severe shortage of shipping. As the war wore on, more and more steamships were drawn into the war effort. In some cases this was the result of their being commandeered into military service, as was the case with one of the Zanzibar government's steamers, which spent the war as a minesweeper. But even vessels that remained in private hands were often busy carrying war material and hence were not available for the more mundane work of carrying rice and kangas (cloth worn by women and usually imported from India) to East Africa. The shortage of shipping, combined with the sudden severing of commercial links with areas that had become enemy territory, created severe food shortages especially in places like Zanzibar which had traditionally relied on imported foodstuffs. This became especially troublesome after Japan entered the war and Japanese and South-east Asian rice supplies were cut off.[25]

In Tanganyika the shipping shortage hit hard and fast. As early as December 1939 the committee that controlled wartime shipping allotted

---

[24] See, for example, Frederick Cooper, *On the African Waterfront* (New Haven: 1987), pp. 57–78 who describes a continent-wide spasm of labour action that largely coincided with the Second World War.

[25] ZNA AB4/494, Dutton to Stanley, 13 February 1943.

Tanganyika 19,400 tons of cargo space for goods destined for the UK at a time when nearly 70,000 tons of goods were awaiting shipment to the UK. Since transferring resources to the UK was probably a priority it seems reasonable to suppose that the shipping shortage for intra-Indian Ocean shipping was equally or more severe.[26] The shortage of coastal shipping was also severe. There are constant references in wartime monthly reports and provincial reports to a coastal shipping shortage.[27] In addition a shortage of fuel meant that lorries that might otherwise have filled in for the missing coastal shipping were laid up.

What was a problem for the authorities was a godsend for dhow owners. Dhows were kept so busy that at times there were shortages of dhow space. In 1943 in the Rufiji district the combined shipping and trucking shortages meant that of the 3480 tons of rice exported from the Rufiji, 2,948 were shipped by dhow.[28] In March 1941, the Rufiji District Officer reported that the mangrove season was going poorly since Arab dhows were too busy carrying foodstuffs between Lindi, Mombasa and Zanzibar to bother with mangrove poles.[29] And as we saw earlier it was dhows that 'saved the situation' in Lindi by bringing food when the rains had cut Lindi off from the interior in 1941 and the conference lines could not supply the town's food needs.

Both the local and the seasonal dhow fleets took advantage of this shipping shortage. Arab vessels got involved in the East African coastal trade and, when food shortages in Arabia made the run north highly profitable, Tanganyika dhows got into the long-distance trade. In 1945 the Tanganyika government noticed that, in addition to suffering from a shortage of coastal steamer services, a dhow shortage was developing. Part of the problem was that local dhows were being cleared for Arabia and then never coming back. The authorities never did figure out what was going on, but they did worry that this practice was using up local shipbuilding materials, was wasteful of dhows when there were too few of them already, and as an afterthought they wondered what was happening to the crews. It did emerge that the freights charged for the northward run were so high that the owners simply wrote off their dhows, but what cargo might offer those types of returns was never established.[30]

What seems to have been happening was that dhows that were cleared for Arabia were actually going first to Mozambique, where they bought sugar. Sugar was in such high demand in Arabia that the profits from one shipload of sugar could easily cover the cost of a new dhow. Since most of this commerce was illegal and the sugar was landed outside of the official

[26] TNA 27552, Information Officer to Chief Secretary, 6 October 1939.

[27] See, for example, TNA 61/3/XIII/D, Rufiji Annual Report, 1943, TNA 61/3/XV/D, Rufiji Annual Report, 1940, and TNA 25407 Vol. II, Provincial Secretary Southern Province to Chief Secretary, 1 May 1941. There are many more such references.

[28] TNA 61/3/XVIII/D, Rufiji Annual Report, 1943.

[29] TNA 61/3/XVI/D, Rufiji Monthly Report, March 1941.

[30] TNA 19039 Vol. III, General Manager Railways, and Ports to Chief Secretary, 9 February 1945.

ports, it was easier to abandon the vessels than it was to explain the arrival of an empty vessel at an official port.[31]

Thus dhows profited from the shipping shortage on the mainland in two ways. By filling in for the missing coastal-steamer traffic, they provided a valuable and no doubt profitable service. The profits of this service were high enough to attract long-distance dhows away from their usual cargoes, and the importance of this service was such that the government began to deny clearance to local dhows that wanted to sail to Arabia for fear they would not come back. This situation forced the government to think of dhows in a new way, less as an archaic nuisance and more as a valuable part of the economy, able to function while fuel was in short supply and ready to fill in when the 'modern' economy was reeling under the strains of war.

The other way in which dhows in Tanganyika profited from the war was by exploiting shortages created by rationing and rules governing the movement of food. The high profits to be had from hauling sugar to Arabia are an example of this phenomenon. Here dhow owners were taking advantage of the fact that the war had created a black market. They had ships well suited to smuggling and did just that. In doing so they made a tidy profit and saw to it that the Arabs got sugar, even if that meant buying it in Mozambique and exporting it illegally, thus subverting a war effort of greater interest to their colonial masters than to themselves.

In Zanzibar the war also caused a host of difficulties for commerce and transport. Zanzibar suffered from an international shipping shortage just like Tanganyika, and, also like Tanganyika, it suffered from a local shortage of shipping. In Zanzibar dhows were able to address both these problems. Since a significant proportion of Zanzibar's international exports were destined for markets within the Indian Ocean (India alone consumed over a fifth of Zanzibar's cloves), dhows were able to fill in for steamers in a way that was not possible in Tanganyika. Thus, during the war, dhows carried the vital clove crop from Pemba to Zanzibar and also, to a surprising extent, from Zanzibar to India. Dhows recaptured their former role as passenger carriers, both locally and internationally. Dhows also brought valuable foodstuffs (dried shark was important, since it fed the poor ,and so was ghee, since fats were scarce) to the Protectorate. Suddenly, colonial officials anxious to ensure Zanzibar's food supply and to keep the clove economy alive, began to see dhows as a useful adjunct to the official economy rather than as a threat to that economy. At the same time, dhows, both local and seagoing, were perceived as a security threat. Since enemy territory in Somalia and neutral territory in Mozambique were accessible by dhow, the authorities started to wonder whether dhows might not be used by infiltrators or saboteurs to gain access to Zanzibar. Thus an increasing acceptance of and dependence on dhows as an economic force was linked to increases in concern about dhows as a threat to security and as a socially disruptive force. During the years between the end of the war and the

---

[31] Interview with Sherali Haji Rashid, 16 October 1994.

Revolution, the main worry about dhows was not keeping them in their economic place but rather maintaining social order and security despite an annual influx of unruly dhow crews.

Zanzibar, of course, suffered from the same worldwide shipping shortage that troubled Tanganyika during the war. In addition, the *Al-Hathera*, one of the two government ships used on the Pemba run, was called away to do duty as a minesweeper and the remaining ship – the *Al-Said* – was expected to provide service to Pemba and to serve the mainland as well. As a result, in 1942 Pemba saw only thirty-one visits by steamers.[32] Even when the *Al-Hathera* returned from her minesweeping duties, fuel shortages, which persisted until the late 1940s, meant that the steamer service, which had always been inadequate, still ran at only partial capacity.[33] As a result, dhows, which were not affected by the fuel shortage and were not likely to be called up for minesweeping duty, filled the gap. As we saw in a previous chapter, whatever bile had motivated the government's earlier worries about dhows in the clove trade was purged during the war, and even the Clove Growers' Association (CGA), the one true bastion of steamer shipment, was forced to ship cloves by dhow. In fact there was so much demand for the carrying space that the local dhows began to be augmented by seagoing dhows, which forwent trips to the Rufiji to carry cloves for the CGA and private shippers. The Pemba mail was sometimes sent by dhow and even government workers were forced, not without protest, to go to their posts in Pemba by dhow (this indignity was limited to native and Asiatic employees).[34]

Dhows also filled in for missing international shipping. Dhows had carried a significant percentage of Zanzibar's foreign trade in the first half of the twentieth century. From the mid-1920s until the early years of the 1930s, dhows carried between 14 and 11 per cent of Zanzibar's foreign trade. During the depression that percentage dropped below 10. But the war suddenly brought dhows back into demand as export cargo carriers. By 1943 19.9 per cent of Zanzibar's exports were moved by dhow and in 1944 that number had increased to 23.6, representing over half a million pounds sterling worth of trade.[35]

During the war several clove-exporting firms bought dhows so that they could send cloves to India. The A.P. Hirji firm bought two dhows during the war to keep its cloves moving and Ghadvi and Co., normally a booking agent for dhows and schooners that operated in Zanzibar waters, developed a sideline in finding space for cloves in dhows bound for India. Shipping by dhow had two appeals. One was simply that there was often space on dhows when there was no other shipping available. But shippers also

[32] ZNA BA36/8, Zanzibar Government, *Annual Report of the Port and Marine Section*, 1942, p. 3.
[33] ZNA BA36/9, Zanzibar Government, *Report of the Port and Marine Section*, 1943, p. 4, and ZNA BA36/15, Zanzibar Government, *Annual Report of the Port and Marine Department*, 1949.
[34] ZNA BA30/22, Pemba Monthly Reports, January 1941, March 1941 and February 1942.
[35] ZNA BA1/7, Zanzibar Government, *Annual Trade Report*, 1928, ZNA BA1/15, Zanzibar Government, *Annual Trade Report*, 1938, ZNA BA1/28, Zanzibar Government, *Annual Trade Report*, 1943, and ZNA BA1/35, Zanzibar Government, *Annual Trade Report*, 1948.

believed that goods travelling by dhow were safer because dhows were less likely to be attacked by the Japanese than steamers. As far as I know, there was no significant submarine warfare in the western Indian Ocean, but in this as in all things it is the customers' perceptions that matter far more than the realities of the situation. So the fear of attack encouraged people to choose dhows over steamers even when there was space available in steamers.[36]

This emerging demand for local and long-distance transport caused a two-part response on the part of Arab and Indian dhow owners. There was a general upward trend in the numbers of dhows arriving from Arabia and India during the war. This was presumably the result of their awareness that there was money to be made in Zanzibar. Interestingly, during this period there was a new trend among seagoing dhows wherein more dhows arrived each year from India and Arabia than went home.[37] So, while Tanganyika was worrying about its dhow fleet being transferred to the north as increasing numbers of vessels went north never to return, a reciprocal process was going on between Zanzibar and Arabia and India.

While the government of Zanzibar no doubt welcomed the assistance dhows provided in easing the shipping shortage locally and internationally, they were still wary. Both seagoing craft and local dhows were scrutinized and regulated closely during the war. Both were seen as potential points of entry for enemy agents, and seagoing dhows were especially suspect since they brought large numbers of passengers each of whom was an added burden to already scarce food supplies and a potential saboteur. Thus the new regulations aimed to control the movements of dhows and the behaviour of their crews and worried less about defining and controlling the economic role of dhows.

In 1940, concern about the number of enemy nationals living in Tanganyika led the government of Zanzibar to pass a regulation (GN170/40) that forbade the movement of ships after dark within 3 miles of the coast of Pemba or Unguja. This regulation caused difficulty for dhow owners, since dhows leaving Pemba with cloves for Zanzibar frequently departed after a full day of loading only to be forced to anchor all night fully exposed to the force of the sea. Alternatively, they might stay in the ports, but Pemba ports were tidal creeks so an overnight stay in one of creeks almost certainly meant that the dhow would be trapped by the low tide. This could mean two things. If the tides delayed the dhow's departure the next morning, then the dhow might not make Zanzibar before dark the next day and might be be forced to anchor overnight. Or, if the fully loaded dhow was beached by the tide, the weight of the cargo would make the seams in the hull work loose, letting water into the hold. Either eventuality – being forced to anchor in rough water or straining the hull in shallow water – meant that the cloves got wet, which in turn meant that the inspectors in Zanzibar

---

[36] Interview with Mohammed Hussein, 17 August 1994, and interview with Vijay Gadhvi, 27 August 1994.
[37] Zanzibar Government, *Blue Book*, 1941, 1942 and 1943.

would reject them. The rule led to complaints by clove shippers in Pemba, but the regulation remained in force for the length of the war.[38] So, even if the government's concerns about dhows had changed, dhow owners continued to suffer economic hardship as a result of a new body of security-minded regulations that applied only to dhows.

Typically there was no real agreement as to how this rule was actually supposed to protect Zanzibar since, as one official put it, if someone wanted to destroy the wireless station at Chake Chake, he 'would do so regardless of the regulations since there is nothing else to stop him ... On the other hand if he really wanted to be punctilious and gentlemanly about it, he would use a fishing canoe ... and so comply with the law.' (Fishing canoes were not subject to the regulation.)[39] So, despite official recognition that the regulation did next to nothing for security and caused the clove dhows great inconvenience, the regulation survived. Irrational concern about dhows as a security threat had replaced irrational concern about dhows as an economic threat.

Seagoing dhows probably posed a more realistic threat to Zanzibar, at least during the early years of the war when parts of Somalia and Ethiopia were still under Italian control. While no specific new regulations were passed to control the growing annual influx of visitors from the north, the movements of dhows before they arrived at Zanzibar and the cargoes they carried were carefully scrutinized and recorded by the police. During the war the shortage of staff led to a general decline in record keeping and reporting. Annual reports and statistics often lumped several years together and were less complete than they had been in the pre-war period. This reflected a shortage of bodies and funds. That a new type of careful and time-consuming record keeping emerged during this period speaks eloquently to the level of concern the authorities felt about seagoing dhows.[40]

The first police reports on long distance dhow arrivals date from December of 1942 but the reports for the remainder of the 1942–3 dhow season were either not continued or lost. Since the records for the 1943–4 season are quite complete, it seems most likely that the paperwork has disappeared sometime in the last fifty years. Likewise, it is not clear whether 1942 marked the inauguration of this surveillance or of the retention of the records.

The early police reports record the arrival of each vessel that arrived on the monsoon. It gives the name, date of arrival, home port, and cargo of

---

[38] ZNA AB45/51a, Koja Gulamhussein Datoo to Resident, n.d. [1941] and ZNA AB45/51a, Commanding Officer, Zanzibar Naval Volunteer Force (ZNVF) to Chief Secretary, 30 September 1941.

[39] ZNA AB45/51A, Provincial Commissioner to Commanding Officer, ZNVF, 2 October 1941.

[40] Cooper, *Waterfront*, p. 2, notes that after 1940 colonial officals began to see Kenyan workers as 'social beings' and as a result began to have panels and committees to investigate their habits, while files concerning workers got larger. This is remarkably similar to what happened in Zanzibar, where sailors went from being virtually unnoticed to being the subject of much handwringing at exactly the same time.

each vessel. It also recorded the size of the crew, the number of passengers and whether the passengers were allowed to land. Passengers needed 'Zanzibar Entry Permits' or they were required to remain on board the ship during its stay in Zanzibar.[41] Instead of becoming perfunctory over time, the records instead become increasingly detailed. By the 1943–4 dhow season the records include information about the ports of call along the way and what portion of the cargo was sold *en route* and for what sort of prices. Also included are running totals of the number of arrivals up to a given point in the season and comparisons with the preceding season. By the 1944–5 season the records include the tonnages of the vessels, the names of the captains and the owners and a detailed account of the cargo, and the passenger lists tell where the passengers are from, for example:

A/R. 64 'Mutsahel' (Arabian):

Arrived on 11-2-45, from Soor via Seihut, Hafun and Mogadishu. Nahodha: Mbarak Ali. Owner: Ali Mubarak. Tonnage: 80. Crew: 20. Cargo: 13 Camels (excluding one died on voyage), 19 goats, 1 horse, 19 oxen, 70 tins of ghee, 80 tins of shark oil, and 2 petrol stoves. Passengers: 8, i.e. 1 from Seihut and 7 from Somalia.[42]

The records go on endlessly in this vein, recording apparent minutiae of the dhows' voyages south. While there is no direct explanation offered in these files as to their purpose, the people to whom they were circulated and the sorts of tallies that were made in the margins and at the end of sections tell us something about their purpose. Each instalment of this record was circulated to the Economic Control Board and to the Military Security Officer.

The Economic Control Board, charged with regulating the Protectorate's imports and exports during the war and for some time afterwards, might well have been interested in knowing what cargoes dhows were bringing to Zanzibar, especially when those cargoes included much needed food. Likewise the constant comparisons of each year's dhow arrivals with the previous season and the attempts to explain shortfalls probably indicate an increasing awareness of the importance of dhows in the maintenance of Zanzibar's wartime food supply.

That these reports were also circulated to the Military Security Control Officer is emblematic of the dhow's new role as security threat. Of most interest to the Military Security Officer would have been the tracking of the movement of the dhows and knowledge of what was happening to their passengers. Passengers were seen as a threat to the limited food supply and also as potential troublemakers. As far as I can tell, no real threat to the security of Zanzibar emerged during the war, but that security consciousness carried on into the post-war period, as did the Economic Control Board's control over what foodstuffs dhows could export. Thus in

---

[41] ZNA AB45/45, 'Police Reports of Dhow Arrivals,' p. 1. It is worth noting that there is no explanation in this file for its existence or purpose. It simply exists.

[42] Ibid., p. 30.

the postwar period, we see a desire on the part of the government to encourage seagoing dhows to come to Zanzibar, and a simultaneous desire to control the often disruptive behaviour of the crews. They succeeded in the first instance. For a variety of reasons, the two decades after the war were a boom time for both the local and the long-distance dhow trades. The government's efforts to control the behaviour of the crews and passengers who accompanied them were only partially successful. Interestingly, the government's efforts to control the dhow crews often involved making economic concession to the owners, captains and agents involved in the trade. These three groups quickly learned to use their relative importance to the Zanzibar economy and the threat of social disorder to force the government to make the concessions they sought.

The boom years

Although records for the early part of the twentieth century are patchy and records from the nineteenth century are even more limited, it appears that the postwar era was the apogee of the dhow trade. Dhow traffic between East Africa and southern Arabia and the Persian Gulf hit new heights and did so with almost no competition from steamships. It was not until the last years of the 1950s that regular steam communication with the Persian Gulf was inaugurated, so any increase in trade between the two regions reflected an increase in dhow traffic. Trade between India and Zanzibar moved mostly by steamship, but the 1950s also saw an increase in the number of Indian dhows coming to Zanzibar. Likewise trade in general boomed in the 1950s. Total annual tonnages of native vessels passing through Zanzibar port exceeded 100,000 tons at least seven times between 1950 and 1960.[43] In the prewar period Zanzibar's native-vessel traffic never reached the 100,000 ton mark.[44]

While the steamship industry also enjoyed a postwar recovery, it did not see the sort of exuberant frenzy that characterized the dhow boom of the 1950s. Annual tonnages for steamships calling at Zanzibar, both coastal and ocean-going, recovered to pre-war levels and occasionally put in a better showing, but never did anything extraordinary. In the prewar period ocean-going steamer traffic fluctuated between 1,238,000 tons in 1926 and 1,695,000 tons in 1937. In the postwar period (1946 to 1959) ocean-going steamer traffic fluctuated between 421,900 tons in 1946 (still the wartime slump) and 1,765,000 in 1959.[45] Thus the increase in the dhow traffic was not limited to participating in the general postwar economic recovery, instead the sectors in which both local and seagoing dhows participated

---

[43] See Zanzibar Government, *Port and Marine Annual Reports*, 1950 to 1960 except 1957. I have not located the *Port and Marine Annual Report*, 1957, so I do not know what the tonnages were for that year. Native-vessel tonnages for that year may well have exceeded 100,000 tons also.

[44] See Zanzibar Government, *Port and Marine Annual Reports*, 1926 to 1949.

[45] Zanzibar Government, *Port and Marine Annual Reports* for 1926 to 1959.

enjoyed a prosperity that exceeded that of the broader economy served by steamships.

As we saw in preceding chapters much of this boom was the result of high demand for mangrove poles in an increasingly oil-rich Persian Gulf. Even Indian dhows seem to have been attracted to this trade. After bringing cargoes from India to East Africa, usually Mangalore roofing tiles – ballast with a resale value, they would load up with mangrove poles and carry them to the Gulf. From the Gulf they collected dates, which they carried to India.[46] In addition to a growing demand for mangrove poles in the Gulf, other factors may have encouraged Gulf Arabs to invest in trade with East Africa. The demise of the Gulf's pearling industry in the 1930s meant that there were labour and capital ready to be applied to other sorts of maritime enterprise.[47] At exactly the same time when the British had come to see dhows as economically beneficial but a threat to security, dhows started to pour into Zanzibar in numbers never seen before.

The seasonal influx of dhow crews into Zanzibar has been part of life there since at least the early nineteenth century. In Chapter Two we saw that in the middle of the nineteenth century dhow crews were occasionally disruptive enough for Consul Rigby to be reduced to begging for a Royal Navy ship to remain in the harbour during the monsoon season, and at one point the American Consul was actually barricaded in his house by the crews of 'pirate dhows'. So dhow crews, like seamen anywhere, have always been a socially disruptive force. The idea that dhows and their crews were more subversive of the social order than of the economic order re-emerged after the war. To prevent dhow crews from causing too much trouble, the authorities attempted to both appease and control them. If before the war the government's meddling in the dhow economy had been high-handed, after the war they were equally careful not to antagonize the seasonal visitors.

During the war the authorities had worried that dhows might harbour enemy agents or unwanted hungry mouths; they now worried that dhow crews would either fight among themselves or react violently to the Economic Control Board's efforts to control the cargoes they took home with them. Of the former problem the 1947–8 dhow season makes a good example. In November of 1947 word reached Zanzibar that rioting in Mogadishu between Arabs and Somalis had left many Arabs dead. Dhow agents in Zanzibar cabled their charges in the Gulf and advised all Arab vessels to avoid Somalia and to come straight to Zanzibar.[48]

Since many Zanzibaris had friends and relatives who were killed or injured during the Mogadishu riots, Zanzibar's Arab merchants resolved to

[46] Interviews with Sherali Haji Rashid, 27 August 1994, and Vijay Gadhvi, 27 August 1994.

[47] This was a long-term trend. The Gulf pearling industry had been losing ground to Japanese cultured pearls since the early 1930s. By the late 1930s Kuwaiti dhow captains were leaving the pearling business and trading to East Africa as an alternative. See Allan Villiers, *Sons of Sinbad* (New York: 1969) p. 349–50.

[48] ZNA AK4/31, Provincial Commissioner to Chief Secretary, 8 November 1947, and ZNA AK4/31, 'Somalis Fight Arabs in Mogadishu,' *Tanganyika Standard*, 4 November 1947.

boycott Somali dhow cargoes that year.[49] Smelling potential trouble between either Arab and Somali sailors or Zanzibari Arabs and Somalis, the Provincial Commissioner recommended that Somali dhows be barred from Zanzibar that year. He argued that Somali dhows carried three to four times the number of men actually needed to handle the ships, and that 'These extra men are really passengers [and] … a fruitful source of trouble.'[50]

On 22 November a committee met to try to coordinate efforts at keeping the dhow season as calm as possible. As far as I can tell, this was the first of what was to become an annual tradition. From 1947 on, each dhow season seems to have been preceded by a series of meetings during which Zanzibar's dhow agents were asked to predict any potential sources of unrest. At this first meeting the Resident opined that 'Somalis in general were known to be a quick-tempered and hasty people,' but since it was not certain that the same batch of Somalis that had been causing trouble in Mogadishu was coming to Zanzibar he decided not to bar Somali dhows from Zanzibar. Instead, the committee decided to take special precautions to head off any flare-ups before things got out of hand.[51]

The plan was as follows: the District Commissioner was to arrange for 'propaganda among the people of the "inflammable" quarters of town (e.g. Funguni and Malindi) to treat the seasonal immigrants as visitors and to keep the peace'. The Customs Department was to search all arriving vessels for weapons and to impound them. The police were to see to it that Arabic-speaking officers were posted in Malindi (the area around the port) and that a reserve force of fifty men were to be kept at the Beit al Ajab, a five minute walk from the port. This same reserve force was to do a weekly route march with fixed bayonets through Malindi just to remind everybody who was in charge.[52]

These elaborate precautions were a partial success. There was no rioting but, by 19 March 1948, a Somali boy had been murdered. Before things could get out of hand, the District Commissioner dragged two Zanzibari dhow agents and five Somali *nakhoda* into a meeting, the upshot of which was that one of the dhow agents paid Shgs. 2000/- to the Somalis on behalf of the murders. This seems to have forestalled further conflict.[53] Disputes of this sort had almost certainly occurred before the war, but the government reacted to this dispute with noteworthy alarm and alacrity. The 1947–8 dhow season seems to have set the tone for the rest of the colonial

---

[49] ZNA AK3/31, 'Report of the PC on a meeting held to discuss the Somali Arab Problem,' 11 November 1947.

[50] ZNA AK4/31, Provincial Commissioner to Chief Secretary, 8 November 1947.

[51] ZNA AK4/31, 'Record of a meeting held in the council chamber … to discuss arrangements in regard to the annual visit of Somali dhows,' 22 November 1947.

[52] ZNA AK4/31, 'Dhow Season Duties' attached to Provincial Commissioner to Chief Secretary, 24 December 1947.

[53] ZNA AK4/31, 'Notes on a Meeting in District Commissioners Office, Held on 19 March 1948.'

[54] The government succeeded in controlling the visiting sailors that year, but as they were leaving in August of 1948 a strike broke out among the dock-workers – arguably the most important labour action in Zanzibar's history. See Norman Bennett, *A History of the Arab State of Zanzibar* (London: 1978), pp. 247–9.

era.[54] From then on, each dhow season was a source of worry to the police and was met with increased police presence, numerous meetings, admonitions to Zanzibaris to welcome the visitors and helpful tips from all quarters on how to deal with the volatile guests. In 1955, for example, the District Commissioner (Urban) advised the Town Mudir:

> As you know some of these peoples are primitive and staying together with different tribes with different languages becomes extremely hard, therefore just a minor dispute or even argument may cause a fight which can involve a whole tribe.[55]

These sentiments were not limited to the government. In 1962 Sheikh Bagurnah, a dhow agent, no less, asked the government to use patience with the annual visitors since the sailors were 'ignorant ... the countries they come from were still backward [and] they therefore regard this country's laws as mere botheration'.[56]

In part, this new tenor in the relationship between the dhow economy and the authorities must be seen in the context of increasing anticolonial agitation throughout Africa in the postwar era. In a colonial world marked by labour actions, Mau Mau, demands for more participation in government and generalized discontent, Zanzibar's annual visitation by large numbers of volatile outsiders, who not only fought among themselves but antagonized their local hosts and who moved freely across various colonial borders, must have looked threatening to the colonial regime. Zanzibaris themselves had misgivings about this annual influx. The presence of a couple of thousand sailors each year, most of whom slept ashore either in makeshift huts or in the streets, was a source of irritation. Dhow crewmen were seen, probably with good reason, as petty thieves, noise makers, drunkards and sexual predators. One resident of the Malindi neighbourhood wrote to the police to complain that he awoke one morning to find that five Somali sailors had broken into the bottom storey of his house to sleep off a drinking binge.[57] So sailors were a legitimate annoyance. This, of course, is not an unusual way for townspeople to perceive sailors. Sailors, who are often young men, are always just passing through and so are not subject to the same sorts of social restraints as long-term residents.

But dhow crews were more disruptive than other sailors. Dhows carried proportionally huge crews compared with ocean-going steamers. Some dhows might carry as many as one sailor per 2 tons of vessel. In comparison, a multi-thousand ton steamer might carry a crew of ten or fifteen men. While a steamer might be in port for a week and its crew would sleep on board, dhows' crews were often in Zanzibar for four to six months, trapped as they were by the monsoon, and their crews preferred to sleep ashore rather than aboard. Further exacerbating the potential for disruption was

[55] ZNA AK4/35, District Commissioner (Urban) to Town Mudir, 14 January 1955.
[56] ZNA AK4/35, 'Dhow Agents Meeting held in the office of the District Commissioner, Urban,' 27 October 1962.
[57] ZNA AK18/13, Permanent Secretary to Senior District Commissioner, 23 December 1961.

153

the ever-increasing number of dhows calling at Zanzibar in the 1950s. By the early 1960s it was common practice for the police to step up their patrols in the Malindi area during the dhow season supplemented by an 'occasional visit by the Gordon Highlanders', which 'had a very desirable effect'.[58] So the threat of disorder during the dhow season was taken quite seriously.

In keeping with their new understanding of how dhows fitted into the economic and social fabric of Zanzibar, the colonial government also tried to encourage dhows to come to Zanzibar and took active steps to avoid antagonizing dhow captains and crews once they arrived. These efforts ranged from the common sense – building a new shark market – to the comical – the annual *nakhodas'* ball. This type of nervous encouragement of the dhow trade by the government is perhaps best illustrated by the Economic Control Board's efforts to get dhows to bring food to Zanzibar, to ensure that the dhow crews did not eat up precious local food supplies, to see to it that they provided dhows' captains with a sufficiently valuable return cargo to entice them to come back the next year and to prevent them from leaving with commodities that were in short supply: all this without making them angry.

The Economic Control Board, although originally constituted during the war, survived into the 1950s. During the war, the Board imposed a system of rationing where food was allotted on a per ship basis regardless of the size of the crew or the number of the passengers. Passengers were required to either remain on board or pay a substantial deposit if they wanted to go ashore, the idea being to discourage excessively large crews from coming to Zanzibar and eating up the local food supply. The Economic Control Board also limited the types of cargoes dhows returning north could take with them. A certain amount of food was allowed to each crew for the return voyage and, when possible, the Board made *sim sim* (sesame), coconut oil or local coffee available as a cargo. These goods were only offered to ships that brought food cargoes with them, ships arriving in ballast had to settle for *boritis*.[59]

These rules were hard on the crews and passengers, who occasionally went hungry and on *nakhodas*, who often wanted food cargoes. The hardship engendered by these rules and the potential for violent reaction did not escape the notice of the authorities. The Economic Controller seems to have made an honest effort to come up with goods that would interest *nakhodas* as return cargoes. Likewise, restrictions on the export of coconut oil and flour were broadcast as widely as possible to avoid potentially explosive misunderstandings. The caution with which the government enforced these rules is remarkable. A 1948 memo from the Economic Controller that details the lengths to which he has gone to obtain millet and maize from South Africa so that the dhows would have something to take home and his effort to put out the word about export restrictions ends with a hopeful: 'I do not anticipate any trouble this season.' This was underlined by

[58] ZNA AK4/35, Senior District Commissioner to Permanent Secretary, 20 March 1962.
[59] ZNA AB4/494, Chief Secretary to Resident, 22 February 1943, and ZNA AB4/494, Chief Secretary to East African Production and Supply Council, Nairobi, 31 July 1944.

someone else, who also wrote 'Insha'llah' in the margin. This is a perfect illustration of the new thinking about dhows. Dhows were economically important enough for adequate return cargoes to have to be conjured up for them. At the same, time the dhow crews were a problem since they were large and hungry and potentially disruptive. Any adverse regulation of dhows had to be carried out as diplomatically as possible and with as many visible concessions as possible.[60]

It did not take long for the dhow agents and the *nakhodas* to sense that a new era was upon them. Dhow owners and their agents, who had fought a rearguard action against colonial interference in the 1930s, began to assert themselves in the late 1940s and 1950s. They used the government's fear of unrest as a lever with which to gain concessions and favours from the government. The best example of how dhow agents used this leverage comes from the construction of a new storage area for dried shark. In 1957 the government set out to build a new shark market and, while they were considering the possible location and dimensions of the new market, demolished the old one. With the dhow season right around the corner, they built a temporary shed, which was small and could not be locked. Not only did the temporary structure lack sufficient space, but *nakhodas* were forced to sleep there at night to keep an eye on their shark. The dhow agents were quick to voice their displeasure. At the annual dhow agents' meeting, they informed the District Commissioner that the shark market's shortcomings were sure to lead to trouble.

> They went on to say that all the people who arrive in the monsoon are of different character and are quarrelsome people and difficult to control… They went on enumerating the character of these dhow people and assured the meeting that trouble is bound to happen, that will then be beyond them to control and wished the Government not to ask of them their cooperation … whatever might happen it will be the Government to be blamed.[61]

The dhow agents knew exactly how to motivate their colonial masters. The next day, Christmas Eve, the Comptroller of Customs ordered that more storage area for shark should be built 'as quickly as possible'.[62] While some of the description above reflects ideas about the wildness of Omani and Gulf Arabs that are still held by Zanzibaris today, it still looks like a calculated attempt to play on British fears in order to gain extra storage space. The dhow agents knew how to put their case and got immediate results.

By the latter part of the 1950s, this sort of convincing was less necessary; instead, the government was bending over backwards to please dhow captains and their agents. By 1960 the authorities were genuinely concerned that the dhows might stop coming. They feared that the trend

---

[60] ZNA AB25/82, Economic Controller to Chief Secretary, 17 December 1948.
[61] ZNA AK4/35, District Commissioner (Urban) to Comptroller of Customs and Senior Commissioner, 23 December 1957.
[62] ZNA AK4/35, Comptroller of Customs to District Commissioner (Urban) and Senior Commissioner, 24 December 1957.

towards the use of steamers to ship *boriti* to the Gulf would undermine the trade. This would be a problem since dhow crews were thought to spend Shgs. 2,400,000/– per annum on food alone, and because the shark and salt they brought were deemed essential to the local economy. If dhows stopped coming to Zanzibar and made Mombasa (Kenya restricted *boriti* exports to dhows) their terminus, Zanzibar would lose the Shgs. 2,400,000/– and be forced to import almost £100,000 worth of shark from Kenya.[63] While this hand wringing never led to concrete action, such as banning steamer exports of *boriti*, to preserve the dhow trade, it did lead to what might be the strangest episode in the long and unhappy relationship between the government and the dhow economy – the annual *nakhodas'* ball.

The *nakhodas'* ball, which the government began to put on at least as early as 1960, was meant to give the *nakhodas* a chance to air their grievances to the authorities in a more congenial setting than a meeting. There was food and plenty of tea. The party met in the Victoria Gardens opposite the Residence. The point in all this seems to have been to reassure the dhow captains that the government took them seriously and valued their contribution to the Zanzibar economy.[64] The *nakhodas'* ball is a fitting place to leave the contest between the government and the dhow economy. The ball was in many respects a cynical public-relations event, but it still represented a completely new attitude towards the dhow economy. That the government actually went to the trouble to throw a party for the visiting dhow captains speaks volumes about the colonial government's acceptance of the importance of dhows to Zanzibar's economic well-being.

Dhows and the Zanzibar economy

The dhow economy was critical to Zanzibar's economic well-being, and it is remarkable that it took the colonial regime so long to recognize this.[65] The informal, entrepreneurial world of the dhow performed two essential functions for Zanzibar. It propped up the official economy, performing the necessary work of moving cloves from Pemba to Zanzibar, providing food and consumer goods for the clove-growing areas and providing critical transport services for the official economy when steamers were not available. Dhows consistently carried between 10 and 15 per cent of Zanzibar's foreign trade and during times of crisis this percentage increased dramatically.

Second, the dhow economy allowed Zanzibar to participate in a western Indian Ocean regional economy. Dhows connected two ecologically

---

[63] ZNA AK18/13, District Commissioner (Urban) to Senior Commissioner, 23 April 1960 and ZNA AK18/13, Divisional Forest Officer, Coast(Kenya) to Senior Commissioner, 30 April 1960.

[64] ZNA AK4/35, Senior District Commissioner to Senior Commissioner, 15 April 1961.

[65] It is no less remarkable that there is only one book that considers the role of the dhow trade in the colonial era, E.B. Martin and C. Martin, *Cargoes of the East* (London: 1978), and this sees dhows as having been on the ropes for most of the twentieth century.

different areas of the Indian Ocean, giving people in the treeless Gulf access to the plentiful mangrove wood of East Africa while East Africans got dates, shark, salt, carpets, ghee and livestock. And the same ecological constraints that made mangrove wood unavailable in the Gulf made dates and dried shark comparatively plentiful and cheap. So for both Arabs and East Africans this trade was a response to the ecological constraints of their respective climates. Social needs also fuelled this regional trade. Much of the texture of daily life on the East African coast derived from the availability of foods and products brought by dhows. Dates, shark, coffee, ghee, carpets and the sundries like rose-water that dhows brought with them are to some degree linked to Swahili social identity. These foods and accoutrements are part of the social complex that sets coastal peoples, and islanders especially, off from the rest of Africa. Likewise the long-term survival of mud and mangrove building technology in the Gulf while mostly due to economics, is probably also related to the fact that architectural styles had evolved for centuries around the size limitations of mangrove poles, and hence mangrove-pole-based construction techniques had social relevance that could not immediately be replaced by concrete and re-bar.

Dhows also maintained social connections between Oman, the Hadhramaut, the Gulf and East Africa. Dhows invariably carried a few passengers, and occasionally carried large numbers of passengers. Some of these passengers hoped to settle or at least to stay a while before going home. Allan Villiers records that the *Triumph of Righteousness* carried passengers both on its southward and northward voyages, delivering what he claims was a whole sub-clan of Bedouin to Mombasa and three Zanzibari teachers to Muscat.[66] Thus, both in the goods they carried and the people they transported, dhows contributed to the creation of a regional economy and in some sense a regional society.

Dhows in colonial Zanzibar carried out the same functions they had performed in precolonial Zanzibar. They moved goods between Zanzibar and the ports of the coast. To be sure, the goods they hauled were different goods from what they had been one hundred years earlier and often lower in value. Although Zanzibar's importance as an entrepôt had waned, it continued to serve as an entrepôt both for cloves and for the goods brought and sought by seagoing dhows. In many ways the clove economy of the colonial era was but a reworking of Zanzibar's nineteenth-century economy. In the nineteenth-century, dhows brought the produce of East Africa to Zanzibar, where it was sold to the global economy. During the colonial period this was translated into an economy where dhows brought agricultural produce from Pemba to Zanzibar where it was sold to the global economy. During the nineteenth century Zanzibar was the point from which coffee, shark and dates – the cargoes of Arab dhows – were distributed to the East African coast. It kept this role in the colonial period. Dhows continued to use Zanzibar as their terminus and the main business of the dhow agents was reselling dried shark to the mainland and arranging

---

[66] Villiers, *Sons of Sinbad*, pp. 71–85, deals with the question of passengers in some detail.

for the collection of mangrove poles from the mainland for transshipment through Zanzibar. Some of the commodities and the ports of call changed, but the overall structure of Zanzibar's economy and the role of dhows in that economy remained remarkably unchanged.

That the bedrock, the underpinnings, of Zanzibar's economy changed so little during the colonial period, despite a huge dirigist effort to modernize, speaks eloquently to the futility of the economic component of the colonial project in Zanzibar. Dhow owners and the merchants with whom they worked undercut or bypassed every colonial attempt to modernize or control their trade. The colonial state partially succeed in defining the dhow trade into marginality. But, even then, dhows continued to play critical roles in the all-important clove industry and in supplying Zanzibar and Pemba with food. By the time the Second World War was over, it was clear even to the British that dhows played a crucial role in the economy. Dhows, which had formerly been associated with everything from slave running to clove stealing to riot, were, by the closing hours of the colonial drama, a central part of Zanzibar's social and economic life. Dhows and the entrepreneurs who owned them and the regional economy in which they operated played a significant, and as yet unsung, role in the subversion of the colonial attempt to reshape Zanzibar. In the same way that the regional cotton economy in the French Soudan served to undermine the colonial state's efforts at control there, Zanzibar's integration into the dhow-based regional economy of the western Indian Ocean meant that Zanzibar's colonial experience was very different from Kenya's or Tanganyika's. There, where trade routes across the vast interiors were more fragile and less entrenched, the colonial state had a much easier time asserting itself.[67]

Rupture

If there was a fundamental continuity between the Zanzibar of 1860 and the Zanzibar of 1960, Zanzibar in 1970 was a totally different place. Only a handful of monsoon dhows continued to call at Zanzibar and these were mostly Indian or Iranian. By 1970 a centuries-old pattern of monsoon-driven trade had finally come to an end. The fundamental economic structures of the western Indian Ocean were transformed by the oil economy that emerged in the Persian Gulf. The Gulf, which for the first half of the twentieth century was impoverished compared with East Africa and which had often viewed East Africa as a source of economic opportunity, suddenly became the wealthiest place in the Indian Ocean. Where once sailors and migrants from the Gulf had come to East Africa to seek their fortunes, now people from the western Indian Ocean to Texas were clamouring for work in the Gulf. Even in Oman, which did not participate in the first rush of oil prosperity, the possibility of working in

[67]Richard Roberts, *Two Worlds of Cotton* (Stanford: 1996), p. 286.

the oilfields attracted labour away from the dhows. And soon the new wealth generated by this boom made the produce of East Africa, especially mangrove wood, less interesting. More than any other factor, the transformation of the western Indian Ocean's regional economy by oil sank the long-distance dhow trade.

But it did not work alone. The Zanzibar Revolution of 1964 overthrew the Arab-dominated government. Thousands, mostly Arabs, died in the mayhem that followed the Revolution, and those who could fled. The attenuated seagoing dhow fleet that still existed in 1964 did their business elsewhere that year. With a few exceptions the dhow agents fled to Muscat and most of the Indian merchant community moved to Dar-es-Salaam. By the summer of 1965 the Revolutionary Government flatly banned port calls by dhows that had called at Arabian ports in the previous year.[68] In effect, they outlawed the dhow trade. Ironically, Zanzibar forcibly severed her ties with the Gulf region just when those ties might have been most useful.

Zanzibar was a different and poorer place for the loss of her regional trade connections. The loss of income from the seasonal influx of sailors hurt everyone from the big merchants who sold hardware and naval stores to street vendors who sold tea and *mandazis*. Related industries, such as mangrove cutting and the transshipment of dhow cargoes like salt and dried fish to the mainland collapsed.

The effects of this change were not limited to the economic sphere. The texture of daily life for rich and poor changed. Dried shark, what Burton called the 'goût' of Zanzibar, was a staple of the poor; it has virtually disappeared from the local diet.[69] Ghee from Socotra and Somalia was also enjoyed across class lines, it too has disappeared. Dates, carpets, brass work and other commodities that enjoyed a slightly more elite market also disappeared. People also ceased to move back and forth between Arabia and Zanzibar.

Having purposefully cut Zanzibar out of the regional economy, the government made Zanzibar even more reliant on cloves. And here too dhows were driven out. The clove industry came to be controlled by the CGA's revolutionary descendant, the Zanzibar State Trading Corporation (ZSTC). The ZSTC was the only legal buyer and shipper of cloves. They relied on the government steamers and, since these could not really carry the whole clove crop, they moved what could not be carried by steamer in chartered schooners. The whole dhow-based clove-transport system disappeared. Carrying cloves in dhows was considered smuggling and hence a capital crime. A few *nakhodas* are said to have been executed after they were caught carrying cloves.

Under the Revolutionary Government, Zanzibar became increasingly isolated from the regional economy, and in time, from the global economy as well. As the western Indian Ocean reoriented itself towards an economy based on Gulf oil and Indian manufactured goods, Zanzibar remained cut

---

[68] ZNA AK18/13, 'Mkutano Hususi Unaohusu Majahazi ya Musim,' 6 June 1965.
[69] Richard Burton, *Zanzibar: City, Island and Coast* (New York: 1967 [1872]), Vol. 1, p. 104.

off from those changes. Zanzibar bailed out of the older monsoon-based regional economy while it was in decline. By the 1970s a new regional economy fuelled by Gulf oil emerged. The Gulf drew labour and investment from places as far-flung as Korea, Scandinavia and the USA. In effect, the new regional economy created a new and different region. At the same time, Zanzibar was developing stronger political and economic links with the mainland and intentionally purging itself of its links to the broader region. Zanzibar, which was probably better positioned to participate in the Gulf's rise to prosperity than any other place in East Africa, instead sank into poverty.

Epilogue

⊙⊙⊙⊙⊙⊙⊙⊙⊙⊙⊙⊙⊙⊙⊙⊙⊙⊙⊙

Dhows in the Economy of Independent Zanzibar

By 1970 the combined forces of oil money and revolution had cut Zanzibar out of the western Indian Ocean economy. The long-distance dhow trade was finished, apart from the occasional arrival of an Iranian or Indian vessel. The local trade also suffered but survived, and now seems to be staging a comeback of sorts.

Ironically the Revolutionary Government of Zanzibar adopted most of the modernizing impulses of the despised colonial regime and carried them through with an enthusiasm and economic destructiveness that their predecessors could not match. By 1965 the monsoon trade was shut down by government order. Mangrove swamps that the British had wanted to declare as forest reserves for twenty years, but hesitated to do so because they worried about taking land held communally by villages, became state property by a stroke of the revolutionary pen. The clove business became a monopoly of the Zanzibar State Trading Corporation (ZSTC), the Clove Growers' Association (CGA)'s successor.[1] The government steamer fleet grew and regained its clove-carrying monopoly. This system worked poorly but acceptably until the world clove market collapsed in the mid-1980s. Then, with no regional economy to fall back on, disaster resulted. Zanzibar's formal economy now limps along on foreign aid and whatever can be wrung out of the tourist trade. But economic liberalization, beginning in the mid-1980s, has triggered a partial recovery in the informal sector (the clove sector and the rest of the formal economy remain moribund) and dhows and schooners seem to be staging a comeback. There are even tentative signs that Zanzibar may yet find its way back into an Indian Ocean economy.

---

[1] The institutional links between the CGA and the ZSTC were so strong that the ZSTC was still using CGA letterhead in the 1970s.

Revolution and modernization

Zanzibar's revolutionaries embraced modernity with a vengeance. In contrast to the more austere socialism of the mainland, with which Zanzibar merged shortly after the Revolution to form the Republic of Tanzania, Zanzibar's leaders wanted the visible signs of progress. While they gutted the private sector, they set up a colour television station and built a luxury hotel complete with what was supposed to be the largest swimming-pool in the world. The pool has since become a swamp, lovely to look at since it is full of water lilies with dinner-plate-sized blossoms, but also a health hazard in that it is an unofficial rubbish dump and mosquito hatchery. Hard currency acquired when clove prices were high was spent on building huge concrete apartment blocks; these are as ugly but fairly practical, despite their many detractors. The government also built amusement parks in Zanzibar and Chake Chake and a couple of football stadiums, with Chinese assistance.

The Revolutionary Government devoted the same zeal to modernizing the economy. This modernizing zeal fell especially heavily on the government's steamer fleet. The Zanzibar government inherited two ships at independence. By 1980 they had acquired another four ships. One of these, the *Mapinduzi*, at nearly 4,000 tons, was more than twice as big as the combined size of the two ships the colonial government had not been able to use to capacity. The *Mapinduzi* is so big that it could not even enter the harbour at Wete, which was the main port on Pemba at the time it was purchased, and could only approach the main wharf in Zanzibar with difficulty.[2] It is a huge, fine-looking ship, and the government, and most citizens as well, are justifiably proud of it. It has recently been refitted but, even more than the smaller ships it has by now replaced, it is more a reflection of the government's aspirations than of the current realities of Zanzibar's economy.

Despite the presence of newer, larger ships like the *Mapinduzi* and a government monopoly on clove transport, dhows have remained an important part of the local transport scene. In 1979 dhows carried 27.4 per cent of the total, officially recorded cargo traffic of Zanzibar, while the state-run steamer service could claim 30 per cent. (The missing 42.6 per cent represents foreign trade carried by foreign vessels.) The steamers continued to attract over 70 per cent of the passenger traffic, much as they did during the colonial era.[3] That even after the important business of moving cloves had been taken away from the dhow sector and handed over to the steamers dhows continued to carry almost as much of Zanzibar's cargo as did the steamers, speaks volumes about the continuing importance of dhows in independent Zanzibar. And these figures represent only legal trade. Dhows

---

[2] ZNA BA37/8, Bish and Partners, *Pemba Harbour Project: Pre-Investment Study*, June 1977. ZNA BA37/9, Engineering and Consulting Firms Association, *Feasibility Study on Port Development*, January 1981.

[3] ZNA BA37/9, Engineering and Consulting Firms Association, *Feasibility Study*.

have also been deeply involved in subverting the postcolonial project through smuggling.

Illicit trade

Dhows were certainly involved in smuggling during the colonial era. Villiers, the British sailor who travelled by *boom* from Aden to Zanzibar, reported that the *nakhoda* was involved in a few illicit currency exchanges in Somalia and only paid royalties on half of the mangrove poles he shipped in the Rufiji and that the crew and passengers were all involved in petty smuggling of clothing, perfume and jewellery.[4] Still, the main source of profit for the voyage was legitimate commerce. Smuggling seems to have been less important a source of income for dhows then than now, in part because there were fewer restrictions placed on their activities then and most of the cargoes that dhows carried were not charged duties. So, while dhows often evaded the authorities just to save time and trouble and probably moved many an illicitly cut mangrove pole, smuggling was more of a sideline than their *raison d'être*. After independence, when virtually all private commerce was either illegal or close to it, smuggling once again became an important source of revenue. Cloves and people seem to have been the big moneymakers. Cloves became popular with smugglers once the ZSTC, the only legal buyer of cloves even now, lowered the producer price for cloves to a fraction of the world market price. Pembans were perfectly aware that they were being exploited and reacted by sending their cloves to Mombasa where they could be sold for substantially higher prices. The ZSTC responded to this not by paying a fair price but by making clove smuggling a capital offence.[5] Despite the high stakes, clove smuggling was apparently widespread into the 1980s, when world market prices fell. In 1994 the ZSTC was paying about Shgs. 200/- per kilo for cloves, at a time when rice was selling for Shgs. 190/- per kilo. Not surprisingly most cloves were left unharvested. I was told that in Mombasa cloves were selling for just over Shgs. 800/- per kilo, a differential that most people thought was not worth the risk of smuggling for. So even the illicit side of the clove business was now lost to dhows. Lately though, with the chaos in Indonesia, the world market price of cloves has gone up dramatically. The ZSTC has not reacted to this development and Mombasa is once again seeing dhows arriving with smuggled cloves.

People too have been a source of illicit income for dhows. After the Revolution dhows helped people who needed to get out of Zanzibar do so. This seems to have been a big business in the years immediately following the Revolution, but tapered off after a while. But even today owners of schooners and dhows talk about them as if they were partly insurance policies against some new upheaval. On several occasions I heard people

---

[4] Allan Villiers, *Sons of Sinbad*, (New York: 1969)pp. 109-112, 135-137.
[5] Esmond Bradly Martin, *Zanzibar*, (London: 1978) pp. 80-1.

mention that if 'something' happened their boats would be their ticket out. So cautious-minded Zanzibaris still see their schooners and dhows as a sort of safety net that not only earns money on a regular basis but could also save their skins.

And they were right. 'Something' happened. In the aftermath of the elections of 2000, there was widespread repression in Zanzibar. The island of Pemba, deemed by the ruling party – Chama Cha Mapinduzi (CCM) – to be an opposition stronghold went through an extended clamp-down that resulted in the deaths of at least thirty people. For young men in Pemba, who were particularly targeted by the police, the most common escape route was over the sea by dhow to Shimoni in Kenya. Dhows came from Kenya to collect refugees and local dhows and even fishing canoes were pressed into service to carry refugees to safety. In much the same way that dhows had served to undermine the economic side of the colonial project they are now playing a role in mitigating the worst abuses of the postcolonial state. Interestingly, in the run up to the 2000 election, when the main opposition party – the Civic United Front (CUF) – was having difficulty getting permission to hold rallies, it held a rally at sea in dhows.

Patterns of ownership

Before the Revolution the ownership of Zanzibar's local dhow fleet was roughly equally divided between Asian and non-Asian Zanzibaris. After the Revolution, as the government took over the clove-carriage trade and made the retail business increasingly difficult and unprofitable for Asians, most of the better-off Asian merchants left Zanzibar. Most seem to have turned their *jahazis* over to their *nakhodas*, and today there is not a single Asian that I have heard of who owns a *jahazi*. Instead the island's sailing fleet seems to be entirely in the hands of people who would call themselves either Arab or Shirazi. The current owners represent an interesting mixture of Zanzibari society. They range from a former dhow agent, who once used *jahazis* to ship the salt fish he bought from the monsoon dhows to the mainland and now uses them to keep his wholesale shop supplied with goods from the mainland and to ship retail goods to Pemba, to owners who live in the rural towns of Nungwi and Mkokotoni, who make their livings off carrying other peoples goods.

Jahazis still supply Zanzibar town with much of its food and cement, and on one occasion I have seen a Toyota arrive in Zanzibar perched on the thatch decking of a *jahazi*. They also continue to carry mangrove poles to Dar-es-Salaam and Zanzibar, and to carry virtually any cargo that is bulky and not in a hurry. Thus timber from the mainland, flour, potatoes, tomatoes, maize meal, lime, laundry soap, etc. all come to Zanzibar by *jahazi*. Interestingly, these same *jahazis* almost always go to the mainland empty. If you sit at the Starehe Club (a prime dhow-watching place and the most pleasant bar in Zanzibar) on the point of Ras Shangani you will notice that while *jahazis* arriving from the mainland come in with their

7.1   *Ancient Swahili aphorism on a Lamu* mashua *that caters to the tourist trade*

7.2   *Manda Beach Club, the final indignity for a Lamu* jahazi.
Note the registration numbers on the stern

gunwales only inches from the water, *jahazis* going towards Dar ride so high that they look as if they might be capsized by a slight gust. The cargoes that the *jahazis* once carried to the mainland virtually disappeared with the demise of the long-distance trade. Salt, salt fish, dates and ghee, which once gave the local vessels a cargo to carry to the mainland to exchange for the food and manufactures they brought back, have all disappeared with the collapse of the regional economy. Now Zanzibar sends money to the mainland, not Indian Ocean trade, so the demise of the regional economy continues to hurt Zanzibar. No locally produced goods have yet emerged to replace the income once derived from Zanzibar's place in the western Indian Ocean economy. Despite the one-sidedness of this trade it must be fairly profitable since new *jahazis* are still being built and older ones repaired.

If the sailing *jahazi* is in danger of being replaced (and I am not sure that it is) that threat comes not from the government and private-sector steamers that compete with them, but rather from motor dhows or schooners. Lots of new money seems to be moving into the motor dhow market. In some cases, the motor dhows belong to descendants of Asians who once used sailing *jahazis* in the Pemba clove trade; in other cases, they belong to people as diverse as Somali émigrés and Zanzibar Chinese. The reason for this explosion of interest in motor dhows has to with the peculiar relationship between Zanzibar and the mainland. Zanzibar is sufficiently autonomous for it to set its own wharfage fees and import duties, but it is also sufficiently a part of the Union for goods entered at Zanzibar not to be taxed upon arrival in Dar-es-Salaam or Tanga.

Zanzibar's wharfage fees and import duties are lower than those on the mainland. To take advantage of this, Dar es Salaam importers began to have their goods sent to Zanzibar rather than Dar es Salaam. Upon arrival at Zanzibar, the shipping containers were opened, duties or some other payment in lieu of taxes was made and the goods were loaded on to motor dhows and sent to Dar es Salaam where they entered duty-free, since they were moving from one part of Tanzania to another. This loophole has been closed recently, but it is an interesting example of the way in which the informal sector takes advantage of opportunities presented to it by government regulations. Just as the informal sector profited from artificial distortions in the East African economy during the Second World War, so too it has found advantages and opportunity in the regulations and distortions of the post-colonial economy.

A new regional economy

In 1994 there were hints that a modified regional economy might be re-emerging. Zanzibaris living in exile in Oman and Europe are returning to Zanzibar, if not permanently, at least for visits, and private capital seems to be flowing to Zanzibar from Oman. Zanzibaris living abroad are financing the restoration of houses in the stone town, and some of the new guest-houses and hotels that are springing up on Unguja and even on Pemba have been financed from Muscat. CUF, the opposition party that captured a number of parliamentary seats but failed to gain the presidency in the slightly suspicious 1995 elections, and lost the even more dubious 2000 elections, is widely thought to favour separation from Tanzania and closer ties to Oman. While CUF would no doubt deny it, it is seen by many as an 'Arab' party, and even more inaccurately as an Islamist party. So it looks as though at least some Zanzibaris are trying to revive Zanzibar's links to the Gulf.

Zanzibaris have also been more conscious lately of their cultural ties to the broader region. A series of film festivals and cultural conferences have been held in Zanzibar that take as their theme the 'dhow countries'. They use the dhow as the symbol of the connections between the countries of the western Indian Ocean rim. While there is an obvious danger of inflaming old ethnic tensions in Zanzibar, especially in the aftermath of the 2000 elections and the repression that followed, some good may come of this new interest in the broader region and its economy. Zanzibar's clove industry is finished. Until recently, Zanzibar's cloves were being left on the trees, and once Indonesian clove production recovers from its post-Suharto slump, they probably will be again. Occasionally, someone will suggest reviving the demand for cloves by getting mainstream smokers to enjoy clove-flavoured cigarettes (as opposed to the all-clove cigarettes favoured by Indonesians and aspiring Bohemians), but this seems unlikely to happen in the first place or to revive the clove business enough to save Zanzibar. If Zanzibar has a future outside tourism and balance-of-payment support, that future lies in a trade revival rather than agricultural production.

While Zanzibar is unlikely to become the Dubai of East Africa (another popular pipedream), it has a great natural harbour, historical links to the Persian Gulf and India, a commercial heritage and a local maritime tradition that would flourish if Zanzibar became a transshipment point again. Re-establishing Zanzibar as a node in the western Indian Ocean economy seems like a better bet than struggling along in the clove business, competing for tourists with all the other sun-drenched islands in the world or trying to become a light-manufacturing centre like Mauritius. It seems a more logical direction to try to revive the structures of an older trade than to invest a fortune in new infrastructure in the hope that a new manufacturing or agricultural economy will evolve to fit the new infrastructure. If nothing else, allowing Zanzibar to be reintegrated into the western Indian Ocean economy might let local (i.e. Indian, Kenyan or Persian Gulf) private capital do the work of creating a light industrial sector, instead of relying on ever-scarcer foreign aid. Western private capital seems to be interested in nothing but beach resorts, so if Zanzibaris hope to attract other types of investment they may have to open up to less risk-averse investors from areas with which Zanzibar has historical links. It may yet turn out that the apparent collapse of Zanzibar's end of the regional economy in 1964 was more in the way of a temporary hiatus than a long-term rupture. Zanzibar's future may yet have more to do with the Indian Ocean than with Africa as it is traditionally conceived.

Bibliography

Archives

James Duncan Phillips Library at the Peabody Essex Museum, Salem, Massachusetts (PEM)
Ropes Papers
Michael Sheppard Papers
Charles Ward Papers
Richard Waters Papers
Various Ships' Logs

Tanzania National Archives (TNA)
Annual Reports
District Reports
Secretariat Files
Forestry Department Files
Port and Marine Department Files

Zanzibar National Archives (ZNA)
International Maritime Bureau Records
Consular Records
Secretariat Files
Clove Growers' Association Files
Annual District Reports including District and Provincial Reports
Photographs

Official documents

Zanzibar
Annual Reports of the Agriculture Department and the Port and Marine Department
Gazette, Blue Books, Trade Reports, and Annual Reports
'Memorandum on Certain Aspects of the Zanzibar Clove Industry,' 1926
'Report of the Commission on Agriculture,' 1923
R. Pakenham, 'Land Tenure amongst the Wahadimu of Chwaka, Zanzibar Island,' 1947

Kenya
Blue Books
Forest Department Annual Reports

Tanganyika
Blue Books
Annual Reports of the Forest Department

Bibliography

Published works

Admiralty, *Instructions for the Guidance of Captains and Commanding Officers of Her Majesty's Ships of War Employed in the Suppression of the Slave Trade*, Vol. 1, London, 1892.

Allen, James de Vere, *Swahili Origins*, London, James Currey: 1993.

Alpers, Edward, *Ivory and Slaves in East Central Africa*, Berkeley and Los Angeles, University of California: 1975.

——, 'Indian Ocean Africa: the Island Factor,' *Emergences*, 10 (2000) pp. 373–86.

Anon., *Periplus of the Erythrean Sea*, London, Hakluyt: 1980.

Austen, Ralph, *African Economic History*, London, James Currey: 1987.

Barendse, Rene, *The Arabian Seas*, Armonk, NY, and London, M.E. Sharpe: 2002.

Bennett, Norman, *The Zanzibar Letters of Edward D. Ropes, Jr. 1882–1892*, Boston, Boston University Press: 1973.

——, *A History of the Arab State of Zanzibar*, London, Methuen: 1978.

——, *Arab versus European*, New York, Africana: 1986.

Berman, Bruce and Colin Leys (eds), *African Capitalists in African Development*, Boulder, CO, Lynne Rienner: 1994.

Berry, Sara, *Fathers Work for Their Sons*, Berkeley and Los Angeles, University of California: 1985.

——, *No Condition is Permanent*, Madison, University of Wisconsin Press: 1993.

Bhacker, M. Reda, *Trade and Empire in Muscat and Zanzibar*, London, Routledge: 1992.

Bose, Sugata (ed.), *South Asia and World Capitalism*, Delhi, Oxford University Press: 1990.

Burton, Sir Richard F., *The Lake Regions of Central Africa*, 2 vols., New York: Horizon: 1961 (1860).

——, *Zanzibar: City, Island and Coast*, New York, 2 vols, Johnson Reprint: 1967 (1872).

Chandra, Satish (ed.), *The Indian Ocean: Explorations in History, Commerce, and Politics*, New Delhi, Sage: 1987.

Chaudhuri, K.N., *Trade and Civilization in the Indian Ocean*, Cambridge, Cambridge University Press: 1985.

——, *Asia Before Europe*, Cambridge, Cambridge University Press: 1990.

Chittick, Neville, 'Sewn Boats in the Western Indian Ocean, and a Survival in Somalia,' *International Journal of Nautical Archaeology and Underwater Exploration*, 4 (1980).

——, *Kilwa: An Islamic Trading City on the East African Coast*, Nairobi, British Institute in East Africa, 1974.

Clayton, Anthony, *The Zanzibar Revolution and its Aftermath*, London, Hurst: 1981.

Colomb, P.H., *Slave Catching in the Indian Ocean*, London, Longmans: 1873.

Cooper, Frederick, *Plantation Slavery on the East Coast of Africa*, New Haven, Yale University Press: 1977.

——, *From Slaves to Squatters*, New Haven, Yale University Press: 1980.

——, ed., *Struggle for the City*, Beverly Hills, Sage: 1983.

——, *On the African Waterfront*, New Haven, Yale University Press: 1987.

——, et al., *Confronting Historical Paradigms*, Madison, University of Wisconsin Press: 1993.

Crofton, Richard H., *Statistics of the Zanzibar Protectorate 1893–1920*, London, HMSO: 1921.

Curtin, Phillip, 'African Enterprise in the Mangrove Trade: The Case of Lamu,' *African Economic History*, 10 (1981).

Das Gupta, Ashin, and M.N. Pearson, *India and the Indian Ocean*, Calcutta, Oxford University Press: 1987.

de Soto, Hernando, *The Other Path*, New York, Harper and Row: 1989.

Devereux, William C., *A Cruise in the* Gorgon, London, Dawsons: 1968 [1869].

Eltis, David and James Walvin (eds), *The Abolition of the Atlantic Slave Trade*, Madison, WI: 1981, pp. 134–5.

Ewald, Janet, 'Crossers of the Sea: Slaves, Freedmen, and other Migrants in the Northwest Indian Ocean.' *American Historical Review*, 105 (2000), pp. 69–91.

Facey, W. and E.B. Martin, *Oman, a Seafaring Nation*, Muscat, Ministry of Information: 1979.

Fair, Laura, *Pastimes and Politics*, Athens, OH, Ohio University Press & Oxford, James Currey: 2001.

Fernandez-Armesto, Felipe (forthcoming) in F. Bethencourt and D. Ramada Curto (eds), *Portuguese Expansion 1400–1822*, New York, Cambridge University Press.

Freeman-Grenville, G.S.P., *The Medieval History of the Coast of Tanganyika*, London, Oxford University Press: 1962.

——, *The French at Kilwa Island*, Oxford, Clarendon: 1965.

Freitag, Ulrike, and William Clarence-Smith, *Hadhrami Traders, Scholars and Statesmen in the Indian Ocean, 1750–1960s*, Leiden, Brill: 1997.

Ghosh, Amitav, *In an Antique Land*, New York, Vintage: 1992.

Gilbert, Erik, 'The *Mtepe*: Regional Trade and the Late Survival of Sewn Ships in East African Waters,' *International Journal of Nautical Archaeology*, 27 (1998).

——, 'Sailing from Lamu and Back,' *Comparative Studies of South Asia, Africa, and the Middle East*, 19 (1999), pp. 9–15.

Glassman, Jonathon, *Feasts and Riot*, Portsmouth, NH, Heinemann & London, James Currey: 1995.

Grant, D.K.S., 'Mangrove Woods of Tanganyika Territory,' *Tanganyika Notes and Records*, 5 (1938).

Gray, John, *History of Zanzibar*, London, Oxford University Press: 1962.

Gregory, Robert, *South Asian in East Africa*, Boulder, Westview Press: 1993.

Griffith, A. L., *Reconnaissance Report on the Forest Problems of the Zanzibar Protectorate*, Zanzibar, 1949.

Guillain, M., *Documents sur l'histoire, la géographie, et le commerce de l'Afrique Orientale*, 2 vols and album, Paris, Bertrand: 1856.

Hallett, Robin, *Africa since 1875*, Ann Arbor, University of Michigan Press: 1974.

Hart, Keith, 'Informal Income Opportunities and Urban Employment in Ghana,' *Journal of Modern African Studies*, 11 (1973).

Hawkins, C.W., *The Dhow*, Lymington, Nautical Publication Co.: 1977.

Headrick, Daniel, *Tools of Empire*, New York, Oxford University Press: 1981.

Hollingsworth, L.W., *Zanzibar Under the Foreign Office, 1890–1913*, London, Macmillan: 1953.

Hornell, J. 'The Sea-going *Mtepe* and *Dau* of the Lamu Archipelago,' *Mariner's Mirror*, XXVII (1941).

Horton, Mark, 'Asiatic Colonization on the East African Coast: the Manda Evidence,' *Journal of the Royal Asiatic Society*, 2 (1986).

——, 'Early Muslim Trading Settlements on the East African Coast: New Evidence from Shanga,' *Antiquaries Journal*, 67 (1987).

——, *Shanga*, Nairobi, British Institute in East Africa: 1996.

——, and John Middleton, *The Swahili*, Oxford, Blackwell: 2000.

Hourani, G.F., *Arab Seafaring in the Indian Ocean in Ancient and Early Times*, Beirut, Kayats: 1963.

Bibliography

Hoyle, B.S., *The Seaports of East Africa*, Kampala, Makerere Institute of Social Research: 1962.

Hugill, Peter, *World Trade since 1431*, Baltimore, Johns Hopkins University Press: 1993.

Iliffe, John, *The Emergence of African Capitalism*, Minneapolis, University of Minnesota Press: 1983.

Ingrams, W.H., *Zanzibar: Its History and Its People*, London, Witherby: 1931.

Jivanjee, Yusufali Esmailjee, *Memorandum on the Report of the Commission on Agriculture 1923*, Poona, 1924.

Kennedy, Paul, *African Capitalism: The Struggle for Ascendancy*, Cambridge, Cambridge University Press: 1988.

Kirkman, James, *The Arab City of Gedi*, London, Oxford University Press: 1954.

——, *Men and Monuments on the East African Coast*, London, Lutterworth: 1964.

Kusimba, Chapurukha, *The Rise and Fall of the Swahili States*, London, Altamira: 1999.

Lanchester, H.V., *Zanzibar, A Study in Tropical Town Planning*, Cheltenham, Burrow: 1923.

Lewis, Martin, and Karen Wigen, *The Myth of Continents*, Berkeley: University of California Press: 1997.

Lofchie, Michael F., *Zanzibar, Background to Revolution*, Princeton, NJ, Princeton University Press: 1965.

Lovejoy, Paul, *Transitions in Slavery*, Cambridge, Cambridge University Press: 1983.

Lyne, Robert, *Zanzibar in Contemporary Times*, New York, Negro Universities Press: 1969.

MacGaffey, Janet, *The Real Economy of Zaire*, Philadelphia, University of Pennsylvania Press & London, James Currey: 1991.

MacKenzie, Donald, *Knowing Machines*, Cambridge, MA, MIT Press: 1996.

McMaster, D.N., 'The Ocean-going Dhow Trade to East Africa,' *East Africa Geographical Review*, 4 (1966).

McPherson, Kenneth, *The Indian Ocean*, Delhi, Oxford University Press: 1993.

Maliyamkomo, T.L. and M.S.D. Bagachwa, *The Second Economy in Tanzania*, London, James Currey: 1990.

Mangat, J.S., *A History of Asians in East Africa*, Oxford, Clarendon: 1969.

Martin, E.B., *Zanzibar: Tradition and Revolution*, London, Hamish Hamilton: 1978.

—— and Chryssee Martin, *Cargoes of the East*, London, Elm Tree: 1978.

—— and T.C.I. Ryan, 'A Quantitative Assessment of the Arab Slave Trade of East Africa,' *Kenya Historical Review*, 5(1977).

Middleton, John, *The World of the Swahili*, New Haven, Yale University Press: 1992.

Myers, Garth Andrew, 'Reconstructing Ng'ambo: Town Planning and Development on the Other Side of Zanzibar,' unpublished PhD thesis, UCLA, 1993.

Mytelka, Lynn, 'The Unfulfilled Promise of African Industrialization,' *African Studies Review*, 32 (1989).

Nicholls, C.S., *The Swahili Coast: Politics, Diplomacy and Trade on the East African Littoral, 1798–1856*, London, Africana: 1971.

Northway, Phillip, 'Salem and the Zanzibar–East Africa Trade, 1825– 1845', *Essex Institute Historical Collections*, XC (1954).

Nurse, Derek and Thomas Spear, *The Swahili*, Philadelphia, University of Pennsylvania Press: 1985.

Osgood, John F., *Notes of Travel*, Salem, Creamer: 1854.

Pearce, F.B., *Zanzibar: Island Metropolis of Eastern Africa*, London, Frank Cass: 1967.

Pearson, M.N., *Port Cities and Intruders*, Baltimore, Johns Hopkins University Press: 1998.

Prins, A.H.J., 'Uncertainties in Coastal Cultural History:the *Ngalawa* and the *Mtepe*,' *Tanganyika Notes and Records*, 53 (1959).

——, *Swahili-speaking Peoples of Zanzibar and the East African Coast*, London, International Africa Institute: 1961.

——, *Sailing from Lamu*, Assen, Van Gorcum: 1965.

——, 'The *Mtepe* of Lamu, Mombasa, and the Zanzibar Sea'. *Paideuma*, 28 (1982).

Ray, Rajat, 'Asian Capital in the Age of European Domination: the Rise of the Bazaar, 1800–1914,' *Modern Asian Studies*, 29 (1995).

Roberts, Richard, *Two Worlds of Cotton*, Stanford, Stanford University Press: 1996.

Scott, James C., *Seeing Like a State*, New Haven, Yale University Press: 1998.

Sheriff, Abdul, *Slaves, Spices and Ivory in Zanzibar*, London, James Currey: 1987.

—— (ed.), *The History and Conservation of the Zanzibar Stone Town*, London, James Currey: 1995.

—— and Ed Ferguson (eds), *Zanzibar Under Colonial Rule*, London, James Currey: 1991.

Shanula, J.P., 'A Survey on the Distribution and Status of Mangrove Forests in Zanzibar, Tanzania', November–December 1989, Commission for Lands and Environments, Zanzibar.

Spear, Thomas, 'Early Swahili History Reconsidered,' *International Journal of African Historical Studies*, 33 (2000), pp. 257–91.

Sullivan, G.L., *Dhow Chasing in Zanzibar Waters*, London, Low and Marston: 1873.

Thomas, J.J., *Informal Economic Activity*, Ann Arbor, MI: 1992.

Toussaint, Auguste, *History of the Indian Ocean*, Chicago, University of Chicago Press: 1966.

Tracy, James (ed.), *The Political Economy of Merchant Empires*, Cambridge, Cambridge University Press, 1991.

Villiers, Allan, *Sons of Sinbad*, New York, Scribner: 1969.

Welliver, Timothy, 'The clove factor in colonial Zanzibar, 1890–1950,' unpublished PhD thesis, Northwestern University, 1990.

Wriggins, W. Howard (ed.), *Dynamics of Regional Politics: Four Systems on the Indian Ocean Rim*, New York, Columbia University Press: 1992.

Index

Printed and bound by CPI Group (UK) Ltd, Croydon, CR0 4YY

13/04/2025

14656525-0001